Rutherford Alcock

The Journey of Augustus Raymond Margary

From Shanghae to Bhamo, and back to Manwyne

Rutherford Alcock

The Journey of Augustus Raymond Margary
From Shanghae to Bhamo, and back to Manwyne

ISBN/EAN: 9783744755849

Printed in Europe, USA, Canada, Australia, Japan

Cover: Foto ©Andreas Hilbeck / pixelio.de

More available books at **www.hansebooks.com**

THE JOURNEY

OF

AUGUSTUS RAYMOND MARGARY,

FROM SHANGHAE TO BHAMO, AND
BACK TO MANWYNE.

FROM HIS JOURNALS AND LETTERS, WITH A BRIEF
BIOGRAPHICAL PREFACE:

TO WHICH IS ADDED A CONCLUDING CHAPTER.

By SIR RUTHERFORD ALCOCK, K.C.B.

WITH A PORTRAIT ENGRAVED BY JEENS,
AND A ROUTE MAP.

London:
MACMILLAN AND CO.
1876.

BIOGRAPHICAL PREFACE.

In January, 1875, the British mission, under Colonel Browne, appointed in the previous year by Lord Salisbury, at the instance of the Honourable Ashley Eden, Chief Commissioner of British Burmah, reached the city of Bhamô, the point of departure for the great overland trade route between India and China. The importance both politically and commercially of the re-opening of this route had long been acknowledged by the Indian Government.

In 1868 a mission under Major Sladen had crossed the Burmese frontier and reached the city of Momien, in the Chinese province of Yunnan. It had returned from that point, unable to penetrate farther in consequence of the jealousy and opposition of both the Chinese and Mahommedan authorities, then struggling for mastery in Yunnan.

Early in 1874 this civil war, which had for nineteen years desolated the splendid western provinces of China, came to an end by the utter overthrow of the Mahommedan rebels, and the authority of the emperor was restored up to the Burmese frontier. Thus a fresh opportunity arose, and was promptly seized on by our Indian Government. Colonel Browne's mission was despatched with orders to cross

China, from Burmah to Shanghae, promises of safe conduct, with the necessary passports, having been previously obtained from the Pekin Government.*

In order to make it clear, however, to the mandarins of the western provinces that the mission belonged to the same nation which was so well known at the capital and the Treaty-ports of the Pacific Coast, the English minister at Pekin was instructed to send an officer across China to meet them on the western frontier. For this perilous and responsible duty Mr. Margary was selected, a young officer of great promise, belonging to the Consular Service, who, during some six years' residence in China, had thoroughly mastered the language, and made himself familiar with the habits and customs of the country.

He left Shanghae on the 23rd of August, and Hankow on the 4th of September, 1874. So much was known to the Indian Government, and little more. As he himself describes it, he had plunged into darkness for six months. It was doubtful whether, even if he succeeded, he would be able to reach the frontier in time; and, as a precaution, another consular officer, Mr. Clement Allan, who could take his place as interpreter to the mission, if necessary, had been sent round by sea to Rangoon.

The mission had scarcely commenced the prepara-

* The question whether fair and full explanations had been given to the Chinese Foreign Office as to the objects of the mission is discussed in the final chapter, which Sir Rutherford Alcock has kindly contributed, and need not be considered here.

tions for their final start from Bhamô, when the welcome news reached them at the Residency that Mr. Margary had accomplished his task, and was already at Manwyne. Two days later, on the 17th of January, he arrived at the Residency, and reported himself to Colonel Browne.

"It may be easily imagined," writes Dr. Anderson,[*] the eminent naturalist attached to the mission, which position he had also filled in that of 1868, "with what feelings we congratulated the first Englishman who had succeeded in traversing the trade route of the future, as he called it, and with what pleasant anticipations we heard of the accounts of his arduous but successful journey, and the reception accorded all along the line of route, crowned by the politeness shown by the dreaded Li-sich-tai," (the warrior Viceroy of Yunnan, who had extinguished the Mahommedan rebellion). "The astonishment and admiration of the Burmese was even greater. In their own minds they had never realised the existence of English officials in China, and now there appeared a veritable Englishman, speaking Chinese fluently, and versed in the use of chopsticks, and all other points of etiquette."

Accordingly, the inhabitants of Bhamô, from the woon (or governor) downwards, were anxious to see and welcome this Petching Mang, or Pekin mandarin, who had so unexpectedly appeared amongst them. Entertainments in his honour were given,

[*] 'Mandalay to Momien,' p. 307.

and for the few remaining days before the mission started, he was the centre of attraction for the natives, while his cheerful and helpful nature gained him the cordial esteem and regard of Colonel Browne and his colleagues.

Looking back to that time, after the repulse of the mission, Dr. Anderson writes:*—" For my own part I desire to record the deep sympathy entertained for those who mourn the loss of one so beloved. Our brief intercourse lasted long enough to win for him the esteem and cordial friendship of us all; and while we deplore the early loss to his country of the services of one whose past career and talents promised to raise him to high distinction, we lament his untimely loss as that of an old and dear friend."

Early in February the mission started from Bhamô, and, on the morning of the 18th, arrived with their escort and train at the last guard house on Burmese territory, in the valley of Nampoung, a deep, narrow gorge, thickly covered with forest trees festooned with creepers, which separates Burmah from China. Here reports met them of danger ahead. The Kakhyens, wild hill tribes, who occupy the wild frontier, were said to be mustering in force to oppose their progress, encouraged by the authorities at Seray, the first frontier town, and of Manwyne, the chief city of this part of the province of Yunnan. A council was held at which Margary made light of the rumours. He had come safely through the Kakhyen hills, alone,

* 'Mandalay to Momien,' p. 450.

he was known to the mandarins at Seray and Manwyne. He would go on ahead, ascertain the truth, and send back instructions for their guidance. This offer was accepted, and he prepared to start. During the afternoon gongs and cymbals were heard along the hills on the Chinese side, and Kakhyens were seen peering down from amongst the trees, but nothing occurred to interrupt their last dinner, or their sitting afterwards, prolonged late into the night, at which the prospects of the mission were discussed.

Early on the morning of the 19th of February Margary crossed the frontier, with no escort but his Chinese secretary and servants, who had been with him through his whole journey, and a few Burmese muleteers. The next morning brought letters from him, reporting all safe up to Seray. He had been well received there and had passed on to Manwyne. The mission followed slowly, reaching Seray on the 21st. No farther news from Margary; but it was remarked that the Seray chief and all his men were armed, and more rumours came in of hostile preparations, and danger. On the 22nd, in the early morning, the storm broke. The mission camp was almost surrounded by armed bands, while letters from the Burmese agents at Manwyne to the chief in command of their escort told that Margary had been brutally murdered at Manwyne on the previous day. But for the staunchness of their Burmese escort—who resisted all offers of their assailants of heavy bribes if they would draw off and allow them only to kill the "foreign devils"—and the gallantry of the fifteen Sikhs, who formed their body-guard, the whole mission must have shared the fate of their comrade. As it was, after a hard day's fighting, they were able to draw off in the evening and recross the frontier with all their baggage, having had only three men wounded. At Bhamô they eagerly sought for all particulars of the murder, but without much success. The most trustworthy account was that of a Burmese who had seen Margary walking about Manwyne, sometimes with Chinese, sometimes alone, on the morning of the 21st. This man reported that he had left the town on his pony to visit a hot spring at the invitation of some Chinese, who as soon as they were outside the town had knocked him off his pony and speared him.

And so ended the second British mission from Burmah, and with it the life and career of one of a class of her sons of whom England has most reason to be proud in these days. As the years roll on, her special work in the world comes out more and more clearly. In spite of herself—often against her will—she has task after task set her in the wild neglected places of the earth, amongst savage or half-civilised races. Scarce a year passes that the work does not become more pressing, and widen out in all directions. The call comes, now from the oldest haunts and homes of men—from India, from China, from Arabia, from the Malay peninsula—now from the wondrous islands of the Pacific—now from the vast unexplored regions of central or southern Africa. Sometimes it is the conscious cry of the oppressed, "Come over and help us," sometimes the unconscious appeal of anarchy and evildoing in regions where we have planted our foot and from which we cannot draw it back; for whatever the cause or form of the summons it is sure to have " vestigia nulla retrorsum " written over it. And the call, however urgent, however exacting, has rarely failed to bring out the right man, whether it were for missionary, or soldier, or merchant, or traveller, ready to spend himself for his country and his country's work; simply, cheerily, unreservedly doing deeds the reading and hearing of which here in England make our pulses bound and our eyes moisten, without a thought that they were anything more than what every Englishman is called on to do in some form or another for the dear old home. How many such have stepped quietly out of the ranks in the last few years, and what a noble swarth they have cut in the world's tangled harvest work? Unlike in their characters, their powers, the tasks that they were set to do, but alike in this, that they did it, one and all, with their might, and paid for it with their lives; a bright bead roll of heroes, of whom their land may well be proud, the Pattisons, Mackenzies, Goodenoughs, Margarys, whose record goes far to redeem the sloth and selfishness of a generation weighted heavily with wealth and luxury, and is sounding again and again in the ears of our youth the grand old lesson, "a long life hath but few years, but a good name endureth for ever."

It is the object of this book to set before his countrymen, in his own words, the story of the crowning work of the last of this band. The journals and letters which tell it are not perfect. Here and there gaps will be found in the narrative which cannot now be filled up, as the materials necessary for this purpose, with other MS. relating to China, were in his luggage at Manwyne at the time of his murder, and have not been recovered. But these are of small account, and do not mar the vividness and charm of the simple story, so pathetic when read with a knowledge of what was to be the end. But in order to enable readers to appreciate the journey across China from Shanghae to Bhamô, they should know something more of the traveller than can be gathered from the history of the last six months of his life. The slight sketch of his early years which follows will, it is hoped, be sufficient for this purpose.

Augustus Raymond was the third son of Major-General Margary, R.E., and was born at Belgaum, in the Bombay Presidency, on the 26th of May, 1846. As a child he was remarkable for sweetness of disposition, courage and intelligence; and his natural aptitude and perseverance were such, that (although he had no instructor but his mother in the tropical climate in which his first years were passed) when sent to school in France, at the age of nine, he took his place with ease among English boys of his own age. While in that country he lived with his grandfather and grandmother, whose loving care was always gratefully acknowledged by him. After some time spent under the care of his uncle, the rector of Swafield, Norfolk, and in attendance at the North Walsham Grammar School, he was sent with three of his brothers to Brighton College, where he remained for upwards of seven years.

Here, as in later life, he made the most of his time, working hard and playing hard, and gaining the respect and love of masters and boys. "He displayed at Brighton College," an old schoolfellow testifies, "the same noble qualities which distinguished him in manhood. He was always in the front in whatever he did. I remember, for instance, that he was the finest swimmer in the school." The chief incident in his school life was a severe attack of brain fever, the consequence of a blow on the head received in a fight between the college and town, the effects of which he felt occasionally till the end of his life.

Alluding to this attack, Dr. Griffiths the head master writes to his parents: "It was a great comfort to me, when I heard of your son's sudden attack, to feel that he was a boy with whom I never had occasion to find fault, though doubtless he, like all of us, had faults, yet they never came to the surface, as in the case of so many others. His good abilities, his cheerful temper, his willingness to work, and his correct conduct, all combine to make him a favourite pupil. I believe masters and boys have joined heartily in our common prayer for his welfare, and there seems now a fair hope of his recovery."

His letters to his parents at this period are full of the most ardent expressions of affection, and an anxious desire to make the most of his opportunities, and to reward their care and affection by yielding to his mother's influence, and following her counsels in the most minute particulars.

While at Brighton his mind was greatly set on a university career, but, with the thoughtfulness and care for others which characterised him through life, he never alluded to this wish without referring to the claims of his elder and younger brothers, whose interests, dear to him as his own, he continually laid before his parents, with a discriminating judgment and tenderness of affection not often met with in schoolboys of his age. A few extracts from his letters will be enough to illustrate these points in his character:

"Brighton College, 1862.

"MY DEAREST MOTHER,—I have two of your letters before me. . . . One of the letters made me so unhappy. I can't bear it, when I have done anything wrong, to think it makes you unhappy, and then I feel the distance between us, and the time it takes a letter to reach you! Sometimes, when I have written a letter and sent it, I feel quite vexed with myself, and would give anything to recall it; that is just my feeling with regard to my last letter, full of complaints and selfishness; then, it will reach you, and before this letter reaches you to tell you how unhappy it makes me to think that I have written it, your answer will be coming to me, which I shall get about two months from this time, I suppose, by which time I may have forgotten all about it. I find I cannot half express my feelings, but you will understand me, dearest mamma. I feel brimful of love and affection for you and dearest papa, and can't bear to displease you.

"We partook of the Holy Sacrament last Sunday, and everything has gone on very pleasantly lately, and I am getting on very comfortably in the first form now and enjoy the work. I wrote a letter just before starting for Swafield to you, and one while at Swafield, that you might get letters by two mails successively, and I hope Jack has written. I enjoyed my visit to Swafield as much as I possibly could, but had I known the extra expense it caused you I should not have been quite so happy.

"I enjoyed my day in London not only pretty well (when Aunt C—— was so soon to leave England) but very much. I hope the letter you were expecting told you more than my return to Brighton only, for I try to give as much news as I can. I went to Miss Roberts' yesterday to see my little sisters, but found them all out except little C——. She told me they were very happy and liked their schoolfellows, and that everyone was very kind to them.

"I have been three times, but found E—— out each time. Aunt C—— will be able perhaps to tell you more about them than I can. As to my brothers, —— gets on very well, better than ——, who is, I am afraid, rather inclined to be idle, but I will do my best to keep him up to the mark."

The Jack alluded to in this letter was his elder brother, John Louis, who afterwards passed successfully through Sandhurst and was posted to the 105th regiment, which he joined in 1864. He died at Dinapore, of typhoid fever, in January 1867.

"Reading, 1863.

"MY DEAREST FATHER,—I was so glad to see your handwriting when I received a letter last mail, as it is long since I had one from you. Many thanks for writing so kindly. You cannot think how much happier it makes me, and invigorated (*sic*) to do better; whereas if there had been a reproach or disapproval of anything I had done it would instantly have thrown a damp over my spirits, not to be got rid of in a hurry, and so I believe it is with ——. I grieve to see him complaining, but pray bear with him (forgive my saying so to you) and he must soon see his faults and will give up all murmuring and be sorry for any undutifulness. —— worked very hard last quarter, I think, and has evidently done much better in the examinations. I think he was top of the form in one or two things, and very fairly up in others; but then again in one or two subjects he was nearly bottom, which of course pulled him down considerably in a general average order. Both of them will certainly be put into the third form, and I have to say with the greatest pleasure that A—— has won another prize for French. I was fifth, but

I have no chance of beating the four ahead of me. I am spending my vacation at the R——'s, at Reading, in company with Jack, whom I had not seen since Christmas. The house is crammed full of visitors, and we are a thoroughly merry happy party. A—— and A—— were to have gone to Swafield for the holidays, as they ought to have a thorough changes but, to our great disappointment, they were prevented going by scarlet fever, which broke out next door to Uncle John's.

"When I forwarded the pieces you inclosed for Aunt E——, I took the opportunity of asking Uncle P—— if they could have my brothers now, as he had asked them before, but without fixing any time. I think he will have them if he possibly can.

"I suppose the best way for me to learn good composition is to read some good writer like Lord Macaulay. I will devote myself to this."

"Brighton College, 1863.

"My darling Mother,—I have just been to see our dear sisters. They are well and very happy. E—— was engaged and did not appear, but they said she was in high spirits. They tell me she plays very well for a child of her age. C—— has the sweetest disposition imaginable. —— is not very well to-day; he is a good fellow, and works very well. —— has such a lively nature that his attention gets drawn off study very soon. I am so anxious that neither of them should waste a bit of time at college."

This anxiety about his younger brothers is a leading feature in these boyish letters, and grows stronger when his elder brother is about to leave. He begs his mother to write to them, urging them to work, and to listen to his advice, for he shall now feel himself responsible for keeping them steady. But the office of mentor is one which he only accepts as a duty, and with misgivings.

Thus he writes at this time, "I do not know whether I am right in speaking my mind about my brothers, for I have plenty of faults myself. I wish Jack or somebody would tell you all about me.

"Please do not scold my brothers. Jack is very anxious to pass his examination for Sandhurst. I shall miss him very much when he does go, for he has always been a kind brother to me. We have scarcely ever quarrelled since we came here. His great fault is hastiness, and many a time he has got into trouble through it; but I have noticed a great change in him, and I think he has a great deal of common sense. Uncle A—— has invited me for Christmas, and I have no doubt I shall enjoy myself exceedingly, except that I shall be so anxious to hear if Jack passes."

After the return of his parents from India, Mr. Margary resided with them in London, and attended lectures at University College. His wish for an academical career seemed likely to be realised, when he received a nomination from his relative, Mr. Austen Layard, Her Majesty's present minister at Madrid, to compete for a student interpretership in China. Of this he immediately availed himself, and, after three failures, passed a successful examination, and was sent to China on the 20th of March, 1867. He was now in his twenty-first year, but retaining the freshness and brightness of his boyhood; in fact, his animal spirits seem to have grown stronger as his character settled. At school the sense of responsibility which weighed on him, in consequence of the absence of his father and mother in India, made him thoughtful and serious beyond his years. But now that he is fairly started in life, with a clearly marked career before him, and the confidence which is born of confirmed habits of hard work, and a well trained intellect to enable him to make the best of it, his natural joyousness seems to have burst out, and coloured not only his own life, but the life of all around him. Indeed, the special charm of his own narrative, as given in the letters and journals, consists in this joyousness, and in the splendid self reliance—wholly free from self consciousness and from self-seeking—with which he meets and overcomes all dangers and difficulties. Sometimes, indeed, he is half ashamed of himself, and inclined to make excuses for these high spirits, which, as it were, force him to take the lead in fun and adventure of all kinds. He doubts whether they may not be a stumbling-block to his companions, whether he may not be doing them harm, by letting himself loose; but concludes characteristically enough that he is "too deeply attached to the loving principles of the Gospel to be an ascetic." And so he goes on his way rejoicing, with a thorough enjoyment of nature, society, adventure, good living, and hard work, which carries us along with him, and makes his narrative the healthiest kind of reading. Indeed, but for this happy temperament he could never have got through his great journey. With it, he can press steadily on even when lying, scarcely able to move, in the tiny cabin of his boat, struck down by " pleurisy, rheumatism, indigestion, very bad neuralgia, toothache, and a lot more," with the thermometer at $96°$, and no European within 1000 miles, and enjoy intensely in the intervals of pain the glorious scenery through which he is passing.

But his high spirits never interfered with work. Soon after his arrival at Pekin he obtained a reward for rapid proficiency in the Chinese language, his diligent study of which, and of the habits and prejudices of the people, gave him in after years his peculiar power of managing and understanding mandarins and chair-bearers with equal success.

In these early days he was accustomed to cure his occasional fits of home sickness by a recipe at which he often used to laugh while speaking of it. Retiring as far as possible out of hearing of his species, he sang all his old songs at the top of his voice, winding up with "God save the Queen." Having thus exorcised the demon, and reminded himself that he was serving his queen and country, he would return to his companions and his studies in his usual happy temper.

It may be added here, that on two occasions in the course of his career in China, he received offers of employment at a salary at least double what he was getting from Government, which he declined, from the feeling that he would rather serve his country as a poor man than make a fortune in any other service. For his own private interests were always last in his thoughts. Indeed, the advancement and success which his good conduct and ability brought surely and quickly to his feet seemed only to quicken his desire to use time, and means, and influence freely for the help of those less able or fortunate than himself; and many a struggler breaking down in life's race owed new hope and courage to his aid and counsel. In fact, his life has been well described as "full from first to last of a devotion to duty, and of delight in serving his Lord through serving the brethren: a power of ready sympathy with every phase of human joy or sorrow, which gained him so rich a portion of what he coveted most on earth, the love and approbation of good men and women."

He remained as a student and attached to the legation at Pekin until 1870, when he was despatched to take charge of the Consulate in the island of Formosa, where he remained for upwards of a year, residing chiefly at Tamsuy and Kelung, but making expeditions to other parts of the island. While here he added botany and geology to his studies, finding progress in the former much the easier in Formosa. For, while the Chinese highly approved of foreigners gathering flowers and plants, they looked with the keenest suspicion and jealousy on the collection of minerals or fossils, and the use of a geologist's hammer, and would dog the steps and watch narrowly the proceedings of any person so equipped.

When at Kelung, he and his friend, Mr. Dodd, a British merchant there, rescued forty-two lives from shipwreck during a violent typhoon, on the 9th of August, 1871, for which both of them received the medal of the Royal Humane Society, and were honoured by the Queen with the decoration of the Albert medal of 1st class. In 1872, he re-visited England, and took part in a discussion on Formosa, at a meeting of the Royal Geographical Society, of which he became a member, and returned to China, viâ North America and Japan, arriving at Shanghae in September, 1873.

Shortly after reaching Shanghae, he was sent to the northern port of Chefoo; to take charge of the Consulate there. Here his genial and sociable disposition led him to promote many amusements and to join heartily in all the social entertainments in the small community, to promote kindly intercourse amongst its various members of different nationalities, and to while away the tedium of the winter months in a port almost isolated during that season. But here again, as all through his life, we find higher motives than selfish enjoyment at work; and his letters show that his first object in all his intercourse with society was to promote general harmony and goodwill, and to leave no opening for the petty misunderstandings which often arise in small and isolated communities.

From Chefoo he was transferred to Shanghae, in April 1874, and in August received instructions from H.B.M.'s minister at Pekin to proceed at once through the vast south-western provinces of China, to await at one of the passes on the frontier of Yunnan the arrival of Colonel Browne's mission, to which he was to act as interpreter and guide through China, as already stated.

His orders were, to start at once, and secretly, and were obeyed with his usual promptness and exactness, though he felt keenly having to leave on such a journey without being allowed even to say good-bye to his friends; for he was under no delusions as to its danger. No one knew better the intense dislike of the Chinese to any such extension of the rights of foreigners in the interior and western provinces as the mission foreshadowed. And so he writes to his mother on the eve of starting: "It is a long and to a certain extent a perilous journey— I can't disguise that fact, and that for three months I shall be beyond the reach of all news from the outer world." But he will not let her dwell on this side of the picture, and adds directly, "You must picture me trudging on through strange cities, stared at by pig-tailed mobs. At times sitting in eastern etiquette with native governors and viceroys, and lastly you may look at the map, and fancy you see a solitary European, standing above the last pass, and anxiously gazing through his binoculars for the advent of Indian helmets from the west. You know, dearest, I have trust in God and fear nothing. Best love to all.—Your own loving Gus." And again to the lady to whom most of his letters had been addressed since his return from England:—" Is it not a splendid mission? What wonderful things I shall see! I shall hope to have grand sport in the forests and mountains, which teem with wild life. It is impossible to say when you may hear from me. I shall try and make use of the native post, which is a very efficient service, but how far it may be safe for foreign correspondence remains to be proved. It may be that not a word may be heard of me for the whole time, in which case all sorts of rumours may arise as to my fate. Let me beg of you not to believe one; rest assured I will make my way there and back, by God's help, as safe as a trivet."

And in this temper he pressed steadily on, a lonely, sorely-tried man, bent only on doing his duty to the last and getting his work through. And so to him—as surely to all such—came the highest strength and power according to his need. " One disease after another attacked me," he writes to his uncle, the Rev. J. Layard, when he had been more than two months on his road, " with relentless rapidity; even dysentery came to add its terrors to my loneliness, and reduced me to a skeleton. All my pride of flesh and muscle speedily vanished beneath its dire influence; but, thank God, all this suffering was invaluable in curing me of a far greater disease. In the midst of my suffering I was drawn nearer to God, and at last, like Christian, the load rolled off my back, and I was another man. I hope you will not think me immediately full of conceit and vanity, and that I think myself an established Christian, but I hope when I get back, please God, to prove the armour I have put on in private, and don't yet know the strength and endurance of. You will probably smile, but it is a fact that I judge distance entirely by the dear old road from Swafield to North Walsham" (his uncle's rectory, where he had spent two years of his boyhood), "and every Scotch fir on the roadside takes me back to the time when poor Jack and I searched for tiny shoots under the old oak with as much zeal as an archæologist for coins and buried remains."

But it is time that the letters and journals were left to tell their own tale, in the appreciation of which it is hoped the slight and imperfect sketch here given will be helpful to readers. It will enable them at any rate to understand the circumstances under which they were written. The first series are from the neighbourhood of Pekin, while he was attached to the British Consulate there as a student.

ITINERARY.

Date and Hour of Arrival.		Place.	Distance (in li) from previous place.	
Sept.			Hankow :—	
4	3.30 P.M.	武昌	Wu-ch'ang	20
5	2 P.M.	金口	Chin-k'ou	—— [ch'ang.)
,,	Evening	冬瓜腦	Tung-kua-nao	105 (from Wu-
6	——	牌洲	P'ai Chou	45
7	12.30	小划欄	Hsiao-hua-pai	45
8	Evening	胡心洲	Hu-hsin Chou	60
9	Evening	六溪口	Lu-ch'i-k'ou	60
11	——	新堤	Hsin-t'i	60
,,	Evening	螺山	Lo-shan	45
20	Evening	君山	Chün-shan	——
21	Evening	——	Nan-chai	180
22	——	——	Ni-hsin-t'ang	60
,,	Evening	——	Yin-ho Hsiang	40
23	11 A.M.	龍陽縣	Lung-yang Hsien	—— [Hsiang.
,,	3.30 P.M.	——	Liao-ya-tsui	70 from Yin-ho
24	6 P.M.	——	Shih-ma P'u	40
25	Evening	常德府	Ch'ang-tě Fu	20
27	3 P.M.	——	Ta-ch'i-k'ou	20
28	2 P.M.	桃源縣	T'ao-yuen Hsien	70
,,	——	白馬渡	Pai-ma Tu	20
,,	Evening	——	Shui-ch'i	5
29	Evening	——	(Small village.)	——
30	Evening	——	(Small village.)	——
Oct.				
1	——	——	——	——
2	——			35

ITINERARY.

Date and Hour of Arrival.		Place.		Distance (in li) from previous place.
Oct.				
3	7 P.M.	府州辰	Ch'êu-chou Fu	70
4	—	溪瀘	Lu-ch'i	—
5	5 P.M.	——	Pu-shih	—
6	7 A.M.	縣谿辰	Ch'êu-chi Hsien	—
27	5 P.M.	府遠鎮	Chen-yuen Fu	—
28				
29		縣秉施	Shih-ping Hsien	12
,,	Evening			
30	—	——	Hsin-chou	30
31	Evening	洞風大	Ta-fêng-tung	—
Nov.				
1	10 A.M.	縣平清	Ch'ing-p'ing Hsien	—
2				
3	—	縣定貴	Kuei-ting Hsien	45
4	6 P.M.	縣里龍	Lung-li Hsien	75
5	—	府陽貴	Kuei-yang Fu	—
8	—	縣鎮清	Ch'ing-chên Hsien	69
9	—	縣溪清	Ch'ing-ch'i Hsien	62
10	6 P.M.	府順安	An-shun Fu	80
11	—	州甯鎮	Chên-ning Chou	60
,,	—		Huang-kuo-su	25
12				50
13	—	廳岱郎	Lang-tai T'ing	60
14	—	——	Mê-k'ou	Short stage.
15	—	——	Hua-king	35
16				

Date and Hour of Arrival.		Place.	Distance (in li) from previous place.
Nov.			
17		Yang-shun	
18	廳安普	P'u-an T'ing	40
19			
20	縣彝平	P'ing-i Hsien	
21	白水	Pai-shui	
22		Hai-tzŭ P'u	Half way Chan-i [Chou.
,,	州益霑	Chan-i Chou	
23	州龍馬	Ma-lung Chou	
24		Pai-tzŭ P'u	40
,,	司隆易	I-lung Ssu	40
25	林楊	Yang-lin	75
26	橋板	Pan-ch'iao	[lin.
27	Noon	府南雲 Yun-nan Fu	105 from Yang-
Dec.			
2	口鷄碧	Pi-chi K'ou	35
3	州甯安	An-ning Chou	40
4	關鴉老	Lao ya Kuan	70
5	縣豐祿	Lu-fêng Hsien	75
6	資捨	Shê-tzŭ	90
7	縣通廣	Kuang-t'ung Hsien	
8	站腰	Yao-chan	
,,	府雄楚	Ch'u-hsiung Fu	
9	州南鎮	Chên-nan Chou	95
10		Sha-ch'iao	35
11		Lien-p'eng	95

Four more stages to Ta-li Fu.

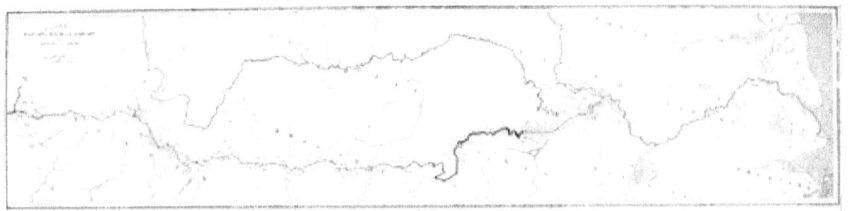

MARGARY'S JOURNEY.

To his uncle, the Rev. J. Layard.

Lung Wang Sang, June 11th, 1868.—I am now, as perhaps you know, at the hills, living in a delightful temple with two friends. . . . I came out early in May, and have got on well in Chinese during the interval. This is a glorious place to work. Although there are seven of us out here, distributed in three temples, we keep apart in order to work, each in our own rooms, and only meet at meal times. I work, on the average, about seven hours a day, and it is wonderful that one can do it on one subject alone. We expect the chief and his family out in a few days. What with picnics in the evenings, and little soirees, we shall probably spend a delightful summer. But work at Chinese will not be hindered, as it is somewhat in the winter, for just now the sun prevents anything else until 6 P.M., when we go out for a stroll about the valley, which is very pretty, full of trees and little gorges. Occasionally somebody drops in from the city. One day our French friends arrived, and carried us off with them to a temple for which they are negotiating. It was a truly wonderful spot on the side of the hills, from its commanding position and the forest of trees with which it was surrounded.

The temple was a sort of head monastery, or school for Buddhist priests, who can be known everywhere by their shaven heads. The temples are everywhere mere ordinary rooms filled with innumerable hideous gods. The missionaries have a fearful task in attempting to convert the Chinese. The difficulty of the language is an obstacle, and the simplicity of their service is less likely to attract the sensuous Chinese than the magnificent cathedrals and gorgeous ritual of the Roman Catholics. Some of the Roman missionaries deserve success. They dress in the native costume, and travel about the country for years and years, putting up with Chinese dirt and Chinese food in a way which, to a European, must be a sort of martyrdom. We want, as missionaries, educated gentlemen, free from narrow-mindedness, and possessing a bearing which will command respect from foreigners. There are some such amongst our missionaries.

You wish to know about our Sundays, and I will tell you, though it may pain you; but if you look at it from a broad point of view, I think you will agree that it is not a very dark picture. Though there is a general sense of keeping the Sabbath Day holy, it is more thought of as a day of rest and enjoyment. No scruples prevent us from taking a ride, or making a picnic, or skating. We have a chapel service every Sunday morning, and most of the people in the Legation go regularly; and, for months past, Sundays have been spent very properly and quietly. Fellows spend the afternoon walking on the wall, or sitting about smoking, or writing letters. They never give a card party or wine on Sunday.

I know enough of my own wickedness to make anything like a religious confession painful to me, but I don't mind telling you that I try to live straight, and trust in God for Jesus' sake; that we are as good as I could wish is too much to say, there is still much to be done.

Poor old C—— is gone! I remember him better than you think, and am really awfully sorry not to see him again. I could not help thinking of Horace's lines:

> "Vixere fortes ante Agamemnona
> Multi; sed omnes illacrymabiles
> Urgentur ignotique longâ
> Nocte, carent quia vate sacro."

I read my old favourite, and Homer, now and then, and am glad to find I do not forget much. We were well grounded in grammar at Brighton College, for which I shall always be grateful to Mr. Griffiths.

To his Parents.

August 18*th*, 1868.—We have had an immense deal

of rain, and with it a very strange kind of thunderstorm, or rather wind and lightning storm; I never saw or read of anything like them. If you can fancy a wide belt of very vivid and incessantly flashing lightning, driving furiously before it wind and rain, I think you can form an idea of it. The lightning always appears low down on the horizon, and is accompanied by scarcely any thunder at all. We were sitting at dessert in our mess-room in Pekin, last Tuesday, about eight o'clock, when the first of these storms that I had seen burst upon us. The only warning it gave was the sudden bursting open of doors and windows; then came a furious wind, followed by equally furious rain; and all this whipped in by the extraordinary lightning, which gave me the idea of a flight of huge eagles flashing fire with each sweep of their wings. We rode into Pekin on Monday, and back on Wednesday morning; that one night's storm had blown down trees right and left, and drenched the country; the tall millet stalks were bent down to the ground, and the roads, which are merely troughs cut through fields and well banked on each side, were simply converted into canals; the water actually running two feet deep. The mud, in some places, was impassable, and I found myself in a fix in one place. I turned off to go up the pass, which is very stony, and not liking to take my pony where he ran a risk of breaking his knees, I determined to follow the road, and for about two miles found good ground on the top of the bank; but, as usual, within half a mile, and in sight of the temple, I came to a dead lock. The road was a broad sheet of deep soft mud, and two trees lay across it. Once I had to jump across a ditch with mud on both sides, and my noble pony jumped after me. I found O—— had got in a little before me, after a difficult ride.

August 20*th*.—I sent in a note to ask after mail letters to-day by my teacher, who has gone in on Imperial business. We often have considerable amusement with our three teachers. After finishing a certain amount of reading, we go out into the terrace and talk or play at chess (Chinese), in which we often hold our own. My teacher, Wen, is a very little man, but very high-bred and very clever. . . S——'s friend is the character of the three. Being a married man, and older than the other two, he invariably asserts his superiority, much to our amusement. He is exceedingly polite. You would be amused to see how precise we all are with each other. He invariably smokes our cheroots, and is altogether very independent. His name is Tau. The first time I saw him he asked me how old I was at once, for it is polite in China to ask any number of questions about a man's family, condition, etc. It is extraordinary how pugnacious the Tientsin men are. The Pekinese seldom fight; but O——'s servant and our groom are both natives of that place, and are constantly fighting with some one or other, and S—— and I have often had to rush out and part them, trying to look excessively angry, though it is difficult to refrain from laughing when one sees a couple of fellows, each hauling away at the other's pig-tail. We rode over to a Tavist temple, yesterday, to look at a natural hot spring, believing, too, though wrongly, that we should find a swimming-bath. The priest met us at the door, and, to my surprise, shook hands with us in a most polite and gentle manner, like a polished gentleman. Returning home, we took several jumps, until S——'s pony stopped on the brink of a ditch, put his head down, and walked backwards, depositing poor S—— in the water up to his neck. However, he soon got on again, and his wet clothes helped him to stick on for the rest of the ride. We laughed a bit.

August 22*nd*.—I must now give you an account of an exciting adventure. Yesterday, about three o'clock, a very bright sky was suddenly overcast, and such a torrent of rain came pouring down, and continued till night, as I have never seen. In one hour the courtyard behind was flooded fully a foot deep. In a few minutes it would have burst into our room. S—— and I stripped ourselves of everything and put on our mackintoshes and rushed out. To tear up some bricks would soon relieve us of a good deal of water by making a way out for it; and I went off to our teachers' quarters, where I found priest, teachers, and servants in a terrible plight. All their rooms were flooded below, and through the ceiling. I pointed out a drain which was stopped up, and made them clear it. While thus engaged we were too deafened by the storm to hear shrieks and cries for help that were being raised outside the temple. An excited Chinaman rushed up, and tried to make us understand something; but he spoke so fast, that it was utterly hopeless to catch his meaning, until I heard the words " two foreigners," when off we went like arrows, through the temple, down the steps, across the road, heedless of rough stones, with our naked feet, until, guided by the shouts, we went about a hundred yards to what in the morning had been a road, but was now a deep, rushing mountain-torrent, and, on the opposite bank, stood B——, shouting, "Brandy, for Heaven's sake, G—— is fainting."

I flew back, filled a flask, and was in the torrent up to my waist before I knew its force, but was stopped in time by B——, to whom I threw the flask. It was almost dark, and for some little time he could not find it, but, when he had got hold of it, he rushed with it into a little hut, where G—— was almost, indeed, as nearly as possible, done. Meanwhile, we had torn our awning ropes down, and I had been trying for five minutes to throw it across, when S—— shouted out that the torrent was more practicable above, where was, most fortunately, a tree, to which our servants tied the rope. S—— dashed nobly in with the other end, and, after a severe struggle, gained the opposite bank. I stood up to my waist, holding the rope next to him; G—— then seized the rope, and he and S—— plunged in, and in a moment were carried out in a semi-circle, G—— completely immersed for a few moments. While hauling away for very life, I felt that one of them must go, but they held on nobly, and we pulled them in with a shout. S—— then repeated his feat, and we brought B—— across in the same way, he all the while rolling over and over like a log. Both of them were fearfully exhausted, and G—— we put to bed. Fortunately it was our dinner hour, and everything was ready for them, and when they were refreshed they recounted their adventures.

About four miles from this, they were overtaken by the rain, and in less than half-an-hour their ponies were up to their knees in water. They were above three hours getting across the last bit of their ride, and it was by a miracle they escaped. There was not a square foot of sound ground the whole way, and they had to flounder through mud up to their knees. The roads, from their nature, were soon converted into rushing torrents, strong enough to carry away oxen like feathers. At one place they saw an ox being hurled away, his head every now and then appearing above the water. At last they reached a house, and, though standing up to their knees in water, the inmates would not give them shelter, thinking they were robbers. A half idiot boy at last came out, and boldly offered to take them to a good road and a ford. But at this ford the boy and the horses were simply carried away by the force of the current, and they never expected to see them again. The boy was fortunately thrown on to a bank, where three streams met, and there he sat holding the rein of one pony which was in the water, and there B—— and G—— were obliged to abandon him. They shouted to him but he answered not a word. The only hope was that he would sit there all night, and so he did, and brought the ponies back safe in the morning. B—— and G—— then continued their way, and pulled each other through three streams up to their necks in water. When they reached a hut below us here, they shouted for help, and were there for nearly an hour, shivering, exhausted, and half frantic, before their cries were heard. G—— at one time threw off everything, and plunged in to swim across, but was pulled back by B—— in the nick of time. At last we came to the rescue, and brought them through all right.

The little hut in which they took refuge was full of Chinese huddled together; one of them, a woman, was washed away and drowned. S—— had nothing on, and I only a mackintosh, so we were not hindered or impeded, and were ready to help. O—— ably assisted from the bank, and once went in with all his clothes on. Our servants behaved well, and were rewarded. I shall not forget the adventure, as it has cost me more than I can express in words. My ring is lost! the twist of the rope wrenched it off my finger. But it was lost to save two lives, and I must fain be proud of my loss. Numbers of men searched for it next morning in vain. *Sic transit gloria!* B—— was exceedingly sorry for my loss, and expresses his intention of giving me a ring to keep in memory of this event.* He was carrying despatches to his chief, at a temple about five miles from this, and we were not a little amused when he produced their pulp from his boots. G—— was also the bearer of letters to O—— and S——, which, fortunately for them, had not been put into his riding boots, and, therefore, were dried and deciphered. B—— proceeded next morning on a donkey. The four horses came back in a sorry plight, but soon got quite right again, and the boy was well rewarded, in fact, a great many people were rewarded, and our heroes did not get off too cheaply. Next day, G—— wished to proceed to the temple where our other fellow-students are staying, being invited to a feast given by W——, in commemoration of his birthday, but though all the water had run away, the roads were too soft, the clouds too threatening, and G—— and his horse too weak to attempt the journey. We had a jolly day here, for the pool was full of water, and clear, so that we had a glorious bathe, and swim in it, and the daily repetition of it adds much to our pleasure.

August 27th.—We all four rode over to the temple of Ta-pei-su, yesterday morning early; the distance was about twelve miles, and I never enjoyed a ride

---

* The ring promised as a memento of the event above recorded was given, and was much prized and always worn by its owner.

more. We had to go round to the other side of the hills behind us, and crossed several pretty little valleys, which ran up from the plain, and contained temples perched among trees. The valley we sought was longer and prettier than all, with a succession of temples, perched one above another, and a mountain brook dashing down between them. This is a favourite valley, and nearly all the temples were taken by members of the different European communities. Here was Sir Rutherford Alcock's, and, close by, another, in which W. H—— and O. B—— were staying; two students were their guests for a week, and another was staying with Sir Rutherford, so we were nearly all together at the moment, there being only four left in the Legation, and they will get their turn at the hills. We found them all in a high state of jollity. They had had a grand dinner the day before, and, upon my word, they gave us one that night that would have done credit to Verrey's. O. B—— can afford to be a little extravagant, for his knowledge of chemistry has gained him a capital appointment, if any of us had studied that noble science, we might have got it. We were hospitably put up for the night, and called, as was our duty, on the chief, and the ladies. They were much interested in the history of our adventures, and we had a long and pleasant visit. We rode back to our own temple early this morning, having thoroughly enjoyed our visit. S—— and I return to Pekin on Saturday, having enjoyed ourselves much in this place, improved greatly in health, and made a good start in Chinese. The rain has filled the lakes and canals in the city, which have lain dry for about five years, and have been an eyesore; so the huge city will be much improved. Since yesterday every cloud has vanished, and the country is just getting dry again. Carts are actually passing us.

To the Rev. J. Layard.

Lung Wang Sang, September 1*st.*—Everyone but F—— has gone into Pekin, some for good, some for pleasure, all to get their month's wages: as my friend E—— will bring my pay for me, I preferred remaining to work as hard as possible, as the examination is very near.

In answer to my invitation to come up to my temple and dine with me, F—— writes to say that, being a determined sportsman, he is unable to pass by the 1st of September without seeking partridges, and he is off on a day's shooting. So *solus ego*. A short time since, as I was reading aloud, a party of five Chinese passed by, "*kwanging*," by which we mean site, or sight-seeing. The former is the more appropriate as applied to Chinamen. On their return, I asked them in with all the politeness I could muster. I saw at a glance that they were above the common herd, but as Chinamen never make any display in mufti, and yet are very punctilious, I had great difficulty in determining which was the right person to address, and, of course, pitched upon the wrong one. However, we had a capital conversation for about an hour, and by asking close questions, which is the most polite thing to do, I determined their several grades. Two of them were members of the Imperial family. This body is so large, that they have a yamen of their own, and all the members are distinguished by a yellow girdle. When the relationship gets very remote, they are transferred to the class of red girdles, and then they sink into oblivion. My friend wore only a very narrow yellow belt like a lady's. Not having seen one, and expecting to see a sash, I never noticed his rank. With these two was a distinguished literatus, a member of the Hanlin, or Forest of Pencils, the highest literary degree.

[The following extracts from Mr. Margary's journals and letters were written during his first official appointment to Formosa, mentioned in the introductory sketch.]

Formosa, 1871.—During the last two or three years, public attention has been drawn with unwonted attraction towards China, but it seems to require events of a very extraordinary or very startling character to fix that attention with any steady interest. It might seem that the enormous European demand for tea and silk would be sufficient to inspire some regard for the country of their source; that the activity of trade in the direction of China, the great prosperity of California, the running of the fine Pacific mail steamers from thence to Shanghae and Hong Kong, and the activity of the Russians ever hovering over China, and improving their fine settlement in the Amur, would have been sufficient facts to rouse the House of Commons; but, in fact, it requires an unintelligible Chinese mission, followed by a Tientsin massacre, which proved its hollowness, to raise public interest. Unfortunately the sad European war soon obliterated the effect, and future troubles may be needed to force people to think of the importance of the settlements here. at Hong Kong, Shanghae, and Hankow.

Democracies have always shown a disregard for distant interests, and there are visible signs, even now, that British commerce will suffer sooner or later from these tendencies, and the power of economical ministers increased at the expense of the efficiency of the public services abroad.

In casting about for objects of retrenchment, a death-blow is being aimed at the mercantile existence of Formosa. The island is obscure and little known. Its trade is small, and employs a mere handful of British merchants, but a firm and well-supported protest has been raised against so unwise a measure, and it begins to appear that the trade, specially at the north of the island, owed its existence and first yearly development to a very remarkable instance of British pluck and perseverance. The pioneers are men who have laid aside comfort and the luxuries of civilised life to rescue this beautiful island from undeserved neglect, and who have passed through years of unprofitable toil to dawning prosperity. In one case they have created the cultivation and reputation of a new and highly-prized tea, and now a decree goes forth to crush them.

I have a vivid recollection of the difficulty I experienced long ago on leaving England in getting information about China. Most people knew the names of the three great cities, but it would have put the good people of Shanghae very considerably out of conceit with themselves, to have been told that very few knew even of their existence as a community.

And yet Shanghae is as wonderful a place as Hong Kong or Singapore.

Now Formosa is as little known to people on the mainland, at least at the more northern ports. Such foreign interest as there is in Formosa is confined to two ports, one at each end of the island, and completely isolated from each other by some two hundred miles of difficult road, path, I ought rather to say, for I doubt if civilisation is sufficiently advanced along any part of the route to have made anything worthy the name of a road. These two harbours are the same places which the unfortunate Dutch occupied two hundred and fifty years ago, and where they built massive forts, which stand to this day, and one of which, viz., that of Tamsuy, in the north, has been very grotesquely adapted to the uses of H.M. consulate. The story of the Dutch occupation is a sad one, and well illustrates the treacherous character of Chinese diplomacy.

Formosa was in those days completely in the hands of the aborigines, but much coveted by the Chinese.

The Dutch, following in the wake of the Portuguese, were hindered by the jealous policy of the latter from gaining any equal concessions from the Chinese Government of that day, which was, by the bye, far more tolerant and progressive than the present Government. The renowned Koxinga, who held the command of the whole Imperial fleet at Amoy, and who had received many mortifying repulses in Formosa, cleverly deflected the power and enterprise of the Dutch in the direction of that island. They succeeded in establishing themselves, and even intermarrying with the natives, but the wary Koxinga pounced down upon the successful colonists in a moment of weakness, from the want of supplies from home, and enacted a very Cawnpore tragedy. Just as Koxinga had made a cat's paw of the Dutch, so did the Chinese Government recompense him after he had strutted out his days of usurped sovereignty, and prepared the island for easy annexation.

Since then, the aborigines have been steadily,

though slowly, driven to the eastward, and at the present day they enjoy possession of fully half this gem of the seas. The country is extremely wild and picturesque, and the very few travellers who have had the hardihood to visit the haunts of the aborigines speak of the hard work they encountered in penetrating the thick vegetation of the pathless hills.

It might be interesting to a Highlander to know that these adventurous pioneers have adopted and recommended the kilt as the best dress for such rough travelling. The Chinese have not pushed their colonies with rapidity, and certainly they had grave obstacles to encounter in the undying enmity of the natives, and in the denseness of their forests.

These thick forests of camphor trees have afforded inexhaustible occupation to settlers for many years past, and vast spaces have been cleared and replanted. The natives distil the camphor themselves, and our merchants buy it of them at the place of production.

The savages, as they are called, occasionally come down from their hills, and attack the settlers with varying and trivial success. This only happens on the borders. All along the West Coast, and for some distance inland, the Chinese have fully established themselves in flourishing villages and towns.

To the Rev. J. Layard.

Formosa, January, 1871.—I was grieved to hear in my last home-letters of your very severe illness and suffering, and I was roused thereby to a consciousness of my neglect in leaving one or two of your welcome letters unanswered; it was not that I had forgotten to do so, but various things conspired to prevent my writing.

It took a long time to get over here from Shanghae, and still longer for my luggage to arrive and enable me to set up in comfort at Kelung, and all this time I was hanging on in a comfortless shake-down-kind of existence in miserable quarters converted out of an ancient Dutch fort, which has stood for upwards of one hundred and fifty years, but of which little is accurately known.

[He here speaks of the kindness of his host.]

I was not long at my solitary post at Kelung before I had to return to Tamsuy to see the doctor, who could not come to me, having hurt himself just as I was in need of him. Heavy rains and storms had made the mountain paths so slippery, and so swelled the rapids, that I came down with some difficulty, but was able to return at Christmas.

I am impatient to get back to my books; Kelung is a solitary place. Only the custom-house and one merchant-house are to be seen, and occasionally sailing-ships come in from Shanghae for coal. The Government have never quite made up their mind to encourage Formosan trade. Hence no proper houses have been built for the officers, and just now we are in expectation of orders to close the consulate, and quit the island. I shall be glad enough to go, for it is a wretched existence in many ways, but it will be a great injustice to those who have stuck to the place, and made the trade, and we are all trying our utmost to plead their cause. The tea trade here is quite distinct from that at any other port. It is the purest and the best, and is just getting such an impetus, that it will very soon eclipse many of its rivals on the mainland. Dodd has played the arduous part of pioneer here for six years. His teas are prepared under his own eye, and packed by him; whereas, on the mainland, this part of the business is done by natives, and the teas brought to the market complete. Unfortunately, Formosan tea is a bitter kind, the Oolong, which does not suit English tastes, but it is what the Yankees like, so nearly the whole of it goes to America. It is curious how each nation has its peculiar fancy in tea. The natives make such a profit by tea that they are cultivating it rapidly on the sides of the hills, and even replacing indigo with tea.

The Chinese agriculture is very striking in one respect, and that is, that it does not shrink from invading the highest summits, and far up the hill-sides you see little patches and terraces carefully cultivated, and in a little hut hard by, the solitary worker is content to live.

Looking upon the vast unclaimed surface of this island, which teems with vegetation all over its hills, it is easy to predict an unlimited increase to the trade without the corroborating evidence of statistics. Kelung is only a coal harbour at present, but this year it will be great in tea also. The customs intend to reduce the grievous duties on coal soon, and when they do this, we shall have ships coming down in shoals. At present, it scarcely pays them. We cannot get them to allow foreign miners to deal with the coal-veins, which is a very great pity, as our Celestial friends make a very clumsy mess of it, and are utterly ignorant of the very rudiments of geology, which would enable them to recover the strata at a fault. It is curious how jealous and suspicious the Chinese are of a geologist. If he wanders with a hammer among the rocks he is sure to be watched lest he should discover gold.

It is firmly believed that a foreigner can see three feet into the ground. If, on the contrary, you gather leaves and plants, you gain great respect from them, for you are supposed to be in search of medicines, and all foreigners are physicians in their eyes, and missionary doctors are especially successful. I have taken up botany and geology; we find progress far easier in the former.

The scenery inland is lovely, but unfortunately for several winter months Kelung and its environs is enveloped in storms and wet weather, which is very depressing, unless one has some absorbing occupation. This I find in the books I am reading. I have also engaged a literatus to brush up my Chinese, for which I have little use in these quiet parts. The language certainly imposes a lasting task on the student, which does seem rather hard after the labour of acquiring it. I am reading through a history, in the original, of a period in the third century A.D. It is merely a history of warriors, and battles, and treacheries, not a word of the condition of the people, save when they are slaughtered for the sins of their betters. The favourite treachery of inviting an enemy to a feast, with many protestations of friendship, and then chopping his head off, is recorded over and over again, and it is a significant fact that this custom still prevails. We have had an instance of it in Formosa quite lately, when a mandarin, friendly to foreigners, was the victim after a sumptuous entertainment.

Lesson to foreigners—Don't trust them too much, which some are foolishly persisting in doing.

January 27th.—I am obliged to close hurriedly, as a Siamese steamer has made its appearance at Kelung, and a messenger is going over to-night, so I will not miss the opportunity of sending this, as we cannot tell when another steamer may appear. A gale is blowing, which may delay the appearance of H.M.S. Zebra.

To his Parents.

Foochow, 1871.—I have some stirring scenes to describe to you, which have occupied our minds to the exclusion of everything else.—I sold all my things satisfactorily within forty-eight hours of the *Elk's* arrival, having sent round a comic circular, which had a magic effect, and raised a great deal of fun at the sale. The *Elk* was going round to Kelung for a trip, and also to lovely Sau-o-bay, on the coast of Formosa, where there was a probability of seeing some of the savages. Hence my hot haste, for I was very anxious to visit their haunts, otherwise I might have leisurely awaited her return, as she had come to Tamsuy for treasure. My friends gave me a farewell dinner the night before, and the song of "Old King Cole" was kept up to such a late hour, that I was in danger of oversleeping daylight, and missing the *Elk*; as it was, I had to pursue her in my crumpled white clothes of the previous evening and minus my baggage. However, I hurriedly wrote a note to have my box sent overland to Kelung, and had just time to throw it into the sanpan, which was being towed nearly under. As sure as the telegraph, my things were over there and nearly as soon as I was, so that I had not to borrow much of my very kind friends on board. W—— was a delightful man, and soon proved himself A 1 in the event I am about to describe, and in the confusion and misery caused by a fearful typhoon which we narrowly escaped. The centre of the storm passed immediately over Kelung harbour. Had it occurred a few hours earlier or later, nothing could have saved us: as it was, I think I did some service to H.M.S. *Elk*, by pointing out the safest berth immediately behind a reef. The entrance to Kelung harbour is very simple, and I know the soundings well. They had got a duffer of a pilot, a native fisherman, who was taking the ship wrong, and W—— sent for me. After that, the pilot was going to put him into a place where, as events occurred, he must have been wrecked by other ships drifting down on him, even if he could have steamed up against the wind, which was awfully terrific. I was again referred to, and advised a snug corner which was very nearly occupied by another ship. I went on shore and could not get back to dinner on board at seven, when the blow began. However Dodd and I and another gentleman sat down to dinner. Very soon the wind began to be troublesome, the house rattled, and large pieces of the ceiling came falling down about us in every room in the most uncomfortable manner. We got out our barometers, and sat regarding them for about half an hour with extreme astonishment. The hands moved down *tenths* at a time, at last they reached 28, and we jumped up, and dressed in flannels to sally forth, and do what we could for the unfortunate ships, which we felt sure must be in distress. After opening the door with some difficulty, we struggled across the verandah and peered out into the darkness. The ship's lights seemed to be strangely mixed up, and soon three masts loomed out of the darkness, right under our noses. Then began the hurried excitement which lasted all that night. We had little at hand to make a light with, until a bright thought struck Mr. C——, and a heap of camphor was thrown into a flower-pot, which made a brilliant blaze, and gave a beam of hope to the drifting ships. The water was now dashing all over the garden, and we attached a rope to the flagstaff. Dodd began frantically throwing his clothes off, and I followed his example. We were soon in the water, sticking together and wading out up to our necks, and then we had to swim; but fancy our mortification in finding the rope short, by at least twenty feet. There was such a roar, that they could not hear on shore our cries for more rope, so we chucked it away, and were soon hanging on to the ship's netting. I tried then to swim back with a rope from the ship, but was obliged to haul back. We then went on deck, and tried to get volunteers, but the men said they could not swim. Two days afterwards they were swimming like ducks. We were perfectly disgusted to find Englishmen behaving so. However we got a boat lowered, which was immediately swamped, but soon baled out again, and we started for shore, with two men to row and a rope attached. No sooner were we on land, than the men skedaddled, leaving us in a pretty mess! Dodd was clinging to the rope with all his strength, and I was hanging on to the boat, when a tremendous sea dashed the boat against our legs, laming our assistants on shore, and then turning her over completely. Dodd and I were underneath like any jack-in-a-box, and we must have been killed, had not the boat turned over again miraculously. I felt it was all over for a moment. We could do nothing more then, and as we had ascertained, while standing shivering on board, that the ship was hard and fast, and so far out of danger, we left them, redressed ourselves, and went to look for two other ships which were ashore half a mile off among the worst rocks. The rocks were fearfully strewed with heaps and heaps of timber and copper bolts, difficult to avoid in the pitchy darkness, and blinding wind and rain. Ever and anon we heard a piteous cry from the angry sea, in answer to our chorus of "all right." Every one fell fifty times, and broke as many lanterns, and made as many journeys back to the house to get more. At last we unearthed a whole heap of Malays perched up on a high bank among the luxuriant brushwood, where they had been thrown up. These were conducted safe home, and we learnt from them that the captain was dashed to pieces. They belonged to the *Westward Ho*, and they told us that a French ship lay close to their's with the crew clinging to the wreck. These unfortunate people we were enabled to get safe on shore some time afterwards.

We renewed our search, and crawling down opposite the dark object, we ascertained that the men were still on it. Here again the gallant Dodd plunged in, and effected a connection. I stood by him up to my shoulders in water to hold the line and life-buoy, and always kept close enough to speak to Dodd, who soon reached a buoy, which the Frenchmen threw over.

We then took the rope ashore, where the others made sure of the end, while we easily got on board. A strange scene then ensued. The old French captain began to cry, and embrace us, and we had quite an angry altercation before we could compel the crew to go over the side and trust themselves to the rope. We found a poor wretch with a broken leg, who behaved splendidly, and helped us with his arms and other leg to hoist him over the bulwarks. I then went down and lay on my back in the water, holding on to the rope, and the man's legs were lowered on to my shoulders, so that I formed a sort of bed for him, and Dodd supported his head and shoulders. In this way, half swimming, half hauling, we two, unaided, carried him to shore. Excuse my egotism, but I cannot help being astonished how we managed it! After this, they said, four men were cut off in the bows of the ship. Her back was broken, and at first it seemed impossible to get them off. However Dodd and I again got on board, and crawled near enough to speak to them, and to see that there really was a safe way down. But they had not the courage to move, until we poured abuse into their frightened ears. Just then a big sea rolled us all up into dumplings; my hand fortunately found something to seize, but, to my horror, old Dodd had disappeared! He turned up again, though, frightfully bruised, and groaning with pain, and from that time I minded no more Frenchmen. We all got on shore, however, with the addition of a black cat, which clung to my naked shoulder with desperate energy, while the waves rolled over our heads. About daylight we had a snack, and fell into a sound sleep, utterly exhausted, but we were glad to find on waking that the gun-vessel and two ships remained safe. We remained for a whole fortnight in frightful confusion. Dodd's house was turned into a barrack, and I am sorry to say many things disappeared. Capt. W—— lent us marines, who lived also at Dodd's, and we sallied forth night after night, to make up and watch by a big fire over against the wreck to keep off the natives; every one had his work cut out for the time. I had to bury the poor captain, and help his mate (who was saved, and proved to be a right good worker) to keep his Malays in order, and victual them, and to save as much property as possible. The gun-boat did her best to pull off the stranded vessel. She steamed away with frightful energy, until we thought she would burst herself, instead of which she cracked the strong hawsers with a report that was astonishing to hear. It was at night that these operations were always obliged to be carried on, and the result was a series of Turner's pictures. The Frenchman turned out to be rather a superior sort of man, but he was too fond of telling us that he was all there, that we had plenty of intelligence, and that the maritime laws were not washed out of his head. If that was so, I think they must have been the only things he saved, for his wits were more or less gone for three or four days. There were many strange episodes during these events, which I cannot describe briefly. I remember shortly before we discovered the Frenchman's whereabouts, we tried to light a big fire in a dead-house that happened to be there. I mean a small joss-house, in which the rustics store their ancestral bones. The heavy driving rain prevented any such attempt outside. We picked up pieces of wreck, and threw them inside, and very soon a blaze was created, and a ghastly scene presented itself; there we stood on the wild shore, with our faces screwed up in the pelting, hail-like rain, and inside, an ancient skull grinned upon us from behind the fire.

The next night, a big fire occurred in the city, and Dodd, with his usual impetuosity, put it out by jumping on the tops of the houses, and hacking away with the sword he carried, until he fell through, and was hauled out by the coolies. He then had a hand to hand fight with looters, and retired amidst the cheers of the honest natives.

A few nights after this, we were all knocked clean out of our beds by a smart shock of earthquake. After settling the wrecks, and clearing off the business, we all went round to Tamsuy, and took in our treasure, and I am glad to say it put something into poor W——'s pocket. By the way, a treasure chest, containing 1400 dollars, belonging to the British ship, was fished up by clever divers, and carried off to a village. W—— landed and searched for it, and we had a good deal of bother with the mandarins.

I said good-bye somewhat sorrowfully to Tamsuy, and we had a beautiful passage over.

Large ships are wrecked all down the coast, and we found no less than forty more unfortunate people, including five women, at Tamsuy, forwarded there by mandarins. Captain W—— brought about sixty over with him. Through all the scrimmage, strangely enough, I was about the only one not hurt in any way beyond bruises. I have made a very long, and breathless yarn of this hurricane, but being as it is *currente calamo*, I hope no hostile criticism will attack my faults of grammar, and absence of coherence.

[In the spring of 1872 Mr. Margary returned to England for sixteen months. The following are extracts from letters written on his return journey to China viâ the trans-continental railway through North America.]

To F. E. R.

Cataract Hotel, Niagara, August 22nd, 1873.—I have this afternoon stood over the mighty Falls, wrapped in a delighted gaze. To-morrow morning I hope to sally forth very early, and go down below to the place where they dress you in oilskin, and conduct you right under the arched water. The Horse-shoe Fall is a mighty cataract indeed, with glorious bands of colour stretching across the water, fascinating the eye. . . We ordered a carriage, and drove to the rapids. The first operation was to pay $1.50. each, and then we were let down some two hundred feet of perpendicular cliff in a regular hotel lift, to a standing point, from whence we overlooked the magnificent rapids, still at some depth below, seething into white foam its bright blue waters wherever a rock intervened. . . It is a stupendous gorge through which it runs, in many places showing up with a rich background of trees.

Our hotel and two others in a line with it are full of visitors. There seem to be more ladies than men among them, and as many of them are fresh and pretty, it is rather a gay sight. The coiffure of the younger women is very new, and somewhat amusing to look at. The hotels have an Oriental look about them, through having verandahs outside, and all the rooms thrown open with free ingress and egress from one to the other, so that what with numbers of people sitting outside, talking and smoking, and ladies flitting from room to room, a very animated scene is presented, and there is no need for a stranger to feel *ennuyé*, or to lounge about alone, as at many English sea-side hotels. In fact the whole place has an unfinished look about it, very much reminding me of a settlement in the East, which of itself produces a very refreshing effect.

We have, in coming here, passed through much grand scenery with our eyes shut, although, I must say, it took a long time to get into that blissful state in the sleeping-car, of which we have had our first experience. The trains are conducted by very surly officials, who will not give you information readily, and, this being a free country, of course, treat you as an inferior altogether.

The sleeping-car is rather a clever contrivance, but does not produce the comfort which is expected. In the first place, the rattling and heaving of the carriages is as though you stood by the engine-room of a steamer in a slight sea. The train regularly pitches and oscillates enough to throw you off your balance at times, and this, although it scarcely exceeds a rate of twenty miles. The first appearance of the car is that of a small restaurant, divided off into recesses right and left, filled with bench-seats facing in pairs, but at night the metamorphosis is magical. The nigger conductor passes along, pulling down an upper berth, which contains mattresses, sheets, and pillows, all smelling horribly musty. However, we were told that the Pullman's sleeping-cars, which we do not meet with on this side of Chicago, are much superior in every way. It is pleasant enough being able to lie down, but it is not so easy to undress in the narrow space, and you have hardly room to stow away a bag, so that in a trip of six or seven days, one has to put up with the misery of not being able to change apparel very often, nor is the luxury of a bath attainable.

The American trains are totally different to ours. You can pass right through from one end to the other, and as it does not matter where you get in, you find nothing of that excited rushing about to find your carriage, so common in England. Another rather amusing thing is to see the cool way in which people jump off, or get on to the train while in motion, and also the absence of gates, or other bars, across the line when it passes through the highways. In many places the line passes along between houses, which have their front doors and verandahs facing the railway, and you see whole families sitting out and gazing at the monster trains passing by their very doors. In America it is the custom for trains as well as carriages to pass each other on the right.

To F. E. R.

Pacific Mail Steam-ship '*Japan*,' *September* 2*nd*, 1873.—This is a line which offers few opportunities or incidents for a sparkling correspondence, and I cannot at present see much material on board to work up into a thrilling history.

A magnificent ship like this, with saloons and cabins and ladies' boudoirs fitted up like a house at Princesgate, is desolation itself, with only fifty passengers to enliven its spacious retreats. If only the long vista of this saloon could be sprinkled with the lively freight of an outward P. and O. ship, we should have some fun to relate. But, as it is, the thought of pounding steadily at only nine knots through this wide ocean for three weeks, without touching at a single island, seems to have sent all the ladies to sleep.

For my part, having formed a resolution to brush

up my Chinese and to read through a few volumes of an intellectual type, I am not sorry that my restless social nature has not too much to distract it. I set to work most resolutely this morning, and for some two or three hours stirred up the muddy depths of oft trodden ground.

I shall have to hark back, and tell you more about our trip across America, but it seemed so barren and uncomfortable, that I did not feel as if I had anything to write about when I was there.

As we rattled over that execrable railway, our minds were not equal to much more than playing bezique; consequently many hours were spent over that imbecile game. We used to get a table fixed up, between the opposite bench-seats, and there, in somewhat close packed comfort, we made ourselves sardine sandwiches, instead of dining off the very uninviting food supplied at the stopping places, for the enormous charge of a dollar. Those weary days tried our patience very much, and there was little to reward one at night, when the greasy-smelling black porter came along the carriage pulling down the berths, making the beds (one above and one below), and hanging the curtains all along, a process which soon changed the appearance of the carriage from a café to a dismal, narrow passage lined with mysterious hangings, which utterly bewildered one as to the probable position of one's own head.

The railway followed the route originally taken by the Mormons in their harassing journey to the "promised land" of Utah, and it was interesting to mark certain points and places, made famous by the history of their march. We passed close under "Pulpit Rock," in Echo Cañon, where Brigham Young addressed the assembled congregation before they took possession of the "promised land." Although we did not find time to run down to Salt Lake City, we were right in the middle of the fine Mormon settlement at Ogden, which was the only refreshing place our eyes rested on for many hundred miles. Pretty little villas dotted the plain, which was spread out like an accidental lake in the hollow of the mountains. The harvest had just been gathered in, and the whole place looked happy, a charming oasis after wearisome lengths of prairie and the conventional "city," which generally consisted of the railway station and a gaming shed.

To F. E. R.

Yokohama, September 29*th,* 1873.—We had twenty-two calm, monotonous days on the passage; and then, all of a sudden, experienced a violent storm, one of those veritable typhoons of this dreaded coast, which delayed us twenty-four hours. The captain was a calm, sagacious man, well versed in these extraordinary tornadoes, and he managed to keep the vessel on the outskirts of the hurricane, and so let it pass by us. But we had quite enough of a gale to frighten many who had not been at sea before out of their presence of mind. Many felt serious misgivings on account of the popular prejudice against the safety of these huge gingerbread ships in rough weather. I stood in the wheel-house for'ard, all day long, by the side of the captain, and watched with interest and admiration the quiet way in which he manœuvred the ship to meet the shifting condition of wind and waves. The great ship, steadied as she was by her enormous paddles, rode over the might waves with dignified motion.

One very remarkable phenomenon, amongst others, which in a smaller ship I should scarcely have been able to observe, without being lashed to a mast, I here saw beautifully displayed. It was the power of heavy rain in subduing both wind and waves. I heard the captain muttering "Just in time," after some manœuvring of the helm, when down came a squall which lasted half-an-hour. It rained majestically, and down came the enormous crested waves, under pressure of this new element, from tempestuous surging to an almost level calm. Not a breaker was to be seen! Down, down, to oily smoothness went the angry waters, and I can picture from it the miracle on Gennesareth. "Two hours more of that," says the captain, "and we shall find smooth water." But alas! it was but a squall, and the sulky wind followed on with redoubled fury. Midnight, however, brought a change, and the last day we steamed through quieter seas. . . We steamed along the Japan coast for some hours before reaching our port, and it was extremely beautiful. The hills were much broken up and covered with trees, which is, to my eye, the richest kind of scenery. We landed with delight, expecting to see many wonders in this strange country, but civilisation has advanced so rapidly, that many of their oddest customs have been swept away.

October 2nd.—We start to-day for Shanghae.... Yedo has greatly disappointed us. We went up by the railway, and spent the whole day running about Yedo in a funny little hand-carriage called a "gin-rick-a-sha." This is a modern invention, emanating from the native brain entirely. It is like a perambulator, only drawn in front, and the men who draw them are perfect marvels in activity. They will go all day with you at a fast trot, sometimes working up into a gallop. Gin-rick-a-shas abound. They stand in rows, like cabs in London, and the moment you put your nose outside the hotel, you are besieged with them. You take one as a matter of course. What need for calculation, when a dirty little slip of paper worth cts 1250, or sixpence half-penny, will make the funny little gin-rick-a-sha man's eyes glisten, and his nimble legs scamper for half a day.

To Mrs. J. LAYARD.

Shanghae, 1873.—Very far from feeling any sort of impatience at your earnest letters, I have been very much gratified by reading them, and you need not fear to speak too strongly. I do feel the value of every kind of spiritual help out here, where it is so easy to let go great truths and to sink down to an easy-going level of morality. My visits to your quiet and much-cherished home were of incalculable benefit to me, and I read the Bible with pleasure and awakened interest.

I was quite touched this morning to see the quantity of marks and notes you have both so kindly and laboriously put in the Bible you gave me. I value the Book immensely, and understand it now by the light thrown on it at S——. What an age seems to have passed since I left home; perhaps if I had had a more interesting journey it would not have seemed such a wearisome blank as I feel it now. After the marvellous Falls of Niagara there was nothing to relieve the monotony of the journey. The first city we came to was a pattern of all the rest, a mere handful of small huts on a dusty plain, with four or five sulky-looking roughs lounging about smoking.

The noble prairie was one close cropped waste of dried-up turf, with the faintest approach to undulation, unrelieved by any novelty. The prairie dog was a miserable little animal about the size of a ferret. The only Indians I saw were degraded-looking ruffians begging at the stations. No buffaloes ever appeared, antelopes kept at a distance. The Rocky Mountains were tame, and the scenery of the Sierra Nevadas was shut out from our view by snow-shed tunnels, which added much to our irritation. Add to all this the discomfort of the sleeping-cars, where there is little privacy and much dirt, and where I was cruelly relieved of some 14*l*., and you will understand the abhorrence with which I regard the American route. San Francisco is a curious city. Some of the streets are paved with long planks of wood, which are generally in a rotten state, and your carriage, which is fitted with marvellous springs, buoyant as a balloon, has to tack about to avoid big holes. Railways are laid through the centre of the streets. Trains pull up like omnibuses at certain distances, and people jump on and off them while in motion. Altogether they show a disregard of caution quite startling to a person who in his own country towns seldom catches sight of a train without craning his neck over a high bridge parapet. Upon all this disappointment we had an utterly eventless voyage of twenty-three days, until on the very shores of Japan we encountered one of those terrible local hurricanes, the much dreaded typhoon. But our ship was so enormous that the dangerous waves passed harmlessly away. We, that is to say, I and an American lady and gentleman, with whom I got very intimate *en route*, stayed a week at Yokohama, hoping to be able to make some trips about the country, but we were foiled by the weather. However, there was so much novelty in the settlement itself, and in the great city Yedo, which we visited by rail, that the visit was very enjoyable I fell in with many old Shanghae friends, and felt quite at home. This was the *bonne bouche* of the whole trip, and we left Yokohama with pleasurable anticipations of going through the far famed inland sea. This, at any rate, came up to our expectations; but we were very near paying dearly for our whistle, for another typhoon, at the very doors of the land-locked sea, put us in great peril for some twenty-four hours. When this was safely passed, we soon found ourselves at anchor before a lovely spot called Kobé, or Hiogo. Having to be here a day and a half, we got up a picnic to a waterfall, and enjoyed the rich scenery of the tree-clad hills. In spite of all these refreshing sights, I was very low spirited until we fairly reached the beastly yellow waters of the mighty Yangtsze. Then a feeling of being near home came over me, and I got such a warm welcome on shore that *atra cura* fled rapidly.

[In November, Mr. Margary was sent to Chefoo, to take charge of that port till the consul arrived, and then to remain there as acting Chinese interpreter. He describes it in his letters as a "cold bracing place in winter." "A little house," he writes, "on the top of a small hill is at my disposal. From its windows, I overlook the town on the one hand, and the curved bay on the other, where the blue water rolls in with a delicious murmur. In the back ground high hills close in the scene, with grand effect."]

Letters to F. E. R.

The great institution of the place is a New Club, which at present comprises more amusement than instruction. The reading room is only so in name, but the theatre is used every Sunday for Presbyterian services. I am told they hold a Church of England service there once a month. The great diversion of the club is bowling. On Wednesday and Saturday nights we all meet there and bowl away till midnight.

Friday, November 28th.—I am afraid we have exhausted our fair weather. Heavy clouds are being blown down upon us from the north, and probably they will soon discharge themselves in snow. I am told in the depths of winter, the advancing tide throws up for itself a barrier of ice, which has been seen to grow several feet. . . .

There are some ten steamers, which continually run up and down from Shanghae, to Chefoo, Tientsin, and as the winter approaches, they hurry them backwards and forwards, in the hopes of getting cargoes into the river, up to the last moment, before the ice bars farther progress. Then Tientsin gets shut out, and all these steamers are laid up, with the exception of one or two, which are run up here about once a fortnight. Unfortunately, we cannot count upon their regularity, so as to be sure of catching the mails.

I have paid two official visits to the local mandarin, called the Tao-Tai, and he has returned my introductory call. I put on my uniform, and went off in a sedan chair, borne by four men in the usual style. We merely had to go about half-a-mile. This is not a walled city, but only a small town, the district city being some twenty miles off. So that after passing through the foreign settlement, and its ridiculous little streets, ambitiously named "Broadway," or "Consulate Road," etc., we had only to thread a very short distance of the usual filthy narrow lanes of a Chinese town, before we reached the magistrate's abode. The streets were full of stalls, and choked with buyers, carriers, coolies, and mules. Most of the people stooped down to stare. Some roared with laughter, some quietly said, "Oh, here are foreign officials," others "Look at the foreign devils." The next time I went, I kept my eyes on a Chinese book, and thereby elicted many a surprised remark of approval. I am in this province quite at home again. Every coolie or peasant I meet, I can converse with intelligibly. This is such a comfort, after Shanghae and the South, where a horrible patois debars one from a single word of intercourse with the natives; whereas, up here, wherever I roam, the familiar old Pekin tongue greets my ear, and the pleasure of a walk is increased fifty-fold. The country people are always nice, chatty, and agreeable. Somehow, the moment they herd together, inside walls, the demon of malice, and mischief, seems to possess them.

The Tao-Tai's house was a miserable place. I passed through three or four dirty little courtyards before reaching the hall of audience, which was, as usual, an open room, with only three sides and a mud floor. The Tao-Tai is a young man for his rank.

He is only thirty-six but looks twenty-one. He has passed the highest examinations, and is a member of the "Forest of Pencils," and as a natural consequence, I find him very stupid, and exasperatingly apathetic. He is the Chinese beau ideal of beauty. First of all, very fat, especially in face; that is a great perfection. Eyes with a good upward slant, a broad thick forehead and pericranium, and a large, heavy, sleek, rounded, placid face; the mouth very pleasing, and showing a good set of white teeth when he grins. His general contour is then well supported with thick wadded clothes. He meets you at the door, seats you with ceremony, puts bits of cake before you with his own hand, which you immediately do to him with yours, and then the conversation begins by a good stupid stare, and absurd questions about your honourable age. I stirred him up well, and planted a joke, which has served to put us on the best of terms. . . .

I am gradually getting into studious habits, and as there is so little work in the office, a very large portion of the day is at my disposal. I generally have a couple of hours over Chinese before going to office. . . . I have been negotiating to-day for a Chinese tutor. A young man was brought to me, and highly recommended for his talents and proficiency in the public examinations, and so I have arranged to try him, and we shall commence work in a few days. I shall have his services, morning and evening, for the sum of ten dollars a month, that is at the rate of about 27*l*. a year. . . . My object in getting an entirely fresh hand is to avoid the danger of learning doggerel Chinese, which those men who constantly undergo the drudgery of teaching foreigners unconsciously fall into.

Chefoo, January 25th, 1874.—The Chinese make a great deal of their New Year; a public holiday of a week takes place, and I shall probably take a run up country. . . . All shops are closed, and no business done for a fortnight. They shut themselves up with their families and friends, and have a regular round of feasting and amusement. Heaps of crackers are fired off, and hideous noises of pan-pipes, gongs, and all kinds of music escape from every house. From about this time up to the end of their year, frantic efforts are made to sell off all their available stock; cash is wanted everywhere. It is the grand settling day. Consequently purchasers find their money goes a long way. Now is the time to buy things cheap. As I went by the other day, I noticed the road lined with rustics bringing anything and everything to market, from food to firewood.

February 1st.—We have been out for about two hours, and enjoyed a ramble in an old Chinese family cemetery, which lies outside the town, about three miles off. These ancestral burying places of men of note are tended with great care. A wall surrounds the inclosure, and dark cypress trees overshadow the grave mounds. This one we have been to see to-day was first made by a distinguished provincial governor, named Wang, who died in the early part of the seventeenth century. His mound occupies the top of the oblong, and many of his descendants lie ranged in order, on each side, down towards the entrance, and, after the manner of those times, an open avenue is left up the centre, lined on each side with figures of animals cut in stone. . . . I deciphered the monumental inscriptions, setting forth what offices and attainments each one acquired. These graveyards often afford the best feature in Chinese landscapes, as in them the trees are preserved, and as a rule in them alone will anything approaching to a grove be found. The people are so poor that they cut everything down for firewood, and we see them every day scraping the ground with long bamboo rakes, to gather grass and sticks for the same purpose. . . .

I am planning a trip through the hills with a young Frenchman, and we intend to visit the gold mines, sulphur baths, and other places. The country round is full of minerals. Garnets, jasper, jade, talc, asbestos, and iron have been picked up in our vicinity, and I dare say we shall stumble upon interesting specimens in our tour. We shall be away from eight to ten days.

Chefoo, February, 1874.—The New Year brings joy to the millions of China, from one end of the empire to the other. It is the prince of holidays! I have just taken an opportunity of seeing its effects upon the country people, a short distance away from a port frequented by foreigners. For this once only in the long wearisome year comes a season of freedom from daily toil. The iron bands of laborious existence are burst with an impetuous leap, and the whole nation seems to breathe a sigh of relief, and snuff the breeze of a holiday. It is pleasant to see these beaming faces, relieved of the stupid air of pre-occupation, which usually sits on their dull features. It is refreshing to meet with spontaneous greetings, and humble unaffected curiosity, from the simple country folk. " A touch of nature" seems to work its spell, and quite a pleasant sense of arriving at a common goodwill creeps over the benevolent heart of the " foreign devil "—then " crash, crash," " bang, bang,"—on every side resound the gongs, and pyrotechnic thunders, which far more justly deserve an " infernal" epithet, and might point out the questionable kinship, but that the stranger feels that his delicate chords of sympathy are crushed in those horrid sounds. He knits his brows and walks away.

In much the same way does an inquirer feel checked on many points when he would like to learn something of the inner life of the Chinese.

Questions are unsatisfactory, for they are met by the superior classes with the lying gloss of their hollow etiquette, and by the inferior with an assumption of ignorance. Hence the most preposterous blunders are conceived and perpetuated about this people in writings of great authority. This soon becomes so evident to our countrymen residing at the ports, and who are thereby enabled to travel short distances into the interior, that not a few feel urged to draw a truer picture of the Celestial character to replace the conventional type known at home. But easy as it may seem at first, they find themselves absurdly baffled at the outset, even though they feel themselves perfectly familiar with many phases of the national character. And it cannot be wondered at, when we reflect upon the enormous size of China, and the great difficulty of the language. We wonder at a different character showing itself in no greater distance than London to York; yet here are eighteen teeming provinces, each able to swallow up the whole of Great Britain. With the exception of the missionaries, our consular officers, and a few Europeans in the employ of the Chinese Government, there is scarcely a resident who can find time to acquire the language. And the language is the only key we can use to get at their thoughts, first by reading for ourselves their books, and next by overhearing the common talk of the people in the streets, or while engaged in their daily occupations. The books throw light on manners and customs which have not the same significance when viewed by the uninitiated foreigner, and express the underlying ideas which are often too quaint for our unassisted thoughts to arrive at. Again, the Chinaman in company and the same man in private are totally different. He is always veneered in your presence. The real article must be viewed in the rough. And there is very much to reward a quiet observer, if he is quick enough to pick up the conversation around him when it is supposed that he cannot understand.

It was partly with a view to picking up knowledge in this way of the extraordinary people among whom some of us in China have to pass a large portion of our existence, that I planned a trip lately with a companion into the hilly districts of the great Shantung province in the north-east. By Chinese custom all business is suspended for a few days at the New Year, and accordingly we found ourselves free from all trammels, official or otherwise, for the space of seven days. The length of this interval is fixed by the local mandarin, and often leads to no small grumbling on the part of foreign merchants who have ships lying idle on their hands. My companion was a young Frenchman who had not yet acquired much of the language, but whose incipient knowledge of various scientific subjects made his conversation very agreeable and useful.

The mode of travelling in this mountainous province is by means of mule litters of the simplest construction. The very sight of them would send Messrs. Thrupp and Maberly, or Holland and Holland into a frantic agitation to have the treaty revised, with a special view to the introduction of their advanced improvements. Two poles with cross bars and a canopy of matting. *Voilà tout!*

"Oh, impossible," says the amiable foreign devil

with a smile—" really I can't go in that." But soon he sees his excellent "boy" spread out a most tempting mattress, which rests on his provision box and portmanteau, the whole under-girded with ropes; and he is obliged to confess what an excellent contrivance it is for the tossed and stone-covered goat track the animals cleverly thread. The muleteer always has a spare donkey to carry his own particular baggage, which includes provender for the animals; for at the inns they seem only to provide chopped straw and water. The poor donkeys had certainly the hardest work of all, for, in addition to the load of the pack-saddles, they were never free of our lazy attendants, whose ridiculous attempts to mount the heap were often a source of amusement to us.

My companion and I, rejoicing in the opportunity of free exercise, would walk for hours at a stretch, while our boys were equally energetic in sitting. Nothing but the frosty air ever drove them on to their feet. And perhaps it is not to be wondered at, when they wear such wool-wadded garments. The Chinaman's system of keeping out cold is not found in exercise or fires, but in heaping on clothes, though at night, they have a way in the north of sleeping on a sort of oven. Our boys, after all, must have got a good deal of exercise in the mere business of mounting. The pack-saddle was so high that they mostly took advantage of a mound to help them up; but as the donkey invariably "moved on" (after the ruling passion of a policeman) before his rider was half up, we were greatly entertained to see the struggles of the boy and his half frightened features as he hung like an animated clothes-bag jolting away from the pack. The drivers walk long distances without wanting to rest. The usual stage varies from forty to fifty li, or fifteen miles from halt to halt, and the regular day's journey is just one hundred li. At the inns all is in bustle at daylight. We invariably rose by candlelight. There was little inducement to linger in such a lodging. Picture it? none but the pen of the "casual" could possibly equal the task. 'Tis a "lodging for man and beast," in very truth. The pretentious gates admit the caravan into a courtyard, which is simply a stable fitted with mangers under a shed. On one side, a magnificent suite of hovels with ill-fitting, barn-like doors, which are dignified with the name of guest chambers. In one of these, on one occasion, we found it so cold that the landlord's ingenuity had to be put in requisition to doctor the door. A cheerful old man he was, that landlord, and most obliging. He soon got a large whisp of straw and stuffed it up beautifully.

Young F—— was much too dainty; he would have the torn paper window patched up with pages from his *Revue des Deux Mondes*. This idea was too much for him. He had created a curio that tickled his fancy vastly. To think of those words of wisdom figuring in such a plight! We actually ate in that room. Its ceiling was blackened with smoke, and spiders'-webs. Its walls were in mourning for mud. Hunger is however a good sauce, but really laughter is a panacea. We never felt such overpowering mirth, which culminated at last in a roar—for scarcely had we rolled ourselves up in our blankets and skins, than a suspicious noise hard by made us gradually conscious of the fact that a pig was actually eating the door. This inn may be taken as a sample of all the rest. Our mattresses were spread on the khang, or oven above mentioned, only we dispensed with the fire underneath. Of course, in every instance, the dust had to be swept off it, and sometimes the dirty old mat covering changed for a cleaner.

Settling up in the morning was an invariable cause of delay. However briskly we might prepare for a start, there was always at first this vexatious question of charges to hinder us. "Dum æs exigitur, dum mula ligatur, tota abit hora." After the second day we paid no more than a Chinaman would and got civility to boot. Firmness at first, though it nearly led to blows, had its effect in the end. The rates are really so ridiculously low, that one must feel mean to dispute them; but for the sake of the missionaries, who cannot be lavish, we stedfastly kept to the rule. A hundred copper cash per head, or about five pence, is all the charge. To meet this crushing demand, a ponderous purse, like a potato sack, has to be hauled out of the litter, and its copper contents reduced; for one of the preliminaries of travelling is to change all one's silver into strings of cash; and, as twelve hundred and sixty, just now, are equivalent to a dollar, the purse is necessarily of a size which would embarrass a pickpocket.

On the second day, we were taken to a more pretentious inn. There were really large rooms, and, to our great astonishment, a regular four-poster for a bed. Here, having an hour of daylight to spare, and being simply inundated with curious children of ages varying from five to twenty, we resolved to stroll out of the town and examine the rocks and local strata. With a rabble at our heels, we were not free to use our geological hammer until a good mile lay between, and the crowd had straggled off. But for long we heard their good-humoured shouts, and as the dusk set in we could still see a few figures perched on the walls, peering at our distant forms, and I thought how their superstitious minds must have shuddered to think what diabolical purpose could be inducing those two queer beings to wander up that uninteresting gully of shale. It was dark ere we made a detour and re-entered the town. A couple of scouts darted off to proclaim our return, but, as I thought, the majority were by this time " whipped and sent to bed," so we found the coast pretty clear. It was New Year time, and all the schools were closed, as I learned from the happy boys when I harangued them on the advantages of gaining knowledge. We were not to enjoy these comparatively comfortable quarters for nothing, and the next morning our "*caupo malignus*" calmly made a demand of 1000 cash; but finding I was perfectly able to argue the question in his own language, he was fain to beat a retreat to his office in the gate, and sullenly refuse all assistance to lift our litters on to the mules.

This might be an excellent plan with a patient Chinese traveller wadded in wool, but a European is unaccountably odd, and our amiable host found we were quite able to do the work for ourselves. As the man still refused a fair offer, I politely asked him his name, and wrote it down. Then, amidst a murmur of "Ai-yahs" from the crowd, I proceeded to copy the Chinese name of the inn. This made a grand impression, and the landlord evidently began to feel "sorry he spoke." Then, with an oratorical appeal to the sense of justice of our audience, we presented our friend with just half his demand, and told him he would probably suffer for his incivility. It appeared to be a sort of market day, and the street was full of rustics, unburdening their donkeys of large bundles of fuel and vegetables. Fearing interruption, we brought up the rear of our procession on foot, but had not proceeded far before a cabbage stump was hurled at my companion. This was the only piece of active insult we met with in the whole of our trip. In any European town it would have lighted up the spirit of mischief at once, and the luckless stranger would have found an uncomfortable reception. But how different here! I mention the incident to show what harmless people the Chinese are in themselves. Turning sharply round, I immediately demanded, "Who did that?" Those standing nearest, of course, at once pointed out some one more remote. I then made a short speech, taunting them with a breach of their boasted "Li" (good manners) and asked them if we were to note that as an example of Chinese "Li." Not a word was said, and we proceeded without the slightest attempt at a repetition of the insult. They are simply a reasonable people, and can be talked into good humour very easily. The question of whether they are a cowardly people is entangled with contradictions. Their soldiers have fought well both in the north and south against European forces in isolated instances, and a whole mob in Canton has been known to gut the governor's residence, regardless of a terrible storm of shot and shell from our ships; while they always submit to surgical operations with a steadiness of nerve that few foreigners could boast of. And yet one or two Europeans may thrash a whole crowd, and their sailors are useless in a storm. The real clue to a Chinaman's action is his settled principle of non-intervention. To move in any matter, there must be some strong circumstance affecting him personally to urge him. He will stand by and stare at a Chinaman killing a foreigner with exactly the same indifference as at a foreigner beating a Chinaman.

Their very laws and customs prevent anything approaching to a disinterested act of any kind. If a man fell down fainting in the streets, and a bystander gave him water, he would render himself liable to all sorts of expenses for maintaining, curing, and perhaps burying the sick stranger. And if a wealthy man starts an enterprise he will surely be mulcted by the mandarins. "Never do a thing you can help, and appear to be poorer than you are," is the safest course for a Celestial. It is very much the fashion to talk of China as if it were a sort of human bee-hive, or ant-heap, overburdened with struggling humanity, but I have never yet been overpowered with a sense of this multiplicity. The walls of Pekin, and indeed of every city, embrace as much waste land and open space as ground which is fully occupied, and the open country is but sparsely dotted with villages. And since 1861, the unhappy central provinces which were devastated by the rebels, have remained a wilderness, where now, in parts, the foreigner can roam at will and bag his game by thousands. Pheasants, deer, and wild pigs, multiply without hindrance. No wealthy sportsman at home can rival the natural preserves which a Shanghae resident freely commands. Of course the whole population of China makes up a big figure; but the European mind, with its contracted notions of territory, is not prepared to conceive the vastness of the country which finds room to disperse this huge census. Thus in our trip we were frequently prone to remark what long distances we traversed without meeting with habitations. Every inch of country, however, was cultivated, and generally denuded, not only of wood, but of grass, shrubs, or anything capable of serving as fuel. The people go forth and scrape everything they can find into bundles for sale, to that end. We looked in vain for vegetables or live-stock, in most instances, among the occasional groups which passed us bound to some market. It was always fuel, and sometimes the donkeys were hidden by their loads. These rustics would always hail us pleasantly with the query :—" Where is it you are going to, elder-born ?" " Oh, I'm taking a stroll," I would answer. " A stroll!" they would say in surprise, and move on, wondering what the foreign devil could mean.

For two days and a half we trudged on through a valley and met with nothing to interest us, not even a variety of stratification. All was of quartz. We got sick of quartz, and longed for a change to granite, or porphyry, or gneiss, or anything. But all of these came to reward us in time, and once we rose in a short distance from a depression of igneous rocks to a plateau of blue lias.

At length we passed over into the southern watershed, leaving behind us a fine series of rugged peaks standing in grand bold outline against the clear sky. These are called the Saw-teeth Mountains. They are known to contain gold. The country began to look more picturesque, and before long a towering object on the plain served to quicken our expectations. It looked, as we approached, the very beau ideal of a feudal stronghold perched on a commanding rock, and the motion of the swaying litter was fast inducing a dreamy romance about some fine old baron up there, who dealt splendid misery all round. And so it was, forsooth! Only the baron was lazy old Buddha, and the misery he shed was moral, and social. The temple was beautifully placed on a solitary rock of green sandstone, of a clear light colour when chipped, which was most pleasing to the eye. We had to climb up some two hundred feet to the summit. Two miserable individuals occupied a hovel at the top, and the temple they looked after was full of hideous, painted idols. Buddhism in China is a dead, morbid superstition. The faith exists; but all zeal or reverence in the worship is entirely wanting. In India, fanaticism guards the sacred idol from profane touch, but in China, you may examine the figure, while the worshipper is on his knees before it; you may point to its grotesque features with your stick, and joke on their expression, and he will join you in the laugh before he has even finished his kow tows. It was a dirty place up there, and sadly in want of repair, like everything Chinese; but a small bridge thrown over a deep cleft at the top, and a very steep flight of steps, leading from it up to the topmost shrine, gave the place an interesting and picturesque appearance. The two incumbents were very civil, and communicative, and after showing a decided liking for my cigarettes, obliged us by pointing out a short cut down, by which we could descend and catch up our litters, which were by this time quite out of sight. We looked back with admiration at this commanding site, and dubbed it " Belle Vue " Temple, which, indeed, is a literal translation of the Chinese name, written over the temple door, and justly commemorates its magnificent view.

We had pushed on this day without a halt for tiffin, as the whole stage was shorter than usual, and we hoped to save time for rambling in the vicinity of a walled city of much interest which we were approaching. It was the last day of the Chinese year (falling this time on our 16th of February), and we were soon made uncomfortably aware of the great importance of the day. Walled towns are built square, with a gate in the centre of each side, facing the four quarters of the compass. Travellers put up at the inns in the suburbs, in order not to be trammelled in their early movements by having to wait for the opening of the city gates. So, we too, sought a like advantage, but moved from one quarter to another in vain. The streets were crowded, and people were bustling about to buy last requisites for several days of idle barricade. A crowd stood round us as we waited at the inn door, and silently stared with evident wonder at our travelling at such a time. Indeed, I was more than once asked *en route*, in a tone of compassion, " whether we too had not a New Year to keep." Strange to say, our boys began to get angry at their want of success in trying to induce the innkeepers to take us in. They were evidently getting hungry, and the day was waning without a prospect of finding shelter. Our spirits, on the contrary, began to rise. We could not help laughing at our plight. I joked with the bystanders, and they joined in the laugh. We were evidently in a fix. I told the muleteers if they did not find us quarters, we should make them push on all night. Some one in the crowd then suggested we might find quarters at an inn within the walls, and accordingly this last hope was reluctantly adopted, but proved like the others a will-o'-the-wisp. Matters began to look serious, and as we were no great distance from the place where last December a mob nearly roasted a missionary, I thought it possible that this determined opposition was a result of hostility, and immediately determined to visit the magistrate, whose yamen happily proved to be close by. Proceeding thither on foot, with an attendant rabble, of course, we waited at the door, while my servant went in with cards and passport, to demand an interview. The rabble was very friendly, and showed a great admiration for the cloth of which my large overcoat was made. We chatted and joked in the most amicable manner, until at length a messenger returned to apologize for the mandarin's inability to see us as he was with his barber!—but that, as all we required was a lodging, he would immediately send a constable to procure one for us. He kept his word, and three men accompanied us to the inn, where we waited outside, while a stormy altercation raged within. The innkeeper appeared to be independent enough to oppose the dangerous myrmidons of the law, and the fight was long and loud; overhearing their words, I soon became aware that there was no hostility, but that we were actually inconveniencing the man very seriously by our presence on this great night of the year. So, taking advantage of a lull, I stepped in, and politely told the man that what the constable said was quite true, and that we were really intending to depart early, and that we should spare him all the trouble in our power. Immediately the man's face changed, like sunshine after rain, and he acquiesced at once. I was greatly struck by the effect a few polite words had on this man, and the confidence he at once gathered, from the fact of having to deal with a quiet foreigner who spoke his own language. Being New Year time, all the employées of the inn were gone for their holiday, and not a scrap of provisions remained for man or beast. But as we had our own food with us, in those paragons of invention, the hermetically sealed tins, this dearth could affect us in no way whatever. Having wasted so much time we could only stroll through the town till dusk, and indeed were well repaid for our pains. I should not omit to mention here a very characteristic phase of Chinese cupidity. As soon as we were ensconced in our miserable quarters, the inevitable cumshaw was demanded, and our three stalwart protectors responded to the profuse liberality of the foreign devil by actually kneeling before him, though the sum only amounted to 500 cash, or say 2s. A special messenger arrived shortly after from the mandarin with his cards, to return our visit and kind inquiries. We begged him to take no more trouble about us, as we had what we wanted, thanks to his aid, and that an early start precluded the possibility of our calling again to thank him. The accident which thus brought us within the walls of "Lai Yang" to spend a night, and that the great night of the year, in the very midst of a city population which was not often favoured by a sight of foreigners, was after all a fortunate occurrence for us. For taking advantage of a couple of hours of daylight, we strolled through the streets, which here presented a richer appearance than most district cities can boast of, and at the same time we gained some experience of the temper of a walled population, which, as a rule, one prefers to avoid altogether. Most of the houses were by this time closed, and the streets looked as dismal as an English town on Sunday; but a group of men, standing under an evergreen porch (one of many put up at New Year by way of decoration), gave us an opportunity of conversing, by their cheerful and civil greetings. They were particularly anxious to understand how many days there were in our year, and why our New Year did not coincide with theirs. An extremely pleasant conversation ensued, with the utmost cordiality on both sides, and a thorough appreciation of my cigarettes. The streets were spanned at close intervals with commemorative arches of stone—some recent, spic and span, some old and almost past identification. A fine handsome man who accompanied us stated there were seventy-two of them, and indeed we could easily have guessed there were more. It was quite an epidemic of arches. Every street had broken out with the complaint, and as each one chronicled a virtuous act, we were fain to believe Lai Yang must have reached a point of enviable moral excellence. Our very civil cicerone walked some distance with us, and politely pointed out the chief public places. There was certainly little to admire in them. A large inclosure inside a temple, where our friend told us fairs were held, looked bare and dismal enough. A group of idlers strolled in with us, and indulged themselves with a good stare, passing at the same time several compliments on our knowledge of their language. It is often amusing to hear the remarks of bystanders upon ourselves. They are usually struck with the fact of a foreign devil speaking their own tongue, and commonly exclaim, "Why he can speak our language! What a capital joke; just hear him, he speaks quite well!"

We returned to our inn, and ate a scratch sort of meal, and got into our comfortless couches, shuddering with dread for crawling demons. Up and ready before daylight, not to lose time, we came upon a domestic scene which was worth witnessing. It was New Year's Day (February 17th, 1874), and the first great duty of every householder was going forward. Master and man were busily engaged in the worship and propitiation of their household gods. I stepped across the yard and looked on. Daylight had not yet illumined the scene, and the weird, fitful glimmer of a few sorry candles threw a mystic influence over the rites, which no doubt influenced their superstitious minds. Both were dressed in the same uniform. I must call it so, for the same form of dress marks an office or a ceremony from top to bottom of the social scale; rank being distinguishable by decorations or quality of clothes. The ceremony consisted in lighting some joss-sticks, and kneeling down before them, frequent kow-tows and posturing. A table beside them was neatly laid out, with a cold banquet, and plates and chopsticks were placed round in order for the spirits to sit, and enjoy. While this silent feast proceeded, our host and his man stood by, like reverend waiters, to attend to the wants of their invisible guests. One almost expected something to appear, so cabalistic did the whole scene look. Having given the spirits a reasonable time to devour these solids, our friends proceeded to fire a *feu de joie*, with fearfully noisy crackers, outside the front door, which must have frightened the spirits, if they had any ears. I pitied the poor ghosts hovering over such, to them, indigestible food, and could imagine their pitiable looks and distressing chorus of, " Oh that this too, too solid flesh would melt,"— in the Chinese version, of course. Every house in China was at that moment doing the same, and the reverberation of crackers here, there, and everywhere, made such an infernal din that the foreign devils belied their origin by the speediest possible exit. Such being the state of affairs, we could not but feel rather adrift where to look for our next lodging. New Year was not the time to travel in China, evidently, and no sympathy could be kindled in the face of such innovation. Reluctantly driven thus to change our plans, there was nothing for it but to return by a different route. The direction was here decided for us by the cheerful muleteer, who promised a *certain* lodging at a particular inn, and though it was a long day's journey, we thoroughly enjoyed the trudge, and were rewarded in the evening by putting up at the hostelry of a very remarkable man. Several villages we passed through were decked out in holiday gala—children freed from school gambolled before their laughing parents, and collected to gaze as we passed. I exchanged kind words and most civil greetings everywhere. It was a pleasure to pass through the village groups. Smiles and natural affability were sure to meet us always. Whatever vices these people have, or however depreciatingly this surface civility may be attributed to fear, or any other ignoble cause, still, it is a fact, that a foreign traveller gains pleasure and comfort from its existence, and that is more than he might find in fifty villages in his own land.

The mid-day halt at a little isolated village on the crest of a hill, gave us a picture of the simplest rustic life, such as delights my memory to dwell upon. There may have been two hundred inhabitants in all, counting women and children, and probably none of them had ever moved out of that dreary little circle. They lived twenty miles from anywhere, and that was a poor place. The excitement produced by the arrival of two such superior beings from the outside world was evidently something transcendent. Imagine what a blow it would be to our enlightened intellects, bursting with modern knowledge, to have a sudden interview with the twenty-second century, *vide* " The Coming Race " for example. However, I hope we should put pithier questions to our mortifying guests than these poor fossils had for us. One of them, pointing with pride to a miserable willow, asked if we had anything like *that* in our country, and for the matter of that, indeed, we may have been botanically incompetent to answer. While preparing for our lunch in the best room of the inn, which, by the way, was no better than a dirty old barn, we had to undergo a close inspection from the whole village. Old and young all crowded into the room, and stood and stared, and wanted to touch everything. The operation of washing our heads and faces with sponge and soap seemed to delight them immensely, as being a capital idea. And on my proceeding to take my nails out of mourning with a penknife, a burst of surprise and laughter broke out. The next thing was to get rid of our very dirty and unsavoury guests, but repeated, mild requests proved quite useless: so addressing two or three of the elders with feigned respect, we begged them to teach their juniors better manners, and make them withdraw, while we ate. The stratagem was successful. Quite taken by our complimentary politeness, they immediately cleared out their neighbours, and left us alone for a time. Such a novel sight as two foreign devils feeding after their own fashion was however too good to be lost, and we were soon conscious of innumerable perforations being neatly executed in the paper windows, and of staring eyeballs framed in every hole. Their curiosity was soon better satisfied by our giving away the pickings, and distributing cigarettes and empty bottles. We chatted and joked in the most cheerful manner, and, indeed, received quite an ovation on leaving. Numbers of willing hands assisted in lifting the litters on the mules, and while passing down the street, we gave an opportunity to the smiling womenkind, who had been peeping from every door, with their usual curiosity, to have a good view of us. I should like to visit that village again. It was extremely pleasant; we looked back at its feeble wall inclosure, as we wound down the valley, and wondered when the light of civilisation

F

would break it down, and set this shut-up people free.

It was dark ere we reached our resting-place, outside the walls of another little city called Chi-hsia Hsien. The latter words being attached to districts of similar size, viz., the third order, we knew at once that Chi-hsia was as large as Lai Yang, but it was very evident from its dilapidated condition that it was neither so rich, nor important. A large summer torrent must have annually swept round two sides of the city, judging from its wide dry bed, full of rounded pebbles, and a bold steep bank, on one side, of waterworn porphyry.

Arrived at the inn door, our doubts of the muleteer's ability to find us a lodging received some strength from the futile result of a great deal of knocking. Tired and hungry, we felt impatient to get in somewhere, and the unpleasant looks of the few loiterers in the street did not favour a prospect of easy admission to any house. The muleteer however disappeared at the back of the premises, and very shortly after the door flew wide, to our intense relief, and a smiling, civil host invited us in. The best room appeared to be occupied by a corn factor, judging by his samples of grain. But our energetic host soon bundled him out, most unceremoniously, and had the mud floor and brick "khang" well swept to humour our whimsical objections to dirt. Our servants speedily spread the mattresses and blankets on the "khang," and we threw ourselves down upon them with a book to while away the impatient interval till preparations for dinner were completed. The khangs are always fitted with a little square table, on dwarfish legs, and thus, with one of these between us, we sat and regaled ourselves—a really comfortable position. I recommend it to invalids and sybarites. They can fill the pauses by reclining back on the couch. Just as we were thoroughly appeased, and began to regale ourselves with a glass of wine and a smoke, in that calm frame of mind which is sure to follow a bivouac under difficulties, our host knocked at the door, and cheerfully sat down to join us. This was such an astonishing piece of affability for a Chinaman that we roused every effort to be agreeable, and soon plunged into a long conversation. He alluded to the existing relations between foreigners and his countrymen, and expressed his conviction that they would be the best of friends, if the natives only knew them better. He, himself, had been much with Europeans, and took every opportunity of talking to them; but the country people had only the means of judging from individuals who passed through the villages of the nature of foreigners. Unfortunately, a hasty man had produced a bad impression in one district by striking a native. The result of which was an obstinate determination to give the cold shoulder to any future visitant of his hated race.

This particular place contained a remarkable sulphur spring, and we were bound thither ourselves, so that his information was not calculated to increase our anticipations of pleasure from the next day's trip. Our host's vigorous and enlightened remarks led me to suspect that he was a Christian, which he immediately acknowledged. He had been round with the missionaries, and taken an active part in preaching. In contrast to his allusion to the pugnacious foreigner, I discussed with him the late outrage at Chi-Ini, where the populace set upon the harmless missionary, and burnt out his house. He deplored the circumstance, and explained it by a local irritation, not against the missionary, but a sect which had long existed among them, and which had apparently, to them, sought the missionary's protection against persecution. It is a curious discovery, which the evangelists made when they reached that district, that a sect has existed there for ages, with a peculiar form of faith and worship, untainted with idolatry, and to all appearances based on a Christian origin. They go by the name of the "Undefined Persuasion," reminding one strongly of the Athenians when St. Paul found them worshipping an unknown god. Our host, as I said, was a remarkable man, and the very energy with which he did everything, even to carrying out his own brisk orders in the yard, where he would rebuke the sluggishness of his man in tethering a mule, or lifting a litter, by showing them how, made me much interested in him, and on my return to our port I learned his history from a missionary who knew him well. In the time of the rebellion, when the mandarins and their feeble troops were repulsed and confined to their walls, this innkeeper, Lin, had filled the whole country side with his fame. He raised volunteers from among the rustics, and led them to victory, until, after things were quiet again and the valiant mandarins began to breathe afresh, he was rewarded by arrest and imprisonment! Although they owed their safety to this over-zealous commoner, yet, as his success would prove but too fatal a comment on their own pusillanimity, they wrested his loyalty into an act of rebellion, under a law which forbids such independent action as his. Poor Lin went near to lose his head, but the rustics loved their hero, and came to his timely rescue. The mandarins then released him, after a series of threats, upon a promise, the only one they could extort from the brave fellow, that he would forgive them, and hold his tongue about the whole affair. Such a man must have a grand influence in furthering the spread of Christianity and enlightenment among his fellow provincials, who are, like most rustic populations in China, well disposed, good hearted, hospitable people, but so superstitious, as to be a ready-made combustible for the use of political schemers, and the arrogant literati class, whose hatred of foreigners is at the bottom of every *émeute*, and who know so well how to launch a mob with a specious placard. Lin has two daughters, whom he takes great pains to educate, both in Chinese literature, and in the knowledge of the Bible, and is generally bringing them up in a careful training which no true Chinaman dreams of ever throwing away on so insignificant a thing as a girl. Some weeks after my visit I renewed this man's acquaintance, when he came to call upon me at my house, and I was much struck with his enthusiastic admiration of the view from my verandah, which he said was a sight which few of his countrymen knew how to appreciate.

Letters to F. E. R.

Chefoo, March 26th.—I have just been looking at a wonderful stone, which lies half way down the cliff, poised on a mere point of rock. Some convulsion severed it from the upright strata and carved it into a fanciful resemblance of a junk, which has procured for it the name of "ship stone" among the Chinese. It is a spot much visited by the literati, and various inscriptions adorn the huge stone. Unlike the hideous scrawls of Tom, Dick, and Harry, Chinese characters look so well in themselves, that they invite praise rather than execration for the nameless tourist who put his mark there. Four magnificent characters, deep cut and bearing date some one hundred and twenty years back, proclaim it a "Freak of Nature," while in small, modest type at the side the name and birthplace of the man who composed and wrote the phrase are commemorated. On another portion an impromptu verse hits off a few epigrammatic ideas on the "stone ship poised in mid air, fearless of storms and winds, outrivalling man's handiwork."

The Chinese pride themselves most on writing characters prettily, and composing pithy stanzas. I have seen a couple of old idiots smacking their lips, and clicking their simple tongues, over a pair of slips hung up like pictures, and bearing only four or five characters written by some swell or scholar. . . .

They have started a series of *soirées*, for the benefit of the Temperance Society, at which various people give readings. They have booked me for something next time. The plan of the society is certainly good. A room is provided with papers and periodicals for loafers and seamen of the better class to spend their time in profitably, instead of getting intoxicated for want of somewhere to go to and something to do. . . .

People are apt to scoff at modern missionaries with their comforts of house and home, but I have an opportunity here of seeing that they really do a vast deal of work. If they do not succeed in making many real converts, they certainly diffuse a great deal of knowledge. Their little schools are full of children, and their chapels crowded with devout worshippers. I hope to be able to form a better opinion on the missionary question here than people are able to do at other places. I have made the acquaintance of some of those in this neighbourhood, who are very charming men, of great culture, education, and sociability. One of them gave up a popular pulpit to come out, and study the Chinese philosophically; he is a man of great reading and a very pleasant companion. They are constantly away in the interior, but they hark back now and then to head-quarters at Tung Shing. There they have a grand mansion, over which Mrs. W—— presides.

The other day, Mr. W—— took his wife into the interior, as far as the capital, and to Confucius' tomb, to see how the people would take the intrusion, and the result proved most gratifying, as everywhere they received the utmost politeness, and met with no molestation. Mr. L—— is a most entertaining man. He has had a number of adventures, which prove him to be a man of courage and determination, and he tells his stories with such humour that we were in roars of laughter all last evening when I was dining with him at the B——'s.

An account of some Chinese troops that he met on the war path was true to absurdity, and illustrates the rottenness of their system.

They were going along at the rate of about a mile and a half an hour, to march to some place one hundred miles off, in order to put down a rising which had taken place months before!

Their direction moreover was due east, while the enemy lay far to the west. He told us he was travelling in Mantchooria once, when the whole country was infested with brigands, and how the robbers could find nothing in his effects but copies of the Bible, which he begged them to take, promising that it would teach them a thing or two, how it condemned all crimes, robbery in particular, and how he puzzled them and then preached to them. We spent a very pleasant evening, sitting round the fire, discussing, besides these adventures, books and the Chinese language.

Often and often, when my high spirits make me prominent among my companions, in fun, frolic, or adventure, I deeply upbraid myself for levity, and feel the danger I incur of encouraging some bad propensity in others, although my innermost heart may be free from any wicked desire. I am often in peril of doing or saying things which may be a stumbling-block to others and a scourge of remorse to myself; but I am too devotedly attached to the love-diffusing precepts of our Saviour to be an ascetic, and so lose the chance of doing real good to anybody in need of it, by withdrawing altogether from general society.

Mr. Margary returned to Shanghae early in 1874. The following letters are dated from that port.

Shanghae, April 1874.— You must not take a sailor's view of Shanghae for *anything*, for such time as they spend in such places as this must be wearisome to the last degree. There being no public institutions for the benefit of strangers, they must pass their time in wretched solitude on board their ships, knowing nobody, seeing nothing, and working in the sun. But, for a resident, it is generally found to be a very delightful place. We have all the best improvements of civilisation, good wide roads, handsome houses, gas-lamps, policemen, a fine theatre, cricket-ground, race-course, racket-court, drives and rides, a large man-of-war in harbour, heaps of shipping, a little volunteer army, an excellent philharmonic society, an Asiatic society, with lectures, a club, a library, a magnificent church, a perfect jail, rates and taxes, fire brigades, police-court, judge, jury, mosquitoes, and dinner-parties. And if all that does not make Shanghae deserve its name of a model settlement, we can still point to docks, river steamers on the American palatial type (a mountain of glass), brigades, bands, telegraph, post-offices, and even the little red post-cart, carriages for hire, and gin-rick-a-shas, which some individual has managed to introduce from Japan. Six of us rattled down in these funny little vehicles, along the bund to the theatre, last night.

Shanghae, May 5th, 1874.—I have to relate a wonderful piece of excitement through which we have passed, and which will, no doubt, have been flashed home by the wires as a startling piece of intelligence. The French have had a scrimmage with the Chinese— a purely local dispute. With their usual pride, they reserved the boundaries of their own concession district distinct from that of the English and other nations; and we have known, for some time, that they were engaged in a dispute with a native guild of Ningpo merchants about a road which interfered with their graveyards, and that the dispute had led to a demonstration of the members of the guild. On Sunday afternoon, while walking in the recreation gardens, we were startled by the alarm of the fire-bell, and in a few minutes, as usual, our prompt firemen turned out with their engines, but, to our surprise, were ordered back very quickly, and disbanded. We then learned that a fight was going on in the French settlement.

I betook myself to the spot with all alacrity. I found the French police at their magnificent municipal hall, fuming and fretting with bayonets fixed, and, on inquiry, learned that they had had a scrimmage with the mob, and had been forced to retire after firing and killing a Chinaman. The mob, they said, had attacked and gutted a foreign house, so I immediately went to see the fun. I found that our excellent English police had quietly effected, unarmed, what the hated Frenchmen could not do with shot and bayonet. They were in possession of the house, and quietly removing all the saveable furniture. I mounted the stairs of the gutted house, and stood on a balcony, looking down on a marvellous scene. Inspector —— stood there giving his orders, and the mandarin stood by him. Below us, on an open green, were the upturned faces of from two to three thousand rioters, and in their midst the body of the victim to French precipitancy. "They mean mischief to-night," quoth Inspector ——. I spoke to Chih Hsien, the mandarin, and remarked that, as he had arrived with a few soldiers, I presumed his presence would prevent any further outbreak, but he replied that he was going to call on the French consul first, of course, to "strāng leāng," which, being interpreted, means to "waste time in consulting." Thinking there would be little more to do, I returned home to dinner at our settlement a mile away. But we had not begun before a big lurid glare in the south set all the fire-bells and gongs going like mad, and everyone rushed out to do his duty, after a hasty meal, the boys muddling the dinner most frightfully. Hastening over to the French side, I met several foreigners returning; each one had some absurd tale about the danger of crossing the creek which divides our settlement from the French. By this time an order had been sent out to call in the volunteers, and they were then forming at head-quarters, in my rear, and most of the community were there, so that as I approached the scene of action, I met scarcely half-a-dozen Europeans. I went up right through the crowd, with three other men, and saw the whole fire. The rioters had set a large block ablaze; the house where I had stood that afternoon was a perfect ruin. The mob had been dispelled somewhere, and, at each corner, stood an excited band of Frenchmen with all sorts of weapons. Passing them, we went beyond, to where we found the crowd, some of whom were breaking a lamp. I stepped up to them and told them it was dangerous to meddle with gas. They laughed at me but did not attempt to assault us. Just then, we saw the French deliberately fire into the mob down a cross street; we were indignant; but, as the proximity was getting a little too hot, we made ourselves scarce. We then went back to our settlement, and found three or four hundred volunteers falling in, the most exaggerated reports of an attack, and I don't know what not! I told them I had just been in the very thick of the mob, and walked all round the spot, unharmed. Meanwhile the consul, who was only waiting for a request from the French for aid, and got it, marched down the volunteers, and restored order in no time. Next day all was quiet. For fear, however, of a repetition of the incendiarism at night, it was agreed that a signal of four guns from the man-of-war should call out the volunteers; and the private signal to the ship was to be the hoisting of two lanterns at the French Consulate. Well, about 9.30 P.M. I was in the theatre looking on at a dress rehearsal of a performance which, by the way, takes place to-night. All of a sudden we were hushed by a gun. The scene was grand. Imagine the excitement; the actors pause, another gun! Blood tingles! In eager discussion, whether it might not be the American mail after all, we are hushed by a third gun. A listening attitude, flashing eyes, and then a simultaneous shout of "Four!" and pell-mell, out we tore, dresses, wigs, and properties flung to the winds; the poor female characters fearfully entangled in skirts and pins, and clawing off their clothes. In less than twenty minutes some four or five hundred men were in line, all equipped in uniform and properly armed. I never saw such magnificent promptitude; a little army raised in twenty minutes, or less. I felt proud, and eager for the fray, but, would you believe it, all this grand excitement, all this life-stirring ardour, was the result of a miserable false alarm! This afternoon, a meeting of the foreign consuls with one of the highest mandarins of the province took place at the consulate, and I interpreted for them. We talked over the riot, and insisted on a proclamation. The Chinese authorities have all thanked us for assisting them to restore order.

The mandarin proved to be a very sensible, jolly fellow; one of the best we have ever had to do with here, and all went as smooth as oil. It is most difficult work to interpret concisely the ideas of another person, when they are put in verbose language. . . . We sat round in a semicircle, as usual, and champagne, tea, and biscuits were handed round. When an interview takes place at the mandarin's "yamen" (or office), we follow their custom, and sit in a rectangular arrangement. The two chiefs of each side occupy a divan with cushions, and their respective staffs range themselves in very square chairs, at right angles to the great men, in due order of precedence, their proximity to the august chiefs diminishing with their nothingness. A square table fits in between each set of two chairs, whereon tea and refreshments are served. . . .

I had nearly forgotten to tell you that I dined *à la Chinois*, on the night of the alarm, with a mandarin who sits in the mixed court of this settlement. He gave a capital spread, and invited every one of us from the consulate, but only three of us went.

May 9th, 1874.—I am going on a little pleasure trip on Monday. We shall run down to a port called Ningpo, close by, and go up the creeks in the consular house-boats all among the lovely hills. . . .

Ningpo, Tuesday, May 12*th*.— It is just a night's trip down here. We went on board yesterday at 4 P.M., and dined at six, as we went up the mighty Yangtsze, and turned in, to wake up at the mouth of this lovely part of the world. . . .

Shanghae, May 21*st*.—We had two boats of the class called house-boats. The ladies occupied one, and the gentlemen the other. These boats are cleverly fitted up with two berths, and a small space for ablutions; and all this is separated by a door from the front compartment, which is arranged for eating purposes. The boatmen filled the rear, where they would pack themselves like herrings in a barrel, with marvellous discomfort. Our programme was to move from place to place during the night, and ramble out among the hills and valleys during the day. We first visited a famous monastery, perched up in a wild mountain, covered with large trees and ferns, azaleas blooming in dazzling profusion. The monks assembled in their great hall, and chanted a weird service through, in a quick monotone. They were all dressed in yellow, like the Lamas of Thibet. Some were very earnest and devotional; others chatted and laughed freely with us, while on their knees, and seemed highly delighted at my reading off some characters which one pointed to in his missal, by way of examining me. We lounged about and sat at the bottom of a gorge, in the middle of a running brook, on some big stones. The road itself to this place was very picturesque. A long avenue filled one part; we had to go seven miles from the boats, and the ladies were carried in mountain-chairs. At one point, we were at the summit of a peak, from which the river flowed down on each side, with a fearful declivity. The Chinese have no simple locks, and, in passing from the river into the canals, the boats are bodily pulled over an embankment, and slid down the other side. It is a curious process. I recollect very well the first time I passed over one was in the dead of night, and I was waked up to a consciousness of standing on my head; my legs appeared to be playing a practical joke on me while I slept; but, being utterly bewildered, it took me some time to find out what on earth was happening to the boat. After visiting this lovely spot, we spent a long wet day in miserable progress to another favourite resort, and, when we arrived there, the weather held up beautifully, permitting us to make daily excursions from our boat for four days. We visited several lovely gorges, and each evening managed to come floating down the rapids in the cool sunset, for several miles, until we reached our boat and enjoyed a good dinner. The night, I must say, I looked upon with horror, for the dreadful mosquitoes never let me close my eyes. . . . There was one particular spot which is perfectly enchanting. After ascending a narrowing gorge for two hours, almost hidden in fragrant verdure and water leaping down alongside, we reached a heavenly spot. A most beautiful wavy, sloping waterfall dropped into a glorious deep pool of clear cool water fringed by a lip of smooth rock, made to sit upon.

Shanghae, June 7th.—I went, yesterday, with our consul, to pay a visit to a large Chinese theatre, where a very clever European conjuror is giving a series of performances. Professor Van Eyk (or a name somewhat similar to that) came here some weeks ago, and amused large audiences in our own theatre. I went and enjoyed his legerdemain very much. He was then offered about 5000 dollars by the proprietor of the large native theatre we have in the settlement, to give about thirty performances; and our object in going was to watch the effect of his tricks upon a Chinese "house," and we were well repaid, and immensely amused by the sight. The proprietor was most civil, and, recognising our consul, at once conducted us with every mark of respect through the seated multitude, and gave us excellent seats in a front gallery, such as would correspond to the position of dress-circle at home; nor would he receive any payment from us. There were two prices, all the best seats being a dollar, and the next, half a dollar. These being very high prices for a Chinese audience, the company before us was very select. I was pleased to see so many well-dressed, well-behaved, and, in many instances, elderly and aged gentlemen patronising the foreign conjuror. The house was crowded, and being arranged in regular rows of seats, I should say there were not far short of a thousand present. Ordinarily at their own theatrical performances little square tables are dotted about the hall, whereon tea is served, and the playgoers sit at these much as English rustics at pleasure gardens. The price is very low, and the poorest coolies flock in to while away the time with their tea and pipes while listening to the horrid din of their characteristic orchestra and the falsetto screeching of their boy songstresses. I have been sometimes to these performances. I dare say you have heard how they go on for hours. Sometimes, in a village, where periodical visits are paid by strolling players, the performance is literally carried on for two or three days and nights. As soon as one play is done, another commences without delay; no scenery or preparation being required, except the actors' dressing. The orchestra of gongs and horrid discordant lutes sits on the stage behind the actors, and attendants run in and out with tea to refresh the actors themselves. It is rather amusing to see the way they take it. An apology for an observance of the proprieties of the stage is attempted by the actor holding up his arm on the side next the audience and imbibing his tea under cover of his hanging sleeve. But the act, though covered, is perfectly patent to all; it makes one laugh. In the present instance, as I said, the price being heavy, we had no coolies in the house, but row upon row of well-to-do Chinamen in clean white silk robes. Their pig-tails presented rather a comical view, shown up, as they were, by the white ground. Chinese never take their women kind to theatres, and I dare say it astonished them to see a couple of foreign women walk in and take their seats among the rest. We recognised them as members of our very limited bourgeoiserie. . . .

We immediately entered into conversation with the men about us. My immediate neighbour was a Tientsin man, and a bit of a philosopher. He gave me his views on the comparison of foreigners with his own countrymen. He was very melancholy over the poverty of his nation. I pointed below, and said, " Just look at that crowd of moneyed men." He shook his head, and said, " They have not much, and if a man has a fortune," added he, " how soon it gets dissipated by the multiplication of relations." I was pleased to get some frank, original ideas from a native. It is very true that Chinese families do not separate. The daughters alone go out of the house. All the sons, with their additional families, continue to live under the paternal roof. Well, the professor was a great success. His pantomimic explanations were intensely amusing to us, and more so his occasional utterances, gibberish incantations, and, above all, his polite appeals to "Ladies and Gentlemen." The spectators showed great appreciation, and often clapped their hands, which is a species of applause quite new to Chinese, but one which they appear to be learning from us and taking kindly to.

June 15*th*.—I have often mentioned the Recreation Grounds, but never described them sufficiently. Between our beautiful grounds* and the river on the other side of the bund road, which separates it from us, is a plot of land which was once a muddy bank of the river, but which the energy and public spirit of the community converted into lawns and flowerbeds, which are now kept up to a high state of perfection, and numbers take advantage of its open position to sit out there on the hot summer nights. An amateur band will soon resume their long-established custom of playing there once a week. All the community stroll about, or sit out on their own, or public chairs, during the performance; and, in the dim glimmer of gas-light, one finds a great deal of amusement watching one's neighbours, and finding out those one knows.

* The gardens of the consulate.

June 30*th*.—I have just returned from a very pleasant evening spent on the water. It was hot, and we quite enjoyed the cool breeze of the river fanning us as we dined; and afterwards we were charmed by the music of our Wednesday band, which came floating over the water to us as we lay anchored close by. Many boats were round us, and we could see the promenade kept up on shore. The musicians played very well. Their winding-up galop made us long for more space to dance on our little deck.

July 3*rd*.—The night before last there was a night parade of the volunteers at 9 P.M. I turned out with my old corps, called the "Mihiloongs," in whose ranks I have not stood for three years nearly. It was hot, but we enjoyed the exercise greatly. They marched us out about two miles into the country, and we skirmished by moonlight, and fired blank cartridges to our hearts' content, and rather to the astonishment of the villagers. I could not help laughing at the puzzled looks of a whole village when we dashed through its streets at that late hour and roused all the inmates out of their beds. They came trembling out to look at us, with very little on to bless themselves with.

I have had my time very fully occupied, and have stayed at home beyond office hours to study questions connected with the trade of the port, as I have been deputed to write a branch of the Trade Report. I like responsible work, and this writing a report on the whole trade of a year is exceedingly interesting to me. I have also undertaken to translate *Pekin Gazettes* for the *Evening Courier*.

July 10*th*.—Last night, a whole party of us went to the circus together, tearing along in a line of gin-rick-a-shas. It is most absurd to see grown-up people getting into magnified perambulators, and being whirled off at full speed by two half-naked coolies. In Japan, they run away with you anywhere, without stopping to ask whither, and a stranger gets rather flabbergasted to find himself whizzed away from the rest of his party, and utterly unable to stop or to guide his runaways. And we are fast getting into that way here; for the usual practice is to turn down the streets you want by just touching your coolie on his right or left arm with the end of your stick. So accustomed are they to your driving them the way you wish, that one or two have lately trundled about for hours with the blissful unconsciousness of their "fare" having fallen fast asleep. . . . The circus was certainly a great novelty, and although we all pointed to the children and enjoyed their amazement, methought that was all very fine, but that we elders frequently stared with all our eyes too. A large sprinkling of Chinese betrayed a considerable amount of astonishment at the feats.

July 13*th*.—I walked out to the cricket ground to get some exercise, but finding some friends at a wicket, I bowled for a while, and got a bit of an innings to boot. A fine breeze was playing across the ground, and a couple of ladies with some attendant gentlemen were attracted by it to come over and sit by the pavilion in easy cane chairs, of which we have an abundant supply for visitors. Our cricket ground is as perfect as anything of the kind at home, and it is in the middle of a wide open space which was bought by a large public fund, called the Recreation Fund, and intended for purposes of recreation only; so that however much they may build all round, this fine space will always remain free and open. Shanghae is growing so fast that this boon will soon begin to be felt. Another safeguard against encroachment is, that the race-course completely surrounds it. It is in an oval shape and measures just a mile and a quarter. People often walk round this and ride too. The drive in from this open space, which lies between the settlement proper and a row of bungalows stretching out for three miles along the Bubbling Well Road, is (ordinarily) a very picturesque street called the Maloo. Fortunately, it was made as wide as Oxford Street, at least, or we should have felt the inconvenience of passing through a Chinese population on our main drive. Chinese shops line both sides of this wide maloo, and customers swarm as busy as bees among them. We are content to relinquish the pavements to the elbowing crowd, and walk along the middle of the road in spite of furious driving to and fro. But in this hot weather I must say this lively street is anything but picturesque, for our Celestial friends have a supreme contempt for false modesty, and prefer comfort to appearances.

July 31*st*.—I have just, by luck, got in for the most delightful expedition imaginable, and I have only an hour to pack up in and appear on board the steamer. A party is just starting to cruise among the Chusan Islands, to find one suited for a sanatorium, and I go to represent the consul. The American Consul-general and others form the expedition, so I hope to have good fun. We shall only be away till Tuesday morning (the 3rd).

August 6*th*.—I rushed off to the Ningpo steamer on Saturday, which, of course, delayed a whole hour in starting, and made me hurry to no particular purpose. I met the American Consul-general, who was the promoter and organiser of the expedition, and after shaking hands with him, proceeded with much curiosity to find out who were members of our party. . . . I observed the Yankees were in great force. . . . All these American steamers are arranged with a view to personal comfort. Unlike ours, the saloon is placed in the bows, a most grateful arrangement in this hot weather, by which the fresh wind blows directly into your cabin, and all the smells and sailors are put aft. . . . Our party to Ningpo by the steamer *Shansi* at first appeared likely to prove dull and staid. But this grave heaviness naturally rubbed off after a bit, and though we never rose to any supreme effort of jollity, there was much quiet enjoyment in store for the party.

We could not go direct to the islands, as the steamer had cargo to deliver at Ningpo; but as she arrived there very early, everything in the way of business was disposed of by half-past six, and then with an accession to our party, the good ship's nose was turned down the river again, and we steamed away for the open sea. The Ningpo river itself is full of interest. First of all, on each side, the eye is refreshed with the rich green and yellow of the trees and fields, and this is backed up by the sombre tints of the mountains. The country lay mapped out before us, and I could easily distinguish the whereabouts of the peaks which overlooked those lovely spots we visited in the spring. Then, as we approached the mouth of the river (it is only a run of five miles from settlement down), we looked down on the forts and the heights, which our soldiers stormed in 1842-52 or thereabouts. A small walled city lies at the entrance of the river, overlooked by a remarkable eminence like the Acropolis at Athens. This commanding mound has a large temple on its summit, and it was up here that we left a small garrison to hold the conquered district. It was so curious to look on the now quiet scene and be told how red coats lined those heights, or swarmed up this hill, in all the excitement of battle. The people round soon learned to pick up a few words, and invented an odd, mixed-up sort of lingo, with which they held some sort of communication with the soldiers. These latter went by the name of "I says." They would say, "Oh! here comes an 'I say,'" which shows how quickly they noted the commonest expressions in soldiers' mouths.

Heaps of big junks lay at anchor. Some carried large quantities of timber, which was piled up on deck, and overflowed the sides in such a way that the boat looked like a huge timber raft, nothing being left to view of the actual hull but her head and stern. There is something exceedingly comical about the look of these timber junks, and one watches them with great interest on every possible occasion. They are very clever in arranging the poles to follow the sweeping lines of the junks, and these are brought up to a point at the head, so as to present no obstacle to the sea.

Islands commence at the very mouth of the river, so that we had the pleasure of moving in and out, for a short space, before laying our course for the open, for a certain Napier Island, which was our destination. The sky was lovely, and the sea as calm as a pond, and of a lovely pea-soup consistency, yellow as mud could make it. These Chinese rivers roll down such volumes of mud and clay in solution, that the sea is discoloured for miles away. We steamed away till 2 P.M., lounging on deck in long easy chairs, talking, or reading. Napier Island was close at hand, and heaps of little islands lay all about. There were no trees on them, only grass covered the high slopes. Teeming villages of fishermen peeped out of sheltered nooks, and one might have envied their calm seclusion, but for the knowledge of their crimes, for it was but a narrow border that lay between fishing and piracy, whenever they got the chance. We pulled up first in a choice bay and landed. The whole party then proceeded to walk up to the top, which was rather hot work. We could not see enough beach to make a good bathing-place for ladies, and there was nothing particular to recommend that place, so back we went on board, racing the two boats which the Chinamen pulled remarkably well; got up anchor and proceeded to Napier Island.

The sea was full of red gelatinous-looking creatures, which looked half worm half sea-weed, and wherever they lay on shore most tempting they looked, with a brilliant ruby hue and barley-sugar-like appearance. We rambled all over the island, and examined it with a view to its fitness for a sanatorium. Many little beaches lay below us on both sides, which we looked at with eager desire, for as soon as the sun went down we intended having a jolly good bathe. Quite a large village appeared all of a sudden in one bend, and the whole population stared with great astonishment at the strange figures in white stalking along on the brow of the hill above them. After strolling all round we returned to our beach and proceeded with feelings of inexpressible delight to prepare for the water. If ever that spot is enlivened hereafter with graceful figures drying their hair, and children digging sand pies with wooden spades, I shall recall with keen amusement the opening scene of the budding sanatorium, a dozen big men scrambling into the water at different points, happy as children. When it got dark we started back for Ningpo and arrived early in the morning, left the same day at four, and got back to Shanghae on Tuesday at 6 A.M.

NOTES

OF

A JOURNEY

FROM

HANKOW TO TA-LI FU,

COMPILED FROM THE OFFICIAL JOURNAL AND PRIVATE LETTERS

OF THE LATE

AUGUSTUS RAYMOND MARGARY,

CHINA CONSULAR SERVICE.

On the 9th of August while at Shanghae Mr. MARGARY received notice of his appointment to cross China, and meet Colonel BROWNE's Mission. In compliance with his instructions, he kept a journal on the route, and the portion of it which records his experiences as far as Ta-li Fu has been saved, and is now published with the sanction of the Government. There are various gaps in it, which have been filled up as far as possible by extracts from his private letters. The remainder was probably with him when he was murdered.

For completeness' sake, an itinerary has been appended to the journal.

Shanghae, August 9th.—A magnificent opportunity of distinguishing myself has just been opened to me, and I am sure it will please you very much to know how great an honour has been lately conferred upon me in connection with it. I am appointed to the very duty I was longing for and wrote about in my last letter to you, namely, that of accompanying the Indian expedition which is to enter China through Burmah and survey a new route for commerce. Direct orders have not yet arrived. Mr. Medhurst received orders to breathe a word of it to no one, and I have instructions to make every preparation with all secresy, and to hold myself in readiness to go to Hankow (five hundred miles up the Yangtsze) and to start from there on or about the 1st of September, so that I have but a short notice to prepare for a three months' trip; for I am afraid it will be as long as that, at the very shortest computation ; but I shall be able to send a letter from the interior now and then, as I proceed, for the Chinese have an excellent postal system all over the empire, so that, I am happy to say, you will not be deprived of all news of me.

And now let me tell you that this order is not final. Its carrying out depends upon the arrival of a telegram from the Viceroy of India to say whether I am to start or not. However, I firmly believe we

H

shall have the telegram in a day or two to say "go ahead," and I shall go with joy and alacrity.

Friday, 14th—A telegram from Calcutta did arrive on Wednesday night, directed, contrary to our expectation, to Mr. Wade, so that Mr. Medhurst had to send it up to Pekin unopened, and we shall not know for ten days what is decided. I am inclined to think the expedition has been abandoned, or the telegram would have come to Mr. Medhurst. Won't it be a horrible sell for me! We have suggested to the minister that it would save time and money to send me by sea to Mandalay, to join the expedition at its starting-point, instead of toiling overland some seven or eight hundred miles through a new country untrodden by foreigners.

To his Parents.

Saturday, 15th.—My instructions arrived this morning with warm and flattering letters from Mr. Wade and his secretaries, together with passports and Chinese despatches from the Imperial Foreign officials. The plan adopted is to send me overland from this side to the Western borders of the province of Yunnan, there to wait at one of the passes for four Indian officers who are to come over from a place called Bhamô near the upper sources of the Irrawaddy or Irawady. I am provided with huge Chinese despatches from the Tsungli yamen at Pekin to three governor-generals who rule the vast territories through which I shall pass. These letters direct them to take every care of me, and to issue orders to all their magistrates and officers along my route to protect and help me on. I shall pass over about nine hundred miles of country, of which some five hundred will be new ground. I have to keep an official journal and an itinerary, and everything will be published. The trip is calculated to last six months. At any rate I shall be completely buried out of sight till the end of November, and shall probably hear no news of you or the world in general till next year. Only think what a glorious opportunity I shall have of seeing this wonderful country, and of bringing to light numerous facts as yet unknown, from regions untrodden by foreigners. It is really splendid; you cannot think how elated I am. I am provided with a cook, an official messenger, and a writer. Every thing is to be kept an entire secret, and I find this the hardest part of the job. I have to buy all my provisions for the journey, and slip away without a soul knowing it outside. Mr. Wade dreads any incaution on the part of the papers, which would seriously hamper my movements by getting wrong notions into the head of the Chinese. I have only a week to prepare in, but that is amply sufficient, and probably next Saturday not one of my friends will suspect that I have gone on board the river steamer to start on my long, long journey. I go up to Hankow first, which is five hundred miles up the Yangtsze. These American river palaces do the trip in three days. Two ports are open between,

Chinkiang, where I have been before, and Kinkiang, where I have not yet been. At the latter place I "stop two turns" to consult the vice-consul, Mr. King, about my route, and then proceed in the following steamer to Hankow. There, my final preparations will be made to start as early in September as possible. You had better get a good map of China. Dr. Williams' is the best, I think, and you will be able to follow my movements very well. The course of the Yangtsze will indicate some six hundred miles of it, probably, so that I shall have ascended some one thousand miles of this mighty river. The return trip through China will be pleasant enough in company with the Indian officers I shall meet. They may however elect to return to Burmah, in which case I shall visit that wonderful country also. I am having some rare old missionary charts of the provinces I pass through photographed. They will be of invaluable use to me. It will be intensely interesting to me to see and speak to some of those great viceroys, who rule their provinces like petty kings; but I doubt if I shall be so honoured; they will probably refer me to lesser lights. In any case, it will be very instructive to carry on correspondence with them. I have only to pray for health and strength to carry me through, and there is no doubt I shall have had the privilege of doing some service to the world at large. I must be off now to see to my equipment. I spend all the day at the stores, making out lists and estimates, and adding this, that, and the other necessary as it occurs to me. To-day I am after medicines. I must also see to a good pair of field-glasses. You must picture me standing alone on the heights of the Momein pass, far away on the Burmese frontier, and anxiously scanning the country beyond for the first glimpse of Indian helmets approaching from the West. Then you can picture the meeting, China and India grasping hands, and awakening those primeval echoes with a British hurrah over the *fait accompli*. As it happens, the telegrams have failed in the most important particular, and we cannot make out which pass they intend to traverse; but I shall find them out somehow, or else I will worry the Viceroy of Yunnan out of all peace and quiet.

Friday, August 21st.—I am going to start off to-morrow night for Hankow, if possible. My orders appear now to be very complete. I have had further despatches to-day from Mr. Wade telling me the names of the Indian officers and the pass they intend to come over. A Colonel Browne is at the head of it, and Dr. Anderson, whose name is familiar in connection with previous expeditions, is one of the party, and Mr. Ney Elias. A guard of thirty soldiers accompanies them to the frontiers of China, after which I am to take charge of them and bring them back by the way I go to meet them. The soldiers are not to enter China.

Shanghae, August 22nd, 1874.—MY DARLING MOTHER, —I am so sorry not to be able to write more this mail. Everything has to be done in such a tearing hurry, and I have to rush about from one place to another buying things. I am going to write leisurely on board the steamer going up the river. I start to night, and it takes nearly four days to get up to Hankow. It is so hot I am hardly able to write, and my boy is packing my books, and I have to keep an eye on him to see that he puts the right things at the top. The M——'s are so kind to me. He has lent me his invaluable servant, a man who knows every inch of the country and is full of expedients. It is a long, and, to a certain extent, a perilous journey. I can't disguise that fact, and that for three months I shall be beyond the reach of all news of the outer world. You must picture me trudging on through strange cities, stared at by pig-tailed mobs. At times sitting in Eastern etiquette with native governors and viceroys, and lastly, you may look at the map and fancy you see a solitary European standing above the last pass on the borders of China, and anxiously gazing through his binoculars for the advent of Indian helmets from the West. You know, dearest, I have trust in God, and fear nothing. Best love to all. Your own loving Gus.

On board the S.S. 'Hirado' up the Yangtsze, Sunday, August 23rd.—I started on my trip yesterday, and am now on board one of those wonderful structures which the Americans first adopted for the navigation of their mighty rivers. The last thing this vessel resembles is a ship. You see no masts, but only two gigantic funnels, which are often placed one in front of each paddle box. Tier upon tier of cabins appear to be built upon the smallest possible hull, and the general appearance of the vessel is that of a gaudy palace of pleasure, full of windows and terraces floating on the water. In the centre you see the great lever of the beam engine oscillating backwards and forwards like a gigantic see-saw. This is what is called the "Walking Beam." The cabins are large and roomy. I see one on the opposite side to mine containing a large four-post bedstead. This mighty river, steeped in yellow mud, is not particularly interesting just here. The banks are low, and almost out of sight, so that I have nothing to attract me up on deck. We shall reach the first river port, called Chinkiang in the middle of the night, but, as I have been there before, it will make no difference to me whether I see it again or not. A wide desolation marks the spot which is very depressing to look at. The Taiping rebels had possession of the place, and their heavy hand is witnessed to by the many acres of brickbats which mark the site of a once busy city. I shall feel no small degree of interest in having a sight of the great and famous old city of Nankin which we shall pass to-morrow. There the rebels established their power, and marked it by knocking down the far-renowned porcelain tower, which we used to read of with wonder at school. By-and-by, as we pass farther up, and the huge river narrows, I am told some beautiful scenery opens out, and I shall perhaps be attracted to the deck the greater part of the time. We shall reach the second Treaty-port called Kinkiang on Tuesday. How wonderful it is that we have now a daily service of large, powerful, comfortable steamers ploughing up and down this great river, for seven hundred miles, which, shortly before I came to China, was hermetically sealed to foreign vessels. Our fleet of mighty men of war first forced its way up in 1842, and nothing could be done till 1862 in the way of fairly opening up the river. They say the Yangtsze carries in its bosom enough mud to give a coating of yellow to the whole of Europe. Islands of no mean size are formed in an incredibly short space of time, and the very passage through which our 74-gun ships passed at Chinkiang in 1842 is now high land, connecting a certain Silver Island with the mainland. I think I had better tell you about my departure from Shanghae now, before plunging into history and geography, but I must first find a quieter portion of the ship, as the vibration is too much to allow of my writing.

August 24*th.*—I have now found a steadier table, and am feeling better myself. I have had a long spell of bad health in Shanghae, without any positive sign of sickness. The fact is, as I know now for certain, that I have been under the wearing influence of Shanghae fever, which is very subtle. It is an intermittent fever, and if one's constitution is strong enough, like mine, to resist it, the silent enemy continues its creeping attacks, until the mischief is detected by loss of flesh, and emaciation. I have been working too hard, and sitting out too much in evening breezes, the result of which was a loss of fourteen or fifteen pounds, which I was startled to discover the other day. It is not pleasant to have to start on my stupendous journey after such a pull down, but every mile away from Shanghae has been adding strength and vigour to my spirits and frame, and I have no doubt, under the quiet, regular regime of a traveller's life, I shall feel as blithe as a lark.

I shall be, perhaps, three months reaching the frontier town of Seng-Yuen-Fu, which you will no doubt find marked on the atlas, as the most westerly town in China. Its other name is Momein. From Hankow, which is in the very centre of China, and which place this steamer will reach to-morrow, I start in a native boat, and follow up the course of the mighty Yangtsze, through the province of Sz'chuen, past the wonderful gorges and rapids of Ichang, on through Chung-khing, lat 29° 30′, long. 107° E., and then bending down to Yunnan-Fu, in lat. 25° 30′ long, 102° E., and from thence almost due west to a Chinese border town, called Yung-Chang-Fu. At this place, where the roads through two different passes converge, I am to pause and determine whether the party has had time to reach Momein, and, if possible, I am to push on there to meet them. I suppose by the time I return, I shall have passed over some five thousand miles of country. The letters and passes furnished me by the Imperial Cabinet will command respect from all the officials, high and low, throughout my route; so that, though no doubt innumerable schemes may be devised to hinder my progress, I shall be hedged around with protection. Is it not a splendid mission? What wonderful things I shall see! Some of the mountain scenery in that marvellously rich province of Yunnan is very beautiful. I cannot cease to regret that my talents for sketching are so very poor.

I have had but little time to prepare for a trip of six months. It may last as long as that, for they hint at the possibility of my waiting for the expedition, perhaps for a whole month, in which case I shall hope to have grand sport in the forests and mountains, which teem with wild life. In spite of the short notice, I think I am pretty well provided with clothes, and tinned provisions, weapons and instruments.

It is impossible to say when you may hear from me. I shall try and make use of the native post, which is a very efficient service, but how far it may be safe for foreign correspondence remains to be proved. It may be that not a word will be heard of me the whole time, in which case, all sorts of rumours may arise as to my fate. Let me beg of you not to believe one; rest assured I will make my way there and back, by God's help, as safe as a trivet.

In spite of all my elation, and the fact of my preparations having been completed, and of my having actually started up the Yangtsze, there is yet a possibility of an order following me to stop. For a very suspicious-looking telegram in cypher came from the viceroy last week, to which we could only get a reply from Pekin about now, and the very next steamer behind me may be bringing up instructions to go no farther.

It was troublesome having to keep all my preparations so secret. I have not been able to say good-bye to heaps of my friends, and on Saturday night, after a quiet dinner at the Consulate, I sneaked down the bund at midnight in a gin-rick-a-sha, holding a new dog in a leash, and followed by Bombazine, my old boy, whom I have picked up again, and employed for this trip.

Mr. Medhurst has kindly lent me an invaluable person, who has been in his employ for many years; a sort of confidential rascal, who will do anything, go anywhere, and is never at a loss for an expedient. He knows the greater part of the country through which I am to pass, having been repeatedly sent out in search of golden pheasants and other rare curiosities. If I should happen to be ill anywhere, or come to grief in any way, this man will be back to Hankow in a twinkling and bring the news. He rejoices in the nickname of Leila, which the children gave him years ago, by mistake for the common call with which servants are summoned in China. Much as if in India one were to call a man Zui-hi. But the name has stuck to him.

After a warm farewell from Mr. Medhurst, I started off with a heavy heart. Leila, in his zeal, had carried off every one of my hats with the luggage, and I had to tie my handkerchief round my head, as the night was damp and miasmatic. Passing by the club, which was flaring with gas at every window, I saw the white-coated figures of the late birds, some poring over the mail papers in their luxurious library, others finishing up their billiards in a higher storey. I hurried on like a fugitive, and hid my face from one or two friends strolling home from a dinner somewhere, for I did not want to waste time in explanations, or to be hindered by post-prandial larks. It was quite painful to feel I was going away on a great journey, and yet could not take a warm farewell of my friends. Arrived at the end of the magnificent bund, which stretches for a mile and a half in front of lordly houses, I had only to step across a pontoon on to one of those American river palaces which plough up and down the huge river, and which I have described to you before. My cabin was big enough to do on shore in England. I was met with marked respect from the officer on watch.

"Are you Mr. Margary, sir?"

"Yes."

"All right, sir."

"Here, steward, show Mr. Margary No. 1 cabin."

"I'll look after your dog, sir."

"All right, good night;" and before I awoke, Shanghae was out of sight. And now we have been "coughing" up the muddy sea for the best part of three days. Mark Twain uses the above expression to describe the peculiar soughing noise which these "Walking Beam" engines emit at every revolution. One almost pities the monster, and feels irresistibly impelled to clear one's throat to help the poor asthmatic creature.

We stopped at Chinkiang on Sunday night to discharge cargo and passengers, and a most disagreeable interruption to one's sleep it proved.

The scenery has been flat the whole way up. This afternoon, however, mountains begin to appear, and there will be much to look at from this point.

I was very much interested yesterday, in gazing on the wonderful old city of Nankin. It was here that the last great struggle took place to eradicate the Taiping rebels. Its mighty, grim, dirty old walls were built into the sides of the hills which skirted the northern front of the city for some miles. Nothing could be seen but these grim battlements; but I could picture Colonel Gordon occupying those heights around, and the fearful and atrocious massacre which the Imperialists subsequently perpetrated around those walls, was enough to sicken one to contemplate. The captain had some stories to tell of fearful sights he had seen going up and down the river at that time in the Chinese service. He pointed to the low lying banks on the opposite side of the river, which was not so very wide at that point, and told us how he had seen thousands stampeding across those plains, and striving to escape in crowded boats from their pursuers, and hacking each other down unmercifully in their selfishness and frenzy to escape.

We have a great man on board, no less a person than the Governor of the Province of Canton. We have had him to dinner, and the captain was very glad I was here to talk to him. The manager of the company had given orders to the captain to show every attention to H. E., but as the latter, with the usual piggishness of his country, rejected the best cabins, and chose to ensconce himself in the after hold! it was not so easy to please him. However he accepted the invitation to dinner, and made himself very agreeable, specially after dinner, when we sat out in the bows, and enjoyed the fresh air. His spirits seemed to rise, and he remarked to his attendant amanuensis, that the foreigners' way of sitting out after dinner, and chatting and laughing was very sociable and friendly. Like most successful well-to-do Chinamen, our friend has an enormous figure and paunch. I wonder they don't expire of heat and apoplexy. Wandering round the ship the other day, I saw him fast asleep in a long chair, and an attendant shampooing his fat legs for him all the time.

I wonder what you will all think, when you hear of my hurrying myself out of sight for all these months in the heart of China. The journey as far as Chung-khing has been repeatedly performed; it will be after that point that my difficulties will commence, and I shall pass through many places in Yunnan where a foreigner has never been seen; at such towns, it will require my utmost tact and caution to prevent trouble and excitement. Do not be apprehensive about me. If I only have health, by God's blessing, I shall not dread anything else.

To F. E. R.

British Consulate, Hankow, Sept. 2nd, 1874.--I have not been able to write during the past few days, for, as you may well imagine, the preparations for such a trip as I am about to undertake requires my constant attention and thought. Talking especially takes up a lot of time, and bargaining with Chinamen wears out one's patience.

I sent a letter from Kinkiang on the 26th. I spent a couple of very pleasant days there. The first afternoon I went out to the bungalow in the hills some nine miles off. Mr. King lent me a chair, and I was carried off by three coolies, who took up about three hours in the transit. After going for about an hour, they set me down in a village, and proceeded after their fashion to imbibe tea and eat some horrid looking compound. Meanwhile, I became a gazing stock to the urchins, as well as men and women, which was odd, considering they see foreigners every day. However, instead of allowing them to take peeps at me through the venetians of the chair, I got out and had a chat. My bearers repeated this operation at the end of another hour, and at length, when I reached the foot of the mountain, and found I had to walk up it for about an hour, darkness was setting in. I could hardly steer clear of the stones in the narrow path which wound up a wild gorge. It seemed interminable, but at last I reached the bungalow, and found four gentlemen, three of whom I did not know, taking a plunge into a fine clear deep pool. A mountain torrent rushes down past the door of the bungalow, and forms this fine pool within ten paces of the house.

I came away again next morning at daylight, before the sun should get too hot, first taking a farewell swim, and the mountain torrent was bracingly cold at that early hour.

To-morrow morning I shall be launched in my boat, and perhaps not emerge into the world again till next year. I am going by boat—the same one —for the first thirty to forty days. This part of the travelling will be comfortable enough. I shall have all my books and luxuries round me, and just recline on an easy chair as I float past strange places. The first big place I make for is Yo-chow, at the point in Hunan where the Yangtsze touches the Tungting Lake. Then I traverse the lake and leave it at the south-west corner by a river which carries me past Changteh, Shenchow, to the borders of the province of Kwei-chou, where I shall bid good-bye to my boat and send it back with letters. I shall then have to travel overland in chairs across the mountainous province of Kwei-chou, and reach the distant Yunnan-Fu, which is just above the 25th parallel of lat. N., in some twenty-five days more, and after that I shall do as circumstances require.

The weather was boiling hot during the first few days of my arrival, but now fortunately it has turned a little cooler.

I am fearfully busy and distracted. The Chinese are making war preparations everywhere. We expect the Japanese will give them a sound thrashing at first, and then, perhaps, afterwards, the tables may be turned, for the average Chinaman is double the size of a Japanese. You will hear from me again in a fortnight, I hope. I feel as if I were going into darkness for six months.

To F. E. R.

Yangtsze, ninety miles from Hankow, Wednesday, September 9th.—I have been five days coming thus far, and do not at all relish the misery of such slow travelling, with the thermometer over 90°. But I am slowing down on purpose, in consequence of an Indian telegram which caught me up on the second night out, which proposes my joining the expedition at Rangoon by sea. Mr. Wade, however, has to decide; and so, in order to give time for his answer to arrive, I have written back to say that I will move slowly on up the Yangtsze, and stop at a place near its contiguity with the Tungting Lake. There I shall be at a point from which I can hurry on or drop down the swift stream of the Yangtsze to Hankow in a quarter of the time it takes to go up, according as Mr. Wade's orders may direct.

So far, I find it extremely monotonous. I cannot get out all day on account of the sun, and in the evening at the halting-place I am obliged to undergo a crowd. However, they are seldom troublesome. My writer is a Christian, and therefore possesses moral courage enough to be free from most Chinese prejudices. He will walk with me through any frequented place, and rebuke the crowd with great energy if their curiosity overcomes their politeness.

We were fortunate in having a thunderstorm the first night out, which cooled the air for two days. Saturday and Sunday were consequently delicious, and I did a great deal of walking along the towing path, accompanied by my writer and servant. There was nothing very attractive in the country. Very rough cultivation of cotton, millet, and sesamum showed how little they could count on the rise or fall of the river. This year they have had no inundation, but it is of almost annual occurrence. Even at Hankow the foreign settlement is frequently submerged. The river rises six feet above the level of the fine stone bund they have made there, and quietly takes possession of all the lower rooms in the noble-looking mansions which the merchants occupy. All their dining-room furniture has to be removed above. Boats become the only means of locomotion, and ladies can be seen canoeing in and out of their houses, and over the bund where they are wont to promenade at other times. It is now 3·30 P.M., and having arrived at a convenient anchorage, we are going to stop here for the rest of the day. Meantime, I have found every occupation distressing. With the thermometer at 90°, in this narrow boat, which I can almost stretch across with my arms, and frequently try to unroof with my head, you may imagine what an exercise it is to my patience. Hitherto I had been too weak to sit up and write, but a course of "tonic" has set me up, and I find this the most agreeable way to spend the next few hours till the fierce sun shall have gone down. I read Chinese till that nauseated me, then I alternated between my bed and my open iron chair, now with a novel of Bulwer Lytton's, and now with a Frenchman's account of the regions I am bound to. Oh, why is the weather so hot? It ought to be breaking up now. Indeed it did for two days. The very first night we were out a thunderstorm came up, and we hurried up a creek amid a swarm of boats of all sizes seeking similar shelter. They raised such a Babel of tongues as I never heard. Every boat had several men, and they all shouted at once. The storm did not take the ugly proportions my boatmen seemed to expect. The result was harmless, but intensely refreshing, and for two days sent the thermometer down to 84°. I had a long walk the last of these two days, and cut across a wooded village, which looked very pretty for anything Chinese. My writer and boy always accompany me. We entered a cottage and rested, talking very amiably all the while to the host, an old man, and his various progeny of many generations who surrounded him. These people had never seen a foreigner before, but curbed their curiosity under politeness No sooner had I resumed my walk, however, than I heard quite a loud cackling, like geese, and turning round saw the girls and boys running after me. They were speedily dispersed by a weighty rebuke from my amanuensis. The village proved a very large one. A schoolmaster stepped down and made some polite inquiries, and I thought we were getting on beautifully; but, alas! for our vanity, no sooner had we turned the corner, and reached the shipping frontage in search of our boat, than all the *gamins* in the suburb rose up, and escorted me some half a mile along the wharves before that blessed boat turned up. I was not in a good humour, so did not attempt to play with them, but walked like a Roman with majestic step, feeling all the time an utter fool. It is rather trying to be followed by a dirty, ignorant crowd, which has the audacity to laugh spontaneously at your superior excellence. Upon my word I never felt more out of place.

JOURNAL.

Having received orders, while at Shanghae, to hold myself in readiness to proceed to Yunnan at a short notice, I set myself without delay to make such preparations as would enable me to start with despatch, yet, at the same time, without definitely incurring an outlay in case of a countermand. The above intimation was received through Mr. Medhurst, on the 9th of August, and on 15th and the 21st, I had the honour to receive full and confidential instructions from H.B.M. Minister, which directed me to start at once, and accordingly I left Shanghae on the night of Saturday, the 22nd, for Hankow. Arrived at Kinkiang on the 25th, I remained at that port two days to consult with Mr. Vice-Consul King about the route, as directed in my instructions. This officer had recently ascended the Yangtsze to Chung-khing, and very readily gave me the benefit of his valuable observations, besides furnishing me with books and papers on the subject, including his own private diary of the trip.

August 28th, 1874.— Reached Hankow in exceptionally hot whether, and unfortunately in a very bad state of health, which continued for several days and retarded my final preparations. Mr. Consul Hughes had called upon the viceroy with the letter from the Tsungli yamen, and found H. E. had already received despatches from Pekin on the subject of my trip. The viceroy in conversation strongly recommended the Hu Nan and Kwei-chou route as that which was usually followed by officials, and was just now selected by the Govenor of Yunnan, who was on his way thither. Acting on this advice, and moreover finding that time and expense were likely to be saved by adopting this road, I decided to do so, with Mr. Hughes's full concurrence. The viceroy was informed on the 31st of this decision, and wrote to say that he had forthwith directed all the officials along the route to aid and protect my progress.

The 31st, 1st, and 2nd were taken up in bargaining for and procuring a boat, hiring servants, and concluding financial arrangements, which at first threatened to become exceedingly troublesome. But an order was at length obtained on a Shen Si branch bank which had been set up in Yunnan very recently, and which was indeed an encouraging sign of returning order and prosperity in that long-disturbed province. The banker who supplied me with this order had the civility to call, and proved to be a man of great consequence and ability. He informed me that the Government of Yunnan was also supplied with funds through his bank. Along with the other a tally weight of brass was given to me, which was to be presented at the bank in Yun-nan Fu to serve as the standard of payment. And four per cent. discount was the rate charged for the accommodation.

My preparations were completed for starting on the 3rd, but unfortunately an attack of illness obliged me to put off the departure till next day. The boat was one of those commonly called a mandarin boat, long and narrow, and divided into five or six compartments which ran the whole length of the craft, the centre being occupied with a somewhat wider and neater space, fitted with chairs and tables, and suited for the reception of guests. Each compartment contained a couple of low berths, one on each side of the passage running down the middle. But as a Chinaman's average stature falls far short of an Englishman's proportions, I found it necessary to lengthen the bedside of my compartment by removing the dividing panel. A similar precaution had to be taken with regard to the floor, whereof the boards were lowered fully six inches, to save my head from the pains and penalties of trying to unroof the not too substantial top. A regular Chinese form of agreement was drawn up by the boat-owner and handed over to me. The main conditions were that he should convey me to Ch'ên-yuan Fu in Kwei-chou for the sum of 110,000 cash, which was to be paid in several instalments at different places on the way, starting with a prepayment of 60,000 cash at Hankow. This sum was to include everything, and to free me from all those incidental appeals on behalf of the crew which so frequently spring up *en route* to delay and annoy the traveller. My party consisted of five, comprising a writer, an official messenger, a cook, and my body servant. With regard to the necessary supplies for daily expenses between Hankow and Yunnan Fu, where alone I had credit for funds, I should mention that I adopted the following plan, which appeared to be the best that any one could suggest. It was to take with me in the boat a quantity of cash sufficient to cover everything as far as Ch'ên-yuan Fu, and to leave a margin wherewith to pay the first instalment for chairs in the land journey, which would commence at that place. In addition to this, I procured a hundred taels' worth of small silver ingots, weighing five taels each, which formed a very convenient parcel, and one easily concealed in a box of winter clothes reserved for Yunnan. These small ingots are called at Hankow *chin sha yin*. The cash was intrusted to my official messenger, whose receipt for the amount relieved my mind of the monstrous anxiety of having to watch over the safety of what seemed a vast hoard when converted into the bulky proportions of copper currency. The whole mass was deposited loosely in strings of a 1,000 cash (called a *tiao*) on the floor of the boat, beneath the servant's couch, and there it might remain without the smallest fear of theft, although within easy reach of a pilfering arm. The

Chinese are no thieves. Their purloinings take a different form, which I might charitably term "commission," but prefer to stigmatise a "squeeze."

September 4th.—Left Hankow at 11 A.M., crossed the river and tracked along under the walls of Wu-ch'ang. Made little progress against the strong current, without the aid of a breath of wind. At 3.30 brought up in a creek facing the southern suburb of the capital, having progressed but 20 li. Boatmen expected a storm from the north-west, and declined to proceed. Numbers of junks, large and small, were running in for shelter. I landed and took a short stroll with my writer, without exciting any incivility, though a good deal of curiosity. Finding my boat jambed in among a myriad of small craft, and deprived of every avenue by which a breeze might be wafted in to cool an atmosphere heated up to 92° throughout the day, I compelled the boatman to retrace our course to the mouth of the creek, where shortly after we found ourselves in a perfect Babel of tongues aroused by the fast approaching wind and thunderstorm. The men began to reproach me for bringing our small boat into such dangerous proximity to larger craft, and for some time, as the wind freshened and the vast flotilla began to swing about in constant collision, the uproar of voices surpassed all description. No harm was done, however, for the storm passed off as suddenly as it came, and left us refreshed by a cooler temperature.

September 5th.—Started with a fair wind, and

completed 105 li. Passed Ching-k'ou at 2 p.m. I was down with fever during the morning, but succeeded in walking along the towing path for some distance during the afternoon. The temperature had been reduced ten degrees by the storm. Country appeared to be low and subject to inundation. A few fields of cotton in the very poorest condition, and large quantities of sesamum which seemed healthy, were the only products of cultivation. A pretty view of hills to the north opened out from time to time. On the north bank of the river, *kaoliang* or *sorghum* was cultivated, as well as small quantities of indigo. Reached Tung-kua-nao [a Lekin Station, and anchorage for junks], in the evening, and remained there for the night. A messenger from Hankow arrived at 9 p.m. with a telegram from Calcutta, forwarded by Mr. Medhurst, to the following effect.—

"*Calcutta, 31st August*, 1874.—To Consul Medhurst, Shanghae.—Interpreter had better join party at Rangoon by sea. I am telegraphing to Mr. Wade. Interpreter had better postpone departure, pending further orders from Pekin."—" Foreign."

In the absence of further instructions, and not being pressed for time by this route, I wrote back to say that I should proceed leisurely on, to a place called Lo-shan, and there wait for further orders. My reasons for taking this course were strengthened by a desire to save time. In the first place the current of the Yangtsze being exceedingly strong, it was better to halt as near the Tungting Lake as possible, so that in case of receiving orders to proceed, I could push on faster. In the next place, I calculated that the time required for an answer to arrive would only necessitate a delay of four or five days at Lo-shan. Yao-chou Fu, at the entrance of the lake, had so often evinced an active hostility to foreigners that I preferred a more comfortable halting place, and selected Lo-shan, which was eighty li short of the former city.

September 6th.—Tracked against a south wind all day. Country flat and dry, cultivated with cotton and sesamum. Only made forty-five li, and anchored at P'ai-chou in company with numbers of river junks. Left the boat and walked across a bend to the village of P'ai-chou, which looked exceedingly pretty, embowered in masses of trees. On a nearer view the village expanded into a large straggling town, full of well built substantial houses, which spoke of considerable prosperity. My writer and messenger were with me. We met with civility at first, and sat down at one house chatting with the host. But as we passed the quarter by the junks the wildest excitement broke out. A mob collected and followed me for fully half-a-mile along the bund until I found my boat. It was not very exhilarating, and I confess I failed to enjoy the fun as much as the rest, for they shouted and screamed with laughter, dancing round me as if they were intensely amused. P'ai-chou lies on the right bank of the river.

September 7th.—Only moved on forty-five li to a place called Hsiao-hua-pai, where we arrived at 12.30, and found it intolerably hot. This place was merely a convenient anchorage for junks, owing to the existence of a creek. The few shops which formed a village were only there for the benefit of the junks; like the Lekin barrier, which was there no doubt with the same benevolent object.

September 8th.—Got over sixty li to Hu-hsin Chou, an island in the big river, separated from the mainland by a narrow channel, which afforded a good anchorage to boats passing up. The district city of Chia-yü Hsien was only removed a few li from this spot, and appeared to be well placed among low hills and a quantity of trees. The island itself was thickly covered with sand, hidden by the luxuriant growth of a grassy weed, which deceived the eye at a short distance with the appearance of a meadow. The heat was very great all day.

September 9th.—Tracked all day against wind and stream. Arriving among the hills. Stopped at Lu-ch'i-k'ou, sixty li from the last stage. Here a clear mountain river flowed down from the Tea hills and went to pollute itself in the muddy bosom of the Yangtsze. I was enabled to have a plunge and swim, morning and evening, in this comparatively clear stream. Lu-ch'i-k'ou, which by the way took its name from the river, was a gunboat station. A large man-of-war junk moored close to shore was used as a depôt hulk and dwelling for the officer in command. Several river gunboats lay alongside. The commander of the station, who held the rank of *yu-chi* (a blue buttoned officer), had a residence on shore. Twenty-one gunboats scattered up and down the river received their orders from his hands.

September 10*th*.—Remained all day at Lu-ch'i-k'ou, wind bound. Met with occasional rudeness while taking walks on shore, not from any grown-up persons, but from boys, who repeatedly shouted out "Foreign Devil," from a safe distance. The night watches were struck on board the naval hulk with the usual measured strokes of a drum, and these again were subdivided into periods of twenty minutes by similar strokes of a triangle. Each new watch was ushered in by a prolonged flourish on the drum, which broke my slumbers unpleasantly.

September 11*th*. — A strong favouring breeze having set in from the north, we sprang along under sail in company with a large fleet of river traders, and reached Hsin T'i, a distance of sixty li, in fairly quick time. Hsin T'i appeared to be a flourishing place, and a great number of river craft was massed in the open unsheltered anchorage which faced the long straight frontage of the town. After stopping but a short time at this place, the boatman, feeling insecure in such an exposed position, again set sail and ran on forty-five li, to Lo-shan, the place I had fixed for awaiting further orders at. Hsin T'i was governed by a *chou-t'ung*. A *Tao-Tai* was also established on the bank of the river whose sole duty it was to collect the timber dues from the rafts, which float down in large numbers. These rafts present a very curious appearance. Seen from a short distance they look like a floating village with a brisk population, and on a nearer view one cannot help admiring the ingenious construction. The larger lengths of timber are closely massed together, forming a compact raft of no mean dimensions, down the centre of which are constructed a series of neat huts for the crew to live in. The head of the raft is shaped off to somewhat of a sharp prow, and at the stern a gallery runs out fitted with steering apparatus. The fast stream of the Yangtsze carries them down with sufficient speed, but they are also furnished with enormous sweeps requiring the strength of ten or twelve men to manipulate. The raftsmen appear to possess a magnificent form. I have nowhere seen such fine athletic frames in China, and could not help stopping to admire the splendid development of muscle, which was so well displayed as they swayed to and fro with the enormous sweeps. Three or four of these rafts generally came down in company, one behind the other, in a long string, and for means of communication a diminutive raft, rowed by five men, answered every purpose of a boat. It had all the appearance of a long-legged fly shooting across the water in spasmodic spurts. It may be worthy of remark that I noticed, first at P'ai-chou, and repeatedly afterwards at other places farther up the river, the use of a cart in agriculture. It is not often that one sees a Chinese farmer make use of anything so handy. But in this instance the form of the vehicle was so novel, and so different to that which is sometimes used in the province of Chih Li, that it deserves to be described. The diversity of shape is itself a striking fact in a country where similar operations are carried on in precisely the same way and with the same implements in provinces far apart and disconnected by dialect. The main difference lay in the fact that, whereas the northern carts, like others all the world over, are built with their wheels outside the body of the vehicle, the centre of gravity of which is placed low down, these Hu Pei carts enclose their wheels, and are consequently raised high above them, like a railway carriage. The cart simply amounts to a wide platform poised above two wheels upon the stout axles which protrude. Dragged along by the water buffalo, of all beasts the most ungainly, its appearance is more quaint than elegant.

The following are extracts from private letters :—

To his Parents.

[*On the Yangtsze*, 130 miles beyond Hankow, September 11th, 1874.—I have been a whole week away from my fellow kind, for I cannot look upon the Chinese always in the light of brothers, yet my journey is not fairly commenced. For on the second night of my sojourn in this boat, a messenger from the Consulate overtook me with important covers enclosing a telegram from Calcutta which stops my farther progress. As there are neither railways nor telegraph to Pekin, at least a fortnight must elapse before Mr. Wade's decision can reach me.

I cannot describe the discomfort and annoyance this delay causes me. My boat is not large, and the thermometer has frequently been over 90°. I have as few comforts as possible, and the plainest fare. Movement alone can make up for my miseries, and I am obliged to "slow down." I had no direct orders, so the strong current decided me to push on to the Tungting Lake and there await instructions. If I am to go back, the rapid current will carry me down in a brace of shakes; and if I am to go on, I shall have saved time by surmounting so much of the Yangtsze as forms part of my course. In order to eke out the time, we have gone very short stages, and hope to have as few days of actual halt as possible. Our last stage afforded me the delicious surprise of a clear stream running down from the hills, so I remained there all yesterday and bathed morning and evening. The sensation of a free swim after being pent up in the boat was something transcendent. The people in this part of the country have seen very little of foreigners, and I have frequently to bear the annoyance of mobbing and the impertinent cries of children, when at a safe distance.

The clouds have been gracious to-day and staved off the power of the sun, and the thermometer only reached 85°. I catch cold now at 83°. The other day a sudden thunderstorm sent the temperature down from 92° to 82° in a quarter of an hour. I was delighted, but caught cold of course on the spot; but in spite of this and a grand mass of clouds which seemed to cover the ends of the earth, I was soon being broiled again at 98°. It is an incomprehensible sky.

To-day there has been as thick a covering of clouds as I ever saw all day long, and now at five o'clock the sky is very nearly blue, and the thermometer will still have a chance of gratifying its sneaking desire of touching 90° once in the day at least. My "useful rascal" has been quite alive to every windfall. It is wonderful how eager he is to be useful; his memory is inexhaustible to suggest necessaries, and his activity never flags in marketing. But my cunning "invaluable" is quietly pocketing all the while above ten per cent. in "commission." I found the rogue had got the boatmen to ask a sufficient price to enable him to receive 12 dollars from them as commission. I shall be down on him when we get back.

18*th*.— Here I have been six days, this is the seventh, waiting orders. I wish I had scattered the telegram to the winds and gone on; they could not have stopped me.

However, I can easily make up my six or seven days, as I have chosen a shorter route than we were aware of, and saved both time and expense. Stopping

K

here all this time would have been intolerable but
for two or three circumstances. First of all there is
a most delicious stretch of scrubby downs extending
some distance, and as I have my boat anchored right
under them I am able to go out very often and have a
shot at the pheasants and grouse which I occasionally
find in this excellent cover. Secondly, a thunderstorm
and rain, which confined me to the boat for three
days out of the six, although I managed to shoot
twice between showers, reduced the temperature from
$97°$ to $85°$, which was a boon in spite of its severity.
Thirdly, I am jolly strong and regaining health
rapidly. I think I told you how much I had been
pulled down by the Shanghae summer. I lost sixteen pounds in a month, and I believe if I had not
been moved I should have drifted into a typhoid.
When I left Hankow I was scarcely well enough to
undertake such a journey, but a course of tonic has
rapidly restored me. The people here are new to
the sight of a foreigner, and my first experiences were
uncomfortable, to say the least. It so happened that
a convoy of recruits for the war with Japan were on
leave ashore, and these young braves with the rollick-
ing devilry that characterises Chinese soldiers stirred
up a hubbub which became mighty annoying to me.
Along the whole route of about half-a-mile from my
boat to the mandarin's wretched abode, my chair was
preceded, surrounded, and followed by a screaming,
shouting, demoniacal mob, crying, "Ha! ha! here's a
foreign devil; beat the foreign devil." I began to

feel sorry I had left my thick stick behind. They got more troublesome, and seized the poles of my chair, the rudest vehicle of the kind I ever saw, to have a better look, thereby causing it to oscillate on the shoulders of the two bearers. I was meditating with a smile on my face whether or not I should spoil the countenances of one or two of them, when a kick delivered by my attendant, the invaluable Leila, right in a fellow's chest, sent him reeling among the crowd and made me laugh outright; the rest soon cleared off.

We reached the official house, and the rabble, as usual with Chinese, burst in, and were spectators of my interview with the mandarin, who proved to be a quiet, agreeable man. We got on very well. He sent two of his lictors to conduct me back safely, and they certainly fulfilled their office well in licking the common herd. On arriving at the boat I harangued them on their want of politeness. They listened in silence, and most of them went quietly away. I have not been insulted since, but walk about and shoot and chat with all I meet in the most amicable spirit, and they are as civil to me as possible. It is the nature of Chinamen to give in to anything which asserts its superiority. A kick and a few words in his own tongue telling him he is an ignorant boor will make a common Chinaman worship you. Singly or in small groups they are the pink of civility, but a mob is rather dangerous. I shall probably have to pass through many similar scenes on my long journey,

September 19*th*.—I have waited here now seven days and have made up my mind to wait no longer. I have paid away large sums to boatmen, and bought native orders on distant banks. The spirit of the traveller is on me and I long to go on. Such a plum does not often fall into our parched-up mouths in these days of inaction in our service.

My writer is a capital good man. We get on famously, and I shall improve in Chinese, for I have nothing else to talk all day long. In about a month hence I shall hope to have another opportunity of sending a letter by this boat, which will return to Hankow after completing the contract of conveyance. I shall then have a land journey of a month more to reach my destination. All is well and promising. I think of you all individually, and many a time the thought of hardship in being so perpetually banished from you all comes over me like a cloud. With affectionate love, a long adieu.]

To F. E. R.

[*Lo-shan, a small naval station on the Yangtsze. Saturday, September* 12*th*, 1874.—I think my friends at home could scarcely refrain from laughing at me in my present ridiculous position, could they only get one peep into my boat. I have the honour of writing to you under the eyes of any number of eager natives, who never had a sight of a " foreign devil " before in all their born days. They have been quite frantic with excitement in this little town. I thought it best to pay a visit to the local mandarin, and claim his protection. He happens to be a military mandarin, and in China the army is held in very low estimation as compared with the civil authority. I was afraid, therefore, that this man could prove of little use to me. However, I found him such a nice straightforward man, that I quite enjoyed my visit (although it was not a comfortable one, as I will explain directly), and told my new friend that I hoped he would come and have some champagne in my boat to-morrow, to which he readily consented. The weather had been so hot that mere existence in the boat was a misery, so long as that cruel sun shone. I waited impatiently for four o'clock to come, which was the time fixed for my visit, longing for the diversion it would cause. I was little prepared for the hubbub my presence was going to stir up. It so happened that there was quite a fleet of junks and small craft, freighted with troops for the war in Formosa, waiting at anchor for a fair wind to proceed on their way; and most of the lawless young braves had leave to amuse themselves on shore, chiefly, I imagine, on account of its being somewhat of a merry-making day in the town, and strolling players had set up their stage in the open air. In the country, the advent of a theatrical troop creates frantic excitement. It is the event of the year, and the whole country round flocks in, and stands from morning till night in gratified amazement, watching the marvellous plays. In these representations, noise is the principal feature. The gestures and movements of the actors are bombastic to an absurd degree, and the dialogue is chanted in their favourite falsetto squeak. In large towns, they go on giving a series of plays which last without interruption for days and nights, but here in the country, darkness stays proceedings, and they begin again in the morning. Strings of people file away when it is over toward their village homes.

We met some last night in the course of our walk. My teacher or writer is quite a companion to me now, and more so as he is a very eager Christian; and in talking to them about the play, we told them what a vast difference there was between the large city theatre companies, and these wretched strolling bands that they so much admired.

Revenons à nos moutons. I got into a most miserable chair, and proceeded to the mandarin's house, attended by my useful rascal Liu, or Leila, as I shall call him, for that is his nickname. A rabble of youths, and these young recruits, immediately surrounded my chair, and danced frantically along, laughing, shouting, screaming, and calling me all sorts of names, including "foreign devil." I happened to be in a good humour, otherwise some of them would have felt my fists; but rather amused than otherwise, I left it to my servant to vent his spleen on them, which he did very effectively, especially in the case of one young wag, who seized the chair-pole, and seemed inclined to upset the whole concern. For just as I was debating with myself whether I should spoil his countenance for him or not, I was intensely amused to see "Leila" deliver a kick from the other side, which came fair and square and straight, just like an Englishman's hit from the shoulder, and sent the young joker reeling among the crowd. Arrived at the miserable abode of the petty mandarin, the crowd, *selon les Chinois*, burst in with us, and flattened their noses against the windows, while I talked to my host. He was a fine soldierlike man, and treated me very civilly. We talked for twenty minutes, and then I left. I found him much occupied with a book written by one of his countrymen, who was sent over to record his impressions of foreign countries, and referring to it several times, he said to me, "Ah, your country must be a fine place!" I asked him to lend it to me yesterday, when he came to return my visit, and he was good enough to send it the moment he got home. What do you think was the sight of all others which most struck our celestial author and critic? Well, it was the appearance of Piccadilly at night, with its double row of gas lamps rising and falling with the inequalities of that noble thoroughfare. It reminded him of a gigantic golden dragon! And this was the finest sight in all Europe! Just imagine how difficult it is to negotiate with people who look at things in a totally different plane to ourselves. My military friend lent me a couple of men with whips, to conduct me back, and they managed to repress the demoniacal mob, which nevertheless followed us to the boat, leaping and screaming like maniacs, shouting to others, " I say, come along, here's a foreigner, what a lark, ha! ha! ha!" And when I alighted from my chair, a dense triple row of cheeky faces stood by to have a good stare. I thought if I did not speak there would be annoyance in store for me. So I stood for a moment closely surveying all their faces, and they shrank from my gaze like animals. Then raising my arm, I harangued the crowd.

"Why do you crowd round me in this rude manner? You do not mean to say you have not seen a foreigner before? Is this your courtesy to strangers? I have heard it often said, that China was of all things distinguished for civility and courtesy. But am I to take this as a specimen of it? Shall I go back and tell my countrymen that your boasted (li) civility only amounts to ignorant rudeness?" I was perfectly astonished at the effect this speech produced. They listened with silence, and, when I had done, walked quietly back quite abashed. Only a few remained; and over and over again, after this, many an irrepressible youngster was severely rebuked, for any sign of disrespect, by his elders.

Yesterday, I had a return visit from the mandarin. He came on horseback, and remained a whole hour. I gave him champagne and soda-water, which he seemed to like immensely, and also cigarettes. These neat Russian manufactures take with the Chinese tremendously. I was very much amused to see the mandarin hand over to his servant the remains of his cigarette. There was barely two puffs left, yet the servant eagerly put it to his mouth, and took the prize outside to go the round of the remaining attendants. I begged him to take a fresh one, and we gave two among the servants; since they were piggish enough to pass them from mouth to mouth, I did not think it worth while to waste more on them. I am supplied with a certain number of things to give away to mandarins as presents, such as scented-soap, liqueurs and cigars, and a case of champagne for interviews. My experience having told me of the value of cigarettes, I brought a large quantity. They are as valuable as that Russian's children, who, when pursued by wolves in Siberia, threw them out one by one to stop the ravenous crowd. So I have only to scatter cigarettes, and slip through a mob unmolested.

I was out yesterday very early, and took a stroll over a line of low grass hills, which surround this rather pretty spot. The view was very refreshing; trees abound, and water too. Looking across the Yangtsze, a fine row of dark mountains filled the background, and a richness of colour blended with the view down to the water's edge, where some rather high cliffs of red sand, topped by a military encampment, added picturesqueness to the scene. I started several small coveys of partridges during my walk, and much delighted at the discovery, made arrangements to start after them with my gun this morning, but I have been disappointed by a thunderstorm and heavy rain. . . . The heat has been dreadful. To have to pass a whole day in this narrow and confined space, with the thermometer at 97°, as it was yesterday, is no joke. . . . We get beautiful cool well-water from a temple hard by. It is a boon in itself to get good water. All along I have had first to put alum in, then boil, and afterwards filter the wretched fluid, and even then I dare not trust it without the powerful safeguard of brandy. There is but one drawback to this nice place, which I am getting quite fond of, and that is the mosquitoes. . . . I amuse myself sometimes after dinner with the boatmen on the junks lying alongside us. They regularly form a cluster and watch my evening meal with running comments which are very entertaining to me. We are good friends and very civil to each other, so I afford them every opportunity of wondering at our superior civilisation. . . I never saw such miserable feeders as these Chinese; beyond fish, eggs, and occasionally some skeleton fowls and ducks, it is impossible to buy anything. I am obliged to fall back on my tinned reserves, which were meant for the provinces of Kwei-chou and Yunnan, which are more or less depopulated and poor in provisions.]

September 12th.—In view of having to pass several

days at Lo-shan, I deemed it prudent to call on the local official, although he had neither position nor authority of any consequence whatever. Of military grade, which is looked down upon in China, and of no higher rank than a *pa-tsung*, or ensign, his position in the place at the head of only eighteen men was nothing more than that of a head policeman. Lo-shan contains something over a thousand families, and its civil government, like that of many similar growing places in the district, lies in the jurisdiction of the magistrate who presides over the head city, ten miles away. Having announced my intention of calling at 4 P.M., I waited through a very hot day for the welcome diversion. But I was little prepared for the hubbub my presence was going to create. Lo-shan had never been feasted with even the sight of a foreigner, and their very ignorance of his conformation put a boldness to the curiosity of the mob, which surrounded me with shouts and abusive language as I proceeded in a hired chair, the meanest of its kind, to the poor abode of the local official. As is usually the case in China, the rabble burst into the courtyard of the yamen, and were with difficulty repressed from filling even the audience room by the whips of the lictors at the door, who plied their arms with a will. An interview is never private in China, any more than correspondence. It is not considered indecorous to take up any written document, whether intended to be confidential or not, and to read it calmly through.

I have seen a mandarin, while making a call on the consul, step up to the writer's table, and, coolly putting on his spectacles, read a letter which had just been prepared for another official on an important subject. So, too, every interview I have had the honour to assist at, has been swelled by the presence of a number of idle spectators, from yamen runners down to the household servants of the mandarin. I found the official in question to be a very civil and obliging man, well informed and well disposed towards foreigners. He was reading a book written by a Chinaman of rank, named Pin, who some years ago had been sent to Europe to record his impressions of foreign countries, and subsequently published the volume referred to. Calling my attention to the book, he frequently remarked that England must be a fine country. On taking leave I complained of the conduct of the people, and the officer immediately ordered a couple of his men to escort me back, but their efforts were barely equal to repressing the excited crowd, which followed us to the boat and stood in a dense mass round my chair. The best way of pacifying a Chinese mob is by talking to them, and showing them at once that you are familiar with their language and literature. Accordingly I addressed a few words to my aggressive audience, which had the almost immediate effect of quieting and dispersing it. The disturbance was mainly owing to the presence of a large number of young soldiers who were on their way to the seat of impending war in Formosa, and also to the fact of its being a sort of public holiday, for strolling players had arrived and set up a *sing-song* which attracted spectators from all the country round.

September 13th *to* 19th.—All this time was unfortunately lost in waiting for further orders with respect to the last telegram from Calcutta. But as no messenger had yet made his appearance, and ample time had passed for letters to have reached me, I resolved to proceed on the 20th. No other course was open to me. Further delay would have made it too late to follow the overland route, and it could only have been abandoned at a considerable cost. Lo-shan proved to be an exceedingly pleasant place to stop at. A stretch of downs surrounded the town and afforded me both exercise and sport. I was able to take many a walk free from intruders, and by permission of the mandarin, I shot over some excellent cover. Immediately behind these downs extended a flat plain, as far as the eye could reach, cultivated with rice, and the lotus. This is a great lotus district, and a very curious special industry has grown out of it for the people of Lo-shan. It appears that the art or knack of extracting the kernel of the lotus nut from its hard shell is only properly understood at this place, and the produce of the whole district is sent to Lo-shan, whence it is distributed in its edible form up and down the river. The view across the river, which was here fully a mile and a half wide, ...

September 20*th*.—Still no messenger. Started at 11 A.M. with a strong breeze from the north-east, which accelerated our progress, but struck me down with fever. Splendid views of green country and mountains in the background extended the whole way along the right bank to Yao-chou Fu. We were stopped by a Leking barrier, which was stationed at a distance of twenty to thirty li from Yao-chou Fu. I immediately sent my card to the official in charge, but in the meanwhile, much to my annoyance, I found a soldier poking about among my boxes with a long javelin. A few words made him desist at once and leave the boat. We then sailed for the celebrated island of Chün-shan, which lies at the entrance of the lake opposite the city of Yao-chou, and some thirty li away from the latter. Here we took leave of the muddy Yangtsze, and entered into cleaner waters of a pale green hue. The panorama of Yao-chou Fu and the surrounding hills, as seen from the island of Chün-shan, is certainly very striking, and the city is placed on a beautiful site. The red sandstone, which seems to be the prevailing formation, crops out in various places, adding richness and colour to the scene. Yao-chou Fu used to be the place of transhipment for the grain tribute of Hu Nan, and in those days of prosperity, the business of the place was very large and the wharves crowded with junks, but since the tax has been levied in coin, all this activity has vanished from the place.

September 21*st.*—The island of Chün-shan is celebrated for producing the finest tea in China. A yearly supply of forty catties is required for the Emperor's use, and about one hundred and sixty catties more are annually appropriated by all the high officials of the province, from the viceroy downwards. The Taiping rebels deliberately destroyed a great number of the shrubs, so that the proprietors have but a small crop to dispose of. The price in former days was as high as 5 dollars a catty. The wind continuing favourable and strong, my boatman took the unusual course of sailing straight across the lake instead of creeping along the shore. We actually accomplished one hundred and eighty li at one stretch, and entered the river at 9 P.M. The lake is extremely shallow, and seems to be very little used, for I only saw one or two junks during the day. Unfortunately I was feeling very ill all day with fever. A perfect plague of flies infested us the whole way from Chün-shan to the other end of the lake. These flies were armed with a strong proboscis, with which they could inflict a sting quite as acute as that of a mosquito, though free from venom. Neither pain nor mark remained on brushing away the insect. The Chinese have a legend that they are the soldiers of the Lake Spirit, who sends them to attack all intruders of his domain. We anchored at a place called Nan-chai.

September 22*nd.*—Started at 6 A.M. and sailed up the Yuan river with a good breeze until we arrived at a considerable town stretching along the face of the river, called Ni Hsin T'ang, sixty li from the mouth. After remaining half-an-hour to procure provisions we proceeded on our way. The army of the Lake Spirit here left us as suddenly as it had come. The scenery of the river is exceedingly pretty. In lieu of bare towing paths and muddy deposits, which invariably meet the eye in many parts of China, here I was delighted to find grassy banks covered thickly with willow trees. I landed and walked as far as my weak state permitted. Everywhere the signs of prosperity abounded. There was neat and careful cultivation of cotton. The homesteads adjoining the little farms were well built and well provided, and men, women and children seemed to be happy and thriving. I met with civility from all. Stopped for the night at Yin Ho Hsiang, having run over a hundred li from our last halt.

September 23rd.—Started at 5 A.M. and progressed slowly. The weather began to change and fall in temperature. Passed Lung-yang Hsien, at a distance, by 11 A.M. I felt very unwell. At 3.30 P.M. rain prevented further progress, and we stopped at Liao Ya Tsui, only seventy li in advance.

September 24th.— Continued to rain all the morning, and the most miserable weather lasted all day. In the afternoon, however, a slight improvement induced the boatman to track on till 6 P.M., when we stopped at Shih-ma P'u, twenty li from Ch'ang-tê. We had only progressed forty li. About midway we came across a small tributary river, which does not appear in three several maps which I possess. I am told, however, by the boatmen that this river communicates with Sha-shih, on the Yangtsze, and also with Tseng-shih and Li-chou. I had remarked on my way up that there were very few boats on the river, but this tributary fully accounted for it, according to the statements of my informants. They say that half the trade of Ch'ang-tê passes up northwards to the great marts I have mentioned, through this connecting stream.

September 25th.—Reached Ch'ang-tê, and had a fine view of the city as we passed along its face on the opposite side of the river. The wall of the city, as I observed after we had crossed over, was built very close to the river side, leaving no room whatever for an open suburb to spring up outside, which was absolutely necessary for the carrying on of trade. The difficulty, here, has been got over by building wooden tenements on long piles, embedded in the very mud of the sloping bank. The result is an exceedingly odd appearance of houses walking on long crooked legs and leaning at all angles.

They continue only where the wall exists, or for about a distance of three li, but the line of houses more substantially built extends along ten li of river frontage, and from first to last are to be seen a host of small junks anchored below, awaiting their cargo. We crossed over to the city, and I sent my card to the prefect. I had scarcely dismissed the messenger before a boat came alongside, and a mandarin wearing a red button stepped into my boat. Not being prepared to receive him I hastily retired to rearrange my dress, but my visitor insisted on my making no change, shook hands with me, and said that the prefect had especially deputed him to attend upon me, and that he should accompany me to the next prefecture. He stayed upwards of an hour and talked incessantly. After he left, I was somewhat annoyed by people coming down to stare. In some cases they would step on the side of the boat to look in through the windows. It was the great full moon holiday, and a number of idle characters were about. No direct rudeness was offered, however, although the crowd showed itself inclined to be "larky."

September 27th.—Left Ch'ang-tê, accompanied by Li Pi-shêng, at 11 A.M. The weather was cloudy and the atmosphere damp. At 3 P.M. the boat was brought up at a place called Ta-ch'i-k'ou, only twenty li from Ch'ang-tê. I imagined that the weather was the cause of stopping further progress, but I was informed later, much to my dissatisfaction, that the newly hired men had to feast and drink before commencing the voyage; else they would not work happily. So that I had to submit to the delay on account of their devotion to all the customs of their class.

September 28th.—Started at daylight and by two o'clock reached T'ao-yuen Hsien, which is a large and flourishing city. Strange to say it possesses no walls, and, I am told, never had any. It is the only instance I know of a magisterial city without walls, though my writer says there are a few more. I exchanged cards with the magistrate and proceeded as fast as we could on my way. The whole frontage of the town was stored up with earthenware water-jars and glazed flower-pots. The place was a depôt for the pottery trade, and large quantities of the above ware was passed on from T'ao-yuen Hsien to Ch'ên-chou Fu, and even on to Ch'ên-yuan Fu in Kwei-chou. It is said that the magistrate who rules over T'ao-yuen Hsien has no easy task to perform. It is the most lawless, independent district in the whole province. The people if roused by a sense of injustice or misrule won't hesitate to carry off their chief magistrate bodily to the governor's capital and demand a change. Proceeded on our way twenty li to a place called Pai-ma Tu, where there is a ferry across to the right bank of the river. From that point a high road runs up to Kwei-chou, and continues on to Yun-nan. A very large trade is carried on with those provinces by this road. It is a considerably shorter route than the river, which bends about in all directions. Since this morning we have been entering mountain scenery of a very beautiful and attractive kind. Everywhere vegetation seemed to spring up in abundance. Trees multiplied, but I could not distinguish many varieties. Pines covered all the hill tops, and several stout trees of the ash kind seemed to exist below. I even came across two palms. We stopped for the night five li further on, at Shui-ch'i, ninety-five li.

September 29*th.*—Started 5 A.M. Li Pi-shêng, the mandarin who has accompanied me from Ch'ang-tê, often pays me a visit and talks on any subject. I have found him an exceedingly agreeable companion. This afternoon, being anxious to take a short stroll, I went on shore, and Mr. Li readily accompanied me. The boatmen, however, tracked on in hot haste to a point much farther than I was quite able to accomplish after my long continued weakness and indisposition. We followed a beautiful path high up the green cliff, which often wound inland for a short distance, and thus added to the length of my harassing walk. Li, with great consideration, insisted on my resting often, and in many ways showed a kindness unusual in a Chinaman and an official. In the course of repeated conversations with this man, I had learnt the history of his career, and he was at no pains to conceal from me the discontent he felt at his present lot. One of Li Hung-ch'ang's right-hand men in the wars of the rebellion, he had been successively rewarded with a number of lucrative posts by that powerful chief, whose confidence he still boasts of possessing. In 1864 he had an appointment at Shanghae, where he acquired a liking for Europeans, which appears to have remained unimpaired. Li Hung-ch'ang continued

to promote his favourite until, with a red button
of the second degree, and the rank of Tsungping or
general, he sent him to an important post in Kwei-
chou. Here, however, the little man fell ill, and
was obliged to obtain leave of absence to his native
city Ch'ang-tê. Since then his woes commenced.
Whether it was that the government were jealous
of Li Hung-ch'ang's power, and noticing with dread
the caution with which that able commander was
filling important posts all over the country with
his own men, had set to work to thwart him; or
whether it was a *bonâ fide* compliment to Li Pi-shêng's
abilities, as they would have him believe, certain it
is that, so soon as he became convalescent, my friend
received orders from the viceroy of Hu Kwang at Wu-
ch'ang Fu to remain at Ch'ang-tê under the orders
of the *chih-fu* (prefect), as his energy and influence
were required in his native district. Thus it came
about that I was honoured with the company of a man
of distinction, whose actual services and decoration of
the red button put him somewhat above the position
of the local prefect whose orders he had to obey.
Of course he was intriguing to get free, and trusted
very much in my being able to give him a helping
hand by reporting his diligent attention and civility
to me, in my letter to H.B.M. Minister at Pekin,
who he hoped would incidentally mention him in
terms of praise to his patron Li Hung-ch'ang. Since
this morning we entered upon a complete change of
scenery. The river, with its beautifully clear water.

was considerably narrowed, and began to wind in and out between fine rocky gorges. The hills were tossed about in strange profusion, yet in something like symmetry of form. They were all conical and of moderate size, not exceeding two hundred feet in height. But the general effect was very grand. It gave me the idea of an encampment of hills. Further on, where the gorge became wilder and the hills approached the river, I was enabled to determine the nature of the composing rock, although, without the possibility of approaching near enough to examine closely the towering cliff, I must speak with hesitation as to the correctness of my conclusions. Isolated here and there along the banks, the very heart and centre of these conical hills was laid bare to view. Cut completely in half from apex to base, as though by some mighty convulsion of nature, the hill still preserved its rounded form on the land side, covered with verdure, while to the river it presented a denuded face of grey sandstone cliff. The rocks rose perpendicularly in a triangular shape out of the shallow waters at their base, with a grandeur which was most impressive. The whole of Hu Nan is an exceedingly good field for geological examination. Nature seems to have run riot in this region at some period in the mysterious past.

Lieutenant Garnier, in his excellent pamphlet describing his trip from Hankow down part of this river and up to the Yangtsze at Fuchou, describes the rivers which disappear and reappear after a subterranean course, and the many evidences of mighty convulsions of nature which met his view. The bed of this river itself and the adjoining banks offer a rich harvest to a scientific explorer. Almost every variety of strata crops out at different points. On arriving at our resting place for the night, I was very much surprised to see a small boat of the very commonest class come alongside, and a couple of disreputable looking rascals emerge from it with the card of the T'ao-yuen magistrate in their hands. He had sent them to escort and protect!! me as far as the next magisterial city. The viceroy's orders were imperative, but the worthy magistrate evaded them as far as he dared. Nothing is done thoroughly in China; the mandarins look to their tenure of office as the golden opportunity for feathering their nests. So our worthy friend carried out his instructions as cheaply and nastily as he was able on this occasion. He despatched a couple of dirty scullions, or some other such menials, out of the needy crowd that infests all yamens, hoping no doubt that fine words and the foreigner's ignorance would hide his mean devices. The village we stopped at for the night had a special industry which occupied every family of its inhabitants. Above this point the rapids commenced, and the bamboo ropes (of the thickness of a man's forefinger) required for tracking boats through them were manufactured and procured at this place.

Extracts from letters.

To F. E. R.

[*Four days from Ch'ang-tê. September* 30*th*, 1874.— I have now an opportunity of sending a letter by a mandarin (a very jolly fellow) who has accompanied me for my protection from Chang Fu thus far, and now returns. I have been passing through lovely scenery. The whole of this province must once have been the theatre of an awful convulsion. There are many cases of rivers disappearing and emerging again. But the country round me is more tossed than anything I ever saw. Clusters of conical hills extend as far as the eye can see. In some places they climb on one another, and all are covered with bright green underwood and tall trees. Nearer the river one or two stand out with remarkable boldness, split in two, and showing the bare face of the denuded sandstone. You may imagine what wonderful shapes are continually occurring. The eye is astonished at every bend. Now and then, perched high up on an almost inaccessible height, you see a little temple. Marvellous beauty everywhere. We went through some rapids yesterday. They were very small and did not delay us much. Ch'ang-tê is a wonderful city. The people would have been troublesome, but the mandarins prevented any annoyance beyond staring. In order to enjoy a walk and be free of the crowd, I ordered the boat over to the other side of the river, which was there fully half-a-mile wide, and the water was beautifully clear. We had to

LI PI-SHÊNG'S DEPARTURE.   153

remain there the next day for procuring extra trackers for the rapids, also to complete ceremonies with the local prefect. He declined my presents with good reasons, and gave my messenger 1000 cash, after which I had to follow suit with his messengers when he sent me fowls, ducks, and fruit. He has been attentive enough to send a very superior and intelligent mandarin with me. Every day the jolly old fellow pays me a visit and has a long talk. I shall be escorted from station to station thus. . . . You would laugh if you could see how the people try to catch a glimpse of me. Sometimes I am lying on my air bed with my back to the two small windows, and suddenly turning round see six or seven noses flattened against them, and many pairs of eyes examining me. Of course, I drive them away at once. It happened to be a holiday when I was at Ch'ang-tê, and several respectable people hired boats and came across to have a look at me. All day long I had the annoyance of all these boat-loads lying off and staring at me.]

September 30*th*.— Li Pi-shêng left me to-day at 2.30 P.M. and returned on his homeward voyage, no doubt with a happy sense of relief from the monotonous duty of escorting a foreigner. He must have felt the *ennui* of toiling after my boat very keenly, for in the first place he did little else all the day but smoke opium; and, secondly, it was his duty to accompany me to the next prefectural city, instead of which he bid me good-bye at the boundary of the district.

which oddly enough coincided with the first set of
rapids we had to encounter. I was now left for
" safe conduct and protection " to the care of the two
miserable menials in their ridiculous boat, whose
frantic efforts to keep pace with us afforded me much
amusement. The sail was a marvel. Every square
foot of it had a hole big enough to pass the head
through, and whatever cloth remained to catch the
wind had no more consistency than very old
muslin.

At about 3 P.M. we passed through several rapids
in succession. There was nothing formidable about
them. Five men tracked along the shore, and the
remainder staved the boat off sunken rocks with
their bamboo poles. The scenery was wildly beautiful, and more compact than that we passed through
yesterday; a continuation of perpendicular cliffs now
and then lined the river side. A mountain path,
which was the highway for foot passengers, passed
in some places along the very face of the upright
cliff. But I noticed a heavy iron chain cable hung
in festoons, from niches cut in the rock, along the
face of this dangerous path. It was the gift of a
philanthropic widow, whose charity may have been
evoked by the loss of a relative on the fatal spot.

October 1st.—The weather during the last ten
days has been most unfavourable and unhealthy,
fully bearing out part of the statement which Li Pi-
shêng made at Ch'ang-tê Fu, in the course of our
conversation, that the two dangerous months in Hu

Nan were the second and the eighth. I have not had a chance of recovering health and strength, and the frequent attacks of fever and diarrhœa have reduced me to a state of emaciation almost and extreme weakness. My boatmen too are attacked with simultaneous vomiting and diarrhœa, accompanied with violent pains in the stomach. I cured the head boatman, who suffered most, with an opium pill, the others fortunately recovering quick, or my slender store of drugs might have been exhausted in one night.

To-day we passed through the most dangerous set of rapids on the river. They extended over thirty li, and are divided into three portions of ten li each by the boatmen, who name them the upper, the middle, and the lower. In these rapids, solitary rocks and rugged ledges appeared everywhere in such profusion that it seemed impossible for a boat to be guided through in safety. The labour was great, but they accomplished it with great skill and success, until we had reached half-way across the middle set of rapids, when a violent collision with a rock produced a leak which compelled them to pull up at a timber station that happened to be near and spend half-an-hour over repairs.

I remarked that in one part the bed of the rapid was composed of slate, which, judging by the height to which it extended on the banks, had suffered a tremendous amount of denudation. The rocks which showed above the stream were of a harder slaty shale.

Farther on, at another point in the rapids, the basement rock was undoubtedly trap. All that was seen was rough, pointed, and jagged. Nowhere had it yielded to the force of the running stream and become smooth. Dykes of it rose out of the water, bold and naked to the air, evidently denuded on both sides of the softer rock which formed its bed once, but had long since succumbed to the torrent. The small village we stopped at to make repairs was a very flourishing timber station. The hills at the back were well covered with fine fir-trees, and a mountain stream flowed down from their inmost recesses, facilitating the transfer of the timber from these backwoods to the main stream.

October 2nd.—This morning I had the misfortune to be completely prostrated with a severe attack of dysentery accompanied by acute pain, which lasted for some hours. I was obliged to stop the boat for four or five hours in order to ascertain the course which the malady was likely to take, harassed all the time with the thought of being compelled to relinquish my mission and return to Hankow crestfallen. However, to my great relief, the disease was quickly and completely driven away by opium and ipecac pills, the efficacy of which in the early stage of this malady I can thankfully vouch for. Having lost so much time, we only progressed thirty-five li for this day's journey. Although the disease was cured, I was left so utterly weak as to be unable to rise without assistance. The events consequently of this day and the following week are written up from pencil notes jotted in my private diary, and from the journal kept by my writer.

October 3rd.—Started at 5 A.M., and reached Ch'ên-chou Fu, locally pronounced Shên-chou Fu, a distance of seventy li, by 7 P.M. I could not rise without assistance. From glimpses of the scenery I noted that high continuous hills on both banks hemmed in the river, and that they were well covered with tall straight fir-trees and thick underwood.

October 5th.—Started early and passed a dilapidated city called Lou-ch'i Hsien, which had not yet recovered from the heavy hand of the "Longhaired Rebels," i.e. the Taipings. At 5 P.M. arrived at Pu-shih, formerly the flourishing centre of the timber trade, but now reduced to insignificance by its treatment under the rebel raid. The people, however, seemed to lack nothing in spirit, for they took all the trouble to make their way over fully a mile to where we were anchored off a stony flat, and upon our moving away they followed us along this most uncomfortable ground, shouting and using unpleasant expressions. Even the efforts of the sub-prefect who accompanied me in a gun-boat were fruitless in quieting them, and as for the soldiers they positively feared the mob.

October 6th.—Started at daylight and reached Chên-ch'i Hsien at 7 A.M. Just stopped long enough to exchange cards with the mandarin, and buy what provisions were procurable. The extreme difficulty of buying food has been a continual trouble to me the whole way. Fowl and duck are the only things to be had, and in many places even these are not to be bought. More than this, such as can be bought are meagre and fleshless, containing no nourishment whatever. Any European, therefore, who attempts this route should provide himself with foreign provisions. At Chên-ch'i Hsien the river takes a most remarkable and provoking bend to the south of over two hundred li, and then flows north, until reaching the line of its original course, it bends to the west again. This deviation forms a complete sack in appearance on the map, and adds greatly to the tediousness of tracking through innumerable small rapids.

* * * * *

Hiatus in official journal.

The following notes to October 25th are from a private journal written in pencil, and hardly legible:

Max. 72°.
Min. 65°.
Dist. 67 li.

October 5th.—At 6 P.M. reached Lou-ch'i Hsien, a miserable place. I was still feeling very weak; boatmen somewhat troublesome. Passed the town and anchored off a stony sandy strip of island not far from the town. People flocked over and became noisy; soldiers proved of no use whatever in keeping them quiet. The boatman wanted to buy things, and hence delay occurred. Having started at length, quite a rabble of young men followed along the stony shore for fully a mile in the vain hope of seeing me. But their noise was disagreeable. Stopped at Ta Wan.

Tuesday, 6th.—Here the mandarin who accompanied me from Ch'ên-chou Fu returned. I gave him presents of cigars and soap, which highly pleased him. He returned the compliment with Chinese confectionery. Exchanged cards with Chih Hsien. He sends two official messengers to escort me to the next Hsien. At some five or six li from Chên-ch'i Hsien I saw a number of coal-mines being worked on the hill-side, on left bank of river, in usual Chinese wasteful method. Only one of the two messengers turn up, and he is a most disreputable looking thin youth of twenty.* Place called Sa-tui; no village or houses at all.

Max. 78°.
Min. 69°.
Dist. 68 li.

Wednesday, 7th.—Started at daylight. High rocky land on right bank; one bold denuded cliff looked quite calcined. At 9 A.M., reached Chiang Kôu; small river runs in here. Chiang Kôu compact little town; cottages by river side. Pretty little pagoda in middle; three substantial buildings towering over all. One Kiang Si guild, one Hukwang guild. Quartz everywhere. Gold washers. Chips off bits of gneiss and quartz and granite from weather-worn and blackened cliff. Difficult rapid; seven or eight hundred feet of rope out to top of cliff; there men descend to level and drag on all fours to stony bank. Men worked hard

Max. 75°.
Min. 74°.
Dist. 55 li.

* A mere street-runner.

all day; anchored at Hsias Lou Tsai, in middle of river, 5.50 P.M. Feel myself getting stronger. Scenery very changing; now bold cliffs, now tame quiet downs, now high hills covered with trees. Witness a curious mode of fishing—stream dammed, naked men in water striking at fish with sickles!

Max. 90°.
Min. 73°.
Dist. 50 li.

Thursday, 8th.—Felt very much better. Boatmen very much done up after their hard work yesterday; often take long rests. With temperature at 89° I don't blame them; but they allege a strong south wind as the main cause of obstruction. Country tame and low; few hills. After stopping at Tungwan, a small town governed by a Ssŭ-yeh.* At 6 A.M. I tried to take a stroll, but my strength was scarcely equal to a hundred yards. I went along the cliff path and found composition of hills all quartz. Tung-wan had a lot of houses on poles, which seems their favourite style of architecture here; a number of empty pens showed where the market was held in the day. Attack of rheumatism in right side.

Max. 91°.
Min. 72°.
Dist. 45 li.

Friday, 9th.—High land covered with underwood, rather bare on right bank. Ravines leading to fine trees. Wood-cutter's cottage at entrance. Bed of rapids, slate and laminated shell; bank, ditto. High land everywhere replanted with young trees. Here still remain some fine trees, which show the damage that must have been done by the rebels, who burnt down acres of forest on the hills. Passed through several rapids. Progress slow; men stopped twenty

* *Sic.*

minutes for food about 3 P.M. Sun behind the hills. Took a short stroll. Bank all sand and shell. Two mandarin boats in company with us. Saw a raft stuck in a rapid. Rheumatism alleviated by fomentation.

Saturday, 10*th*.—Pass through tame scenery ; hills recede, and a great deal of plain, cultivated, appears. Now and then cliffs occur, and we cross two or three rapids, stop at———, where there is a gun-boat station. We are only five li from Hung Chiang Ssu, a flourishing place of trade ; feel much stronger. Max. 80°.
Min. 66°.
Dist. 70 li.

Sunday, 11*th*.—Reach Hung Chiang Ssu. Boatman borrows 10,000 cash ; has to hire men and buy provisions. Remain all day. Flourishing place. A Ti-tu and Ssû-yeh ; latter sends four men to look after me. A boat with messengers from Chien Yang Hsien arrives, sent to meet me with civil messages. Large crowd collects opposite boat. I open doors and let them see me reading with teacher. Dense mass of heads. Gradually they become noisy. Boat moved to quieter spot. Send letter to Ti-tu reminding him of his duty to quiet the mob. He does so, and beats the ringleaders. Ni-Ssû-yeh calls and ko-tows, much to my astonishment ; brings his son Tuin Qun. Ssû-yeh wants to send four men with me to Chiang Yang Hsien ; I decline, having already four protectors. Hung Chiang Ssu has a big trade in wood. Rebels destroyed Pu Ssu, where the great timber depôt was, and drove trade down to Hung Chiang Ssu. Rice was grown, though I don't know where. Hill surrounding town. Confluence of river which carried its trade to Chiang Hsi.

Monday, 12th.—Scenery very poor from this point; the river takes a very provoking bend. Ill. Reach Chiang Yang Hsien.

Tuesday, 13th.—Wretched scenery all the way; long stretch of stony flats. Ill.

Wednesday, 14th.—Scenery flat and poor. Ill.

Thursday, 15th.—

Friday, 16th.—Started early in the same cold, muggy damp, one spread of white vapoury canopy, which we have enjoyed for some days past. Scenery has become very tame; low grass-covered lands, and in the river-bed long stretches of stony acres. Rounded stones of no mean size among them. Reached Yuen Chow Fu before dark. Fine bridge. Send cards and letters to mandarin. He sends four soldiers, and Hsien sends three of his own men to look after me!

Saturday, 17th.—A day of misery at Yuen Chow Fu; wasted a whole day. Crowd collected, and got very noisy. No. 2 boatman got into a row with them. A rush on the boat; crowd driven back. Two men, however, remain on board boat. Shoved off into mid-stream. Two men prisoners. Crowd furious. One man escaped, and waded ashore. I sent my card to Chih Hsien. Meanwhile, boat full of citizens comes alongside, and make a great noise. I go out and protest that being ill, I could not stand that noise. They beg me to be at ease, as their

Margin notes:
Max. 72°. Min. 68°. Dist. 60 li.
Max. 88°. Min. Dist. 40 li.
Dist. 30 li.
Max. 60°. Min. 59°. Dist. 50 li.
Max. 61°. Min. 56°. Night 59.
Max. 60°. Night 62°. Dist. 55 li.

quarrel is with the boatmen. Just then Chih Hsien's messengers arrive, in answer to my card, and the boatful make off. No. 2 prisoner escapes and wades to other shore.—N.B. River very shallow. The Tao-Tai of Yunnan Fu and his son, Hsien Niao, are travelling in my company. To-day the son called with his father's compliments, and said he hoped we were to be fellow-passengers to Yunnan Fu, and that in that case, he suggested we should keep our boats together; I agreed at once. Young Niao is a nice young fellow my age. We have become great friends.

The Chih Hsien called, having previously sent presents, which I had reciprocated. He had gone some distance out of his way to see me, for we had moved on. He was a Pekinese, and had a brisk, jolly manner, and a very pleasant face. He thought he had met me before, but he is mistaken. He paid me a long visit, quite exhausting my strength.

Sunday, 18th.—Difficult rapids. River very shallow, and not so clear. Tao-Tai's boat lying below the last. His son borrows my revolver, and sends it to the Tao-Tai for defence if wanted. Son and uncle visit me, and stop an hour chatting. *Max. 67°. Min. 62°. Night 60°. Dist. 35 li.*

Monday, 19th.—Heavy rain half the night, and through great portion of the morning. Could not move during some hours. Shrubs on hills looking beautifully green and fresh after the rain. Received a note from Niao returning my revolver, and begging me to keep my boat near theirs, as there were *Max. 67°. Min. Night 60°. Dist. 25 li.*

large bands of robbers giving trouble ahead, but that his father, the Tao-Tai, had sent a letter ahead to the gun-boat commander, to send one down to protect us. Attempts at murder by the second boatman, who came in drunk, and seizing a chopper, hacked away at one of the poor old boatmen; Lin collared him.

Max. 71°.
Min. 65°.
Dist. 48 li.

Tuesday, 20th.—Sun shone out and lighted up the hills—beautiful sight. Weather warmer and more genial. Passed through a great many rapids. One large one requiring all the boats to aid each other. Fifteen men tracked us through; they had hard work all day. Stopped at San Men Tân.

Max. 68°.
Min. 60°.
Night 72°.
Dist. 25 li.

Wednesday, 21st.—Started early. River very shallow, and full of small rapids. Reach Hwang Chow at about 8 A.M. Wretched place, without even a wall, and apparently only the size of a small town. Exchange cards with Chow, who sends a couple of messengers to accompany me. Scenery diversified. 11 A.M.: Hills recede far off. Pretty dark isolated rocks in the foreground. The Tao-Tai delayed a good deal trying to procure gun-boats and a guard. We moved on three li to Lung-chi-kou. People very well disposed; a camp of soldiers here. At 2 P.M. the Tao-Tai arrives, and after some delay we eventually start with one gun-boat (which fires ostentatiously) and about twenty soldiers on foot. Hwang Chow is full of officialdom and soldiery. No shops. Have to get all their provisions from Lung-chi-kou.

Thursday, 22nd.—At 9 A.M. crossed border of Hu Nan and Kwei-chou at a place called Hsin Tsai Táng. Early this morning Tao-Tai's boat came to grief in a rapid; so he had to go back to Lung-chi-kou, and his son of course waited for him. We went on in company with another boat carrying a mandarin's family. Expect to fall in by night, so that gun-boat and soldiers, and flags and fuss, are got rid of for a time. High rocks, much weather-worn, this morning. Some looking twisted and gnarled like old timber.

Max. 68°.
Min. 65°.
Night 62.
Dist. 40 li.

Friday, 23rd.—Reach Yü-ping Hsien. Have a salute of three guns. Meet old Ching at Hsien. Takes me to his yamen. We have a long talk, and I dine with him. Fine sunny day. Feel strong and well. Arrive at 1 P.M., so only lose half a day, and give Mao Ta-jin a chance of coming up. This Hsien was a fine place, but in third year of Tung-chi the Miaotze swept down from the mountains to the north, and put thousands to the sword. The Hsien can now scarce vie with a village. Chinese government had only kept about 180 soldiers to guard so fine a city. The family who have accompanied us, and who had lost their mother, Man-yang-hsien, received a letter to-day from Yunnan announcing their father's death. The three poor orphan girls cried bitterly all day. They return at once, and have entrusted us with a letter to their brother, who is awaiting them at Ch'ên-yuan Fu. He smokes opium, and is a good for nothing.

Max. 76°.
Min.
Night.
Dist. 20 li.

Max. 78°.
Night 69°.
Dist. 70 li.

Saturday, 24th.—Start about seven. Received a salute of three guns; had proceeded some three or four li when I heard three more guns, and very soon after three more; evidently Mao Tao-Tai had arrived and started; we shall meet to-night. Country flatter. Innumerable water-wheels, size of those of a good large steamer. By-and-by wilder bold rocks; sometimes laminated as regular as brickwork. Anchored in middle of river.

Extracts from letters.

To F. E. R.

[*Three days from end of boat journey*, October 25th, 1874.—We should have been at Ch'ên-yuan Fu, my destination in this boat, five days ago, but various delays and *contretemps* have occurred to prolong our voyage; and when expectation gets so rudely disappointed travelling becomes painfully tedious. However, I trust three days will see us commence our land journey, and I shall hail the change with great relief.

Although this marvellous river, full of rapids, passes between beautiful mountain gorges, I have not half enjoyed its wonders, for I have been ill the whole time. . . . Unfortunately Hu Nan is a most unhealthy province in October, and as it proved, we scarcely saw the sun once in a fortnight. The low cloudy atmosphere was charged with damp, and the thermometer marked tremendous changes. . . .

It is sickening to ring the changes on fowl, duck,

and tinned beef (which is horrid). You cannot buy anything. The country seems quite destitute of meat and vegetables. During the last few days, however, a delightful change has come over the meagre routine. We have actually procured some very nice goat mutton, and some pommelos, and oranges (of course quite unripe). The latter I have either squeezed into lemonade or keep to ripen.

The day before yesterday a most delightful surprise awaited me. I found in the chief magistrate of the city an old friend: a man who used to be head writer in the legation all the time I was at Pekin. He gave me a salute of three guns, and came down in full fig to my boat. After a long talk he asked me to come up and spend the rest of the day with him in his yamen. I accepted, and he then took his departure, and in a short time sent down his chair to fetch me. I put on full uniform and went. The sad sight of a desolate city met my view. About ten years ago, certain rebels, half wild men who inhabit these hills to the north, made a descent on the unfortunate city and massacred over twenty thousand people. Since then it has remained like a city of the dead. Only in one small corner a few shops had got together, and the city had barely the dimensions of a village. I sat with my friend for hours talking over old times, and we walked on the grass plot in front enjoying the sun, which favoured us that day. A Chinese reception hall is open in front to the day, and there congregate a rabble of curious spectators watching the foreigner. It is a curious custom. Even in transacting business you cannot get rid of that annoying crowd of starers and listeners. I always wonder why the mandarin himself does not turn them out. But he seems on the contrary to regard them with complacency. A divan is placed facing the open end of the chamber, and a number of chairs with red cushions face each other, with small teapoys in between each, arranged in prim ceremony at right angles to the divan. The big man is conveyed to the divan seat, and his suite occupy the chairs on his side in order of seniority, while they are faced in like order by the lesser mandarins on the opposite row of seats. That is the order of an official interview. But in my case of course the chairs stared at each other in empty dignity, and I should think they never had occasion to do otherwise. By-and-by, about 4 P.M., a square table was placed in the centre of the hall and dinner was served. It was a very nice little dinner, and being hungry I set to work with my chopsticks with all diligence. Everything is served in bowls. Four small and four large bowls of different kinds of food is the correct thing for a guest, and that is just what we had. First came mushrooms very nicely cooked in a sort of gravy. Then mutton in two forms, then fowl in two forms, then a strange dish of some part of a fish, which was like eating so much lace. This and the last, *pork*, I left alone. The wind-up is always a large bowl of dry boiled rice, which is shovelled down the throat with marvellous rapidity, with a pause in the middle to add titbits from your favourite dish. I took my rice, and being accustomed to that method enjoyed it.

October 26th.—We are moving along in spite of a continual drizzle. It is a melancholy day. I do pity the poor trackers. There are eight of them toiling along quite indifferent to the wet, and I don't believe they have a change of clothes. However, they are accustomed to it, like the eels to skinning.

It is not easy to write in the motion caused by tracking. Three boats like my own (they are called mandarin boats) have been in company with us for upwards of a month, threading this tortuous stream. Two of them belonged to mandarins going to Yunnan. Of the third boat I have to tell you a sad romantic story. It contained the family of a mandarin, who had gone on ahead to take up his post in Yunnan. The family consisted of wife and three daughters between twelve and eighteen, and they were travelling under charge of an uncle. Somewhere about the 23rd of September, on the other side of Ch'ang-tê or Chang-Teh, the mother died, and the poor girls bewailed her loss with loud and bitter cries. Often I have heard their sad moan long, long after the event. Well, on arrival the other day at the city ruled over by my old friend, a letter met them from Yunnan saying the father was dead too. You may imagine the bitter grief of the poor orphans. Those pitiful wails fell on my ears for hours, and I felt for them very keenly. Things being so, there was no object in their going on, and having entrusted us with a letter to the brother who is awaiting them at the end of this water journey, they turned back to go to their own home in Shantung. Fancy what a long journey before them. They must have been three months in that boat coming down, and now all in vain they have to plod back in grief.

The mandarins have been very civil to me, and handed me on from one city to another with an escort. So much for their etiquette, but I am sorry to say their messengers were of no use either in the way of protection or show. You would have laughed to see one set sent by a parsimonious magistrate. They had hired the cheapest boat they could get. It had a marvellous sail. Every square foot of it had a hole big enough to put my head through, and the remainder was thin as muslin. Their frantic efforts to keep up with us were truly ridiculous. Such scandals as this only occurred in a few instances, for I often had a fairly respectable escort. The mobs in some places were very troublesome, collecting in large masses near the boat, and trying to peer in at me as I lay on my couch unwell. Frequently I had the annoyance of seeing faces staring in at me through the narrow windows, and as often drove them away with strong abuse, which rather astonished them, not expecting me to know Chinese. The mandarins in the other boats called upon me and we have arranged to travel together overland. We shall have twenty-five stages in chairs to Yunnan

Fu, the position of which I have described to you in a previous letter. I cannot write again till I get there. . . . I have excellent servants with me. My own boy Bombazine I trained myself, and he is very faithful.]

To his Parents.

[*October* 26*th*, 1874.—One day from the end of my boat journey.

You are no doubt getting very anxious to hear some news of me, and I am equally distressed not to be able to supply it oftener. It is only in large cities that any facilities exist for posting. I have not been able to write before simply because I had not strength to do so. For a month or more I have been ill with fifty different maladies. Fever, diarrhœa, and at last dysentery on October 2nd utterly routed me. It is the first time this dire disease has ever approached, and as I lay for half a day in violent pain, I wondered how it was to end. Ipecacuanha and opium checked the disease at once, but my strength was gone. For a week I could not raise myself. My boy pulled me up when I wanted to see the scenery and make notes. I was reduced to a skeleton, and have remained a pitiable object till within a day or two ago, when the effect of a voracious appetite began to tell, and my bones are clothed with flesh again; but, alas for my muscles, I don't know where they are. After I had almost recovered from this, and began to think I was going to be better than ever, down I went again with some complaint of which I could not form a diagnosis. After this I fell an easy victim to half a dozen diseases: pleurisy, rheumatism, indigestion, very bad neuralgia, toothache, together with a lot more. Of course in between were days when I felt better, and was able to enjoy the glorious scenery. The river winds through marvellous gorges, and is crammed full of rapids. We have, up to the present time, ascended over two hundred large ones, and innumerable small ones. Sheer cliffs of weather beaten rocks hemmed in the stream in many places, but, although the convulsions of nature have played strange pranks with the surrounding hills, yet everywhere the most profuse vegetation has sprung up to hide the roughnesses. Forests of fir trees covered the higher peaks, and for miles of its course the stream passes only woodcutters' stations. Rafts are formed of the timber and floated down to Hankow, cottages for the crew being neatly constructed of wood in the centre. Whenever we reached a large city, I sent my card to the magistrate, which he reciprocated, and sent a couple of men to escort me to the next city. Sometimes the mandarins would come and visit me, which did me, in my weak state, no good; and sometimes they sent presents of fowls, ducks, biscuits, cakes, candles, and ham, which was a greater nuisance, as I had to give their messengers a big "cumshaw" out of my slender purse, and I scarcely brought enough cash in hand; then I had to return the gift with some soap, liqueurs, or cigars. A few days ago I had a pleasant surprise in meeting with an old friend in the magistrate of the city. He gave me a salute of three guns on my arrival and departure, and carried me off to his yamen, saying that after so many days in a boat I should be more comfortable on shore, and that I must come and stretch my legs, and have a long talk with him. I spent the whole afternoon with him, talking over Pekin. He was the head writer in the legation, and Miss L——'s teacher.

There are two other boats in company with mine, conveying the Tao-Tai of Yunnan Fu and his son the Chih Hsien, or magistrate. The latter is a very nice young fellow, just my age, and we are great friends. It has been of great advantage to me being in their company, except that they have delayed me some time. We hoped to travel overland together, but in discussing our arrangements last night, young Mr. Bird, for that is their name, said they wanted to spend five days in Ch'ên-yuan Fu, which does not suit my book at all. I shall not waste more than one if I can help it. He protested that I could not possibly get off under three, but we shall see. I am dreadfully behind time as it is, and can scarcely now reach the borders by November 30th, but I shall make frantic efforts to do so if I can. How glad I shall be when I meet Colonel Browne's party, and get some European news, it will be seven weeks later than anything I have heard. I hope we shall

all return to Yunnan Fu, and spend five or six days in that fine city, buying curiosities, and making trips on the lake, and then will come the return by the big river. How glad I shall be to get back! My servants are all busy packing up everything for removal, so that I am writing under many difficulties, continual shaking inside, and the boat continually heeling over from too great a strain on the track rope; besides it is so cold that I am obliged to put on a kid glove, or I could not hold the pen, conditions somewhat harassing to write under. I often think of you all, and long to be with you. Perhaps I shall demand leave home to recruit.]

October 27*th*.—Reached Ch'ên-yuan Fu at 5 P.M. At the entrance of the city a good bridge of five or six arches, which would not disgrace a railway in England, spans the river. Rocky heights completely surround the town and lend a grandeur to its position. The gorge of the river for the last mile of our approach was very picturesque. On one side the rocks extended with such even regularity that they looked like the ancient walls of some Titan city, and the boatmen pointing upwards laughingly called them the city walls. On arrival, I immediately proceeded on foot, with my attendants and four men sent by the magistrate at my request to protect me a very short distance, to inspect an establishment in which I was intended to pass the night. It was not an inn, but a sort of forwarding house, of which several existed in the city, where travellers are not only lodged, but provided with chairs, bearers, and ponies, for the overland journey. These rival establishments even take the trouble to send touts down the river in light swift boats to meet and secure probable customers. We were thus accosted the day before reaching Ch'ên-yuan Fu, but the person who presented the card disappeared as quickly as he came, instead of remaining with our boat. A circumstance which excited the comments of my attendants at the time, and somewhat puzzled me, though I thought nothing more of it. Although I had but a short distance to walk from the boat, a crowd quickly formed round me, principally consisting of soldiers, the fruitful source of trouble everywhere, and attempted to follow me into the house. But the very unsubstantial door was closed upon them, and it severely taxed the energies of the four yamen men to keep it so. I examined the place, and found a number of clean compartments made of new wood and divided off like horse boxes. Knowing the filthiness of Chinese inns, I thought the place a paradise, and immediately gave orders for the luggage to be brought in. But, to my utter astonishment, I was told that the mob in the rear would not permit a single box to be moved; at the same time excited shopmen rushed in by some back entrance, and protested that the mob in front had completely blocked in their shops and put a stop to all business. Under the circumstances I resolved at once to go to the Hsien (magistrate) and demand protection. Accordingly the door was opened, and the press fell back on seeing me advance. I walked through the mob unmolested, and entered the yamen, which was not a hundred yards away from the scene of disturbance, yet no effort had been made to repress the mob! I was shown into a small room, and had not to wait long before the magistrate came in. His manner was rude, and a glance at his face told me that he was a type of the worst class of mandarins. He sat with face averted, and directly I began my complaint in quiet civil tones, burst out into a hoarse laugh and began to make excuses for the people. I immediately assumed an angry tone, and told him it was no laughing matter, that he was magistrate, and I expected him to disperse the mob and find me a quiet lodging. I then showed him my passport and the yamen's letter to the governor-general. His manner instantly changed, and he gave orders to his men to go down and guard the house in question. He then prepared a chair for me, in which I made an attempt to return. The crowd, however, was too great and aggressive for all the magistrate's men, and we had to beat a retreat to the yamen again, in which ignominious flight I had to be carried backwards through the mob. I was put under the necessity of breaking one man's nose who had the temerity to put his head inside the curtain of the chair to insult me. Attempts were made to upset the chair, but these were frustrated by my escort. As an example of

Chinese official apathy, I may as well mention that at the very spot where I was being insulted by the mob, a military mandarin of high rank was passing by, under whose very command were half the rioters around, and yet he made no more effort to repress them than a private individual. The result was that I had to sleep in the magistrate's yamen. Under cover of night, bedding and food were brought up from the boat, and my cook soon provided me with a scratch dinner. "It is an ill wind," &c. But for the disturbance, I should have had two days to waste in the city making preparations for departure, and striking ruinous bargains for men and conveyances. All this trouble was taken off my hands, for the Hsien was so anxious to get rid of me that he hired the men and ponies that very night so that I might start early. In fact, he wanted me to go on ahead and leave them to forward my luggage. But I would not hear of such a plan, and arranged instead to move up beyond the city in the boat to a safe point where the carriers could meet us, and the luggage be removed without hindrance.

October 28th.—Rose at daylight and went on board the boat before the city was astir. Moved up to the rendezvous, and had everything safely transferred to the carriers by nine o'clock. It rained the whole day, and the high road, which was a narrow ill paved path, became dangerously slippery. In many places the highway to the capital was in a most disgraceful state of neglect. We met a great number of carriers and several strings of ponies returning from the capital, mostly empty-handed and unladen, whose presence, nevertheless, and the well worn path, indicated a brisk trade along this route. Indeed, I was told by more than one mandarin that large quantities of opium, and the mineral products of Kwei-chou and Yunnan were conveyed by this road into Hu Nan. But the expenses of carriage are very heavy, and neither road nor river, above Ch'ang-tê Fu, can ever be of any use for foreign commerce. The whole country showed signs of having been recently devastated by the wild Miaotze. All the villages had a new appearance. The cottages and shops were faced with clean fresh looking woodwork, and in the more prosperous houses, which were principally inns, carpenters were busily employed adding rooms and accommodation. The latter was of the rudest description, for I could see the sky at dawn, as I lay on my couch, through fifty gaps between the roof and the sides of the tenement, which added to the bitterness of turning out at daybreak with the thermometer at about 50°, and discomfort all around.

October 29th.—After proceeding about twelve li, we arrived at Shihping Hsien, where I went straight to the magistrate's yamen, and was well rewarded for my visit. An exceedingly agreeable and gentlemanly man the magistrate proved, and in the course of half an hour we became great friends. He begged me to stay and spend the day with him, but I was obliged to excuse myself on the plea of extreme urgency to continue my journey. He regaled me with some delicious sweetmeats, made by his womenkind, and was good enough to present me with some on leaving, in return for which I gave him cigars. The city was like the rest, reduced by devastation to a straggling hamlet. The yamen itself was newly built, and stood alone as it were out in the country, on a site once surrounded by a busy population.

October 30th.—The road was fortunately dry to-day, for it wound through many dangerous places. The surefootedness and endurance of the chairbearers, who had frequently to carry my weight up long steep inclines and down precipitous paths, in which the stones were so irregular that I could not have walked down myself with their speed, often fairly astonished me, although I had been frequently carried over far worse places in Formosa in a similar manner. Two men bore the front shafts of the sedan, and one alone with a long leverage of poles sustained the weight behind. At a distance of thirty li, I reached Hsin Chow and stopped at an inn to have my lunch, intending to call on the mandarin afterwards. But just as I had finished, a messenger arrived from the yamen to say that a room was ready for me, and with a request that I would go up, which I immediately complied with. There being no resting-place ahead which could be reached to-day, I readily accepted the hospitality of the very civil mandarin, with whom I had a most amicable conversation. He was a Canton man, and had both seen something of foreigners, and travelled by steamers. I omitted to mention an important incident which occurred yesterday. About mid-day two of my late boatmen appeared on the scene with a story that the mob at Ch'ên-yuan Fu, finding their bird flown on the morrow, wreaked their vengeance on the boat which had assisted in my escape. They had, according to their account, burnt all the covering and panelling of the boat, and besides this had destroyed three boxes belonging to me, which I had intrusted to the head boatman to take back to Hankow in order to lighten myself for the land journey, which was expensive in direct ratio to the weight of one's luggage. They also had a story to the effect that one of the rioters had let out that they intended to attack us down the river, but were prevented by the sight of the Tao-Tai's gunboat. The man who gave us the hotel card, and made off so suddenly, had an armed boat's crew in ambush to attack us at night. The head boatman came up with us in the evening, and gave a truer version of the story, by which I learned that my boxes were safe. I wrote a letter to the magistrate at Ch'ên-yuan Fu, inclosing the boatman's deposition, and requesting him to examine into the matter, punish the offenders, and send me an answer at Kuei-yang. This outrage would not have occurred a few days earlier, before the late prefect left, on promotion to the rank of Tao-Tai. His successor had only been in office two days, and was as yet unknown to the citizens of Ch'ên-yuan Fu. This turbulent place appears to have given trouble to many successive prefects, until the above mentioned officer, whose name is Wu, proved himself to be the only man able to rule the place, and this with so much popularity that the people would scarcely let him leave the city when he was promoted. I had heard of him at Ch'ang-tê Fu, and obtained an introduction to him from a friend of his, but unfortunately I arrived just too late to benefit by his magnanimity.

October 31*st*.—The road passed at a very high level for nearly the whole of to-day's stage. The valley below seemed to be sparsely cultivated with rice, and large tracts of land remained in a wild state of nature. Slept at a place called Ta-fêng T'ung.

November 1*st*.—Shortly after leaving Ta-fêng T'ung, or the Cave of the Winds, we came upon the cave, which gives its name to the village. It had a very wide entrance, and I penetrated fully a hundred yards before it began to narrow. Water flowed down an artificial course from its inmost recesses to irrigate the fields outside. I had neither the time nor the means to penetrate farther. The Chinese said it extended several li, and it was full of water. In the course of two or three hours we reached Ch'ing-p'ing Hsien, which like the other was also a city of the dead, but had recovered itself in a much greater degree. Double the number of houses had risen up in comparison with the previous cities I passed through. I went to call on the magistrate, but he was away. His servants, however, pressed me to go in and rest, an offer I readily accepted, as the chair-bearers were about to have their breakfast, an operation which generally took up more than half an hour. They brought me tea, and three or four bowls of food, which I hungrily devoured with the help of chopsticks. On leaving the town I noticed a large heap of good coal exposed for sale, which clearly indicated the existence of mines in the neighbourhood. Every village I passed through showed sad signs of the savage havoc caused by the raid of the Miaotze. Everywhere extensive remains of good substantial stone houses pointed out the prosperity that must have been, and in their stead twenty years of peace and quiet had only produced a huddled group of poor straw-thatched huts, inhabited by emigrants from Ssŭ Ch'uan and Kiang Si. Curiously enough there are signs of a sudden impulse of prosperity now taking place, for in every village, town, and city, new houses were either just finished or in course of construction. Of trade there is nothing to speak of in any of these places, and every house is an inn with a small shop facing the street. I certainly benefited by the building mania, for I was sure of clean fresh quarters at night, although the mud floor could not, to use a simile employed by a mandarin who was eulogising Shanghae to me, be compared in cleanliness to the very streets of our model settlement.

November 2*nd*.—The road passed through a very fertile and beautiful, but wholly deserted, region. Large tracts of good arable land were given up to grass and wild weeds. This fact alone speaks very plainly of the wide-spread desolation, when we consider how accustomed the Chinese are to cultivate their very mountains up to almost inaccessible heights, and if the desolation is so great on the main road, what must it be in the less frequented interior. The Miaotze have been taught many severe lessons by the imperial troops since their day of triumph, and indeed many of them now live in the cities I have passed through, mixed up with the Chinese population. I saw several of their women about the streets. A wild fearless look was in their faces, and withal a very attractive expression, such as I have seen in the countenance of the Pepohwan tribe in North Formosa. But whether thoroughly subdued or not, the settlers in the rising villages have little to fear from their lawless neighbours, for a chain of forts has been erected at distances of five li apart, each containing five soldiers, which serve as watch towers, while the whole route is chock full of soldiery. This system is entirely owing to the energy and vigorous administration of the late Prefect Wu, of whom I have spoken above.

November 3*rd*.—Just as the cities grow in size, and

start into more active life as we approach the capital, so the country becomes less neglected, villages appear in secluded hollows off the main road, and every level plot is cultivated with rice. One crop had just been gathered in, and the patient peasant was everywhere engaged in ploughing up, with aid of the lumbering buffalo, the diminutive basins into which their paddy fields are divided, and preparing the ground for a second or third crop. I noticed a few men thrashing out the in-gathered grain with the very identical old flail which our farmers had to use before machinery drove it out of use. The only other object of cultivation which I could see anywhere was the tobacco plant. It was in blossom with a pink bell-like flower. I must not omit to remark that we met several hucksters on the road, carrying live stock, and among them were not a few baskets full of nice fat young puppies. On remarking to my head servant that they were evidently for market, and that I was not aware his countrymen ever indulged in dog flesh, he replied with considerable scorn, "I should think not indeed; these young pups are for the Miaotze, who do eat them." At the end of forty-five li, or say fifteen miles, we reached a city called Kwe-ting Hsien, which was, as usual, somewhat in advance of its neighbour in resuscitation. I went straight to the yamen and was very civilly received by the mandarin, who had been at Shanghae and Tientsin, and could not refrain from praising up everything that was foreign. We were to go on to-day a long stage of sixty-five li, so, in order to save time, I hurried away, thinking my baggage was well on its way. But what was my astonishment on descending to the main street to find the whole crowd of bearers in a regular mutiny. I had to get out and expostulate with them, surrounded all the time by fifty or sixty of the town's-people, who rather took my part and were exceedingly civil. I am surprised to find that here, as elsewhere, all along the route, the Pekin dialect was thoroughly intelligible, and that I could understand the people far better than I did in Hu Nan. The populace so far has proved itself quiet and harmless, always excepting Ch'ên-yuan Fu, which is a very pandemonium. My expostulations resulted in the headman writing out a guarantee that they should carry me to the capital in exactly the same time under penalty of a heavy mulct. With this security I was content to remain, and having found comfortable quarters, revelled in my spare time to write up my correspondence.

To F. E. R.

[*Province of Kwei-chou, November 4th,* 1874.—It is half-past five, and rather cold, so I cannot write very steadily. I have got up early in order to begin a letter to you at any rate, for to-morrow we enter the capital of the province, and I shall be full of business the whole time. . . . This travelling by road utterly prevents one from writing letters. I am hurried along all day in a sedan chair carried by four men.

and when we arrive late in the evening at an inn, I just have time to write up my official journal, dine, and go to bed. Any spare time is in general provokingly wasted by visits from literati or fellow-travellers of mandarin rank, all of whom are excessively polite and "conducive." My mid-day meal is a very scratch sort of affair. The cook hurriedly turns out an omelet, and fries a bit of fowl, and I have to eat at a rickety table seated on a very narrow bench exposed to the full view of many staring eyes. As for starers and gazers, it is a daily work to clear out a crowd from one's very room. There is so much to attract them that I make full allowance for their curiosity, and treat them like small children. First of all there is my air bed which completely flabbergasts them, and then there are fifty other wonders, from my marvellous tin-box to the knives and forks, to meet their magic gaze. The road is a miserable affair, and although it is the highway to the capital and a principal trade route, yet such a ragged, rough path is it, that it would not be tolerated in the poorest English village. But the scenery is splendid. We were nearly always at a high level, and could overlook the valleys far beneath. Glorious pine-clad hills rose up on the opposite side, surmounted by dark rugged rocks, peeping out where the profuse vegetation ceased to climb.

12.15 P.M.—Having just arrived at our mid-day stage, I propose to fill up the half hour during which the cook is preparing my breakfast by adding all I can in the time to my letter. I bought a kid last night, and am about to have a great treat in change of diet after many days of fowl and duck. This province is certainly an improvement on the last in its vegetable products. Besides the universal rice, I rejoice in the enjoyment of tomatoes, brinjals, and a sort of artichoke. Of fruit, too, there is any quantity of persimmons to be had. This is a fruit you are probably ignorant of, I never heard of it before I came to China. But although it is held in very cheap estimation by foreigners, I have often enjoyed its cool luscious pulp. It has a brick-red colour, and a smooth bright skin which peels off very easily, and then the whole of the inside like the prickly pear is edible, only the pulp, though sweet and palatable, is certainly somewhat coarse. This province of Kwei-chou is sadly devastated, all the cities are reduced to mere villages, and the villages to a mere collection of straw huts. Everywhere ruins of good substantial stone houses abound, and show what a prosperous region this once was, before the wild men of the hills came down *en masse* and butchered the whole population. This occurred twenty years ago, and still the devoted cities remain as cities of the dead, with extensive walls surrounding acres of ruins.

These wild tribes, called Miaotze, have since been severely punished by the imperial troops. They are to be seen, as I saw them, dwelling peaceably in the very cities whose ruin they compassed, and sprinkled among the very foes they cruelly invaded.]

November 4th.—In order to keep their promise, my troublesome carriers would have me rise unusually early, as they intended to " do " seventy-five li this day; of their accomplishing which I certainly felt very sceptical. However, they did complete the long stage by 6 P.M., and I soon found myself in the yamen of the magistrate of Lung-li Hsien.

This gentleman seemed to dread a meeting with the foreigner, and coolly sent a message of " Not at home," going into his back garden meanwhile with mistaken conscientiousness. However, a note explaining my mission speedily brought him to his senses, and he not only sent a couple of men to escort me, but came himself in mufti, late at night, after I had finished my dinner, and smoked a few cigars with me, besides imbibing a little wine and some coffee, which he tasted for the first time in his life and seemed to enjoy. The road, for the greater part of the way to-day, passed through narrow ravines where the grass-clad hills approached very close and no room for cultivation intervened. Thick hedgerows lined the highway, composed of what in other countries are forest trees, but here meanly doing duty as stunted shrubs. There were the oak and the horse-chestnut, of which I could not see even a moderately grown tree anywhere. Fine young Scotch firs were springing up everywhere, and crowning the hills with a fine deep green. Willows and ashes, sycamores and poplars (not the English kind) filled the lower slopes, and now and then I came across a magnificent Spanish chestnut. But the glory of the plain was the persimmon tree, all ablaze with the brightest yellow autumn tint. Wild flowers abounded everywhere, including the camellia, bluebells, marguerites, in splendid variety and profusion, and the violet. The whole road was a perfect paradise of ferns, and grasses flourished in marvellous variety.

To F. E. R.

[*November 5th.*—I have ringing in my ears the old old (beautiful?) refrain of "Remember, remember the fifth of November; gunpowder, treason, and plot," which, much as it used to annoy me as a student, I would give worlds to be at home now to hear once more. The delights of home, and the pleasures and comforts of dear old England are always rising up before me, and my heart yearns too often for the fleshpots of Egypt. I am again snatching a tiffin half hour, and I am seated in a queer barn-like sort of eating-house at the half-way village to the capital. The place is open to the street, and a stray starer or two is gazing at my marvellous proceeding with wide-open eyes and mouth.]

November 5th.—To-day we have completed our last stage and entered the capital of Kwei-chou. I am delighted with the place. The people are most civil and not in the slightest degree troublesome. Although the streets were crowded, none attempted to follow or stare. A look of astonishment passed over their faces, and that was all, while I more than once heard the civil expression used, " Oh, here's a guest arrived." The main street, through which I had to pass on my way to the inn where my servant had secured lodgings for me, was exceedingly picturesque with its sign-boards, and dyed cloths exposed for sale, and coloured umbrellas spread out to tempt the rain with glittering red or blue or green. The first view of the city from the top of the last pass is very beautiful. It rests on an uneven plain well supplied with trees and completely surrounded by high hills, many of which stand solitary on the plain in remarkable forms. There were natural fortresses faced with smooth black rock at the top, otherwise clothed in rich vegetation, and which had been cleverly seized upon by bonzes to build imposing temples up in the air. Then again there was a perfect plum pudding and several pyramids with remarkably pointed apexes. The inequalities of the ground raised all the imposing buildings above the veil of the walls, which everywhere in China provokingly hide every vestige of a city from the traveller's approaching view. The last mile of the road was literally overloaded with memorial arches of white marble, or other substitute, in perpetual honour of maidens distinguished for piety, and widows constant to the memory of the deceased. Their distant effect certainly added to the liveliness of the scene.

To F. E. R.

[*November* 6*th*, 6 A.M.—Well, I only had ten minutes after all to write the above in. I am now lodged all of a heap with luggage and all sorts of articles surrounding me in a small room at a crowded inn of Kwei-yang Fu. A number of Chinese swells are occupying the best rooms, and last night we hob-nobbed till midnight over my cigarettes and wine. The former they think marvellously good. The city magistrate sent me a polite message last night to say that he would have the official travelling quarters got ready for me to-morrow. . . . To-morrow, or rather to-day, I have a busy programme before me. As soon as I have had my bath and breakfast, I shall pay coolies off, etc. I then proceed in my pretty little sedan chair to visit the magistrate and arrange about moving over to the more commodious quarters, for I fear I must stay two days. Not that I should object to remaining a week, for there is much to see, and the townspeople are very civil, but I am in a hurry. I was so astonished to find on entering so large a city and passing along its main thoroughfare crowded with purchasers, and gay with every imaginable kind of shop, that no excitement whatever prevailed, and as I passed quietly along, only an astonished look settled on a few faces at the sight of me. At eleven o'clock I go by appointment to visit the governor, which is a great undertaking. These magnates are seldom accessible to small fry, but I have got an open Sesame in the shape of an Imperial passport and letters from the Chinese foreign office at Pekin. I shall somewhat astonish the governor by requesting a loan of taels 120 or about 40*l*., for I have run dry to my last cash and have not the means to proceed. I have also a grand bone to pick with him about my treatment at Ch'ên-yuan Fu, of which I will tell you shortly. My Chinese volubility has been much benefited by two months' complete isolation from every other tongue save and excepting the horribly mongrel pidgeon English whereby Bombazine and I interchange our thoughts. But an interview with a high official requires many varied forms of etiquette language with which one is not quite so familiar, as though viceroys and governors were served up with breakfast every morning; and in using these forms of speech, which are fulsome and exceedingly obnoxious to English straight-forwardness and bluntness, one requires a good deal of cool nerve. This I have been preparing myself for, and indeed I have been preparing my lesson like a good boy, committing to memory dialogues composed by my writer under my directions, which have supplied me with a good stock of grand phrases. I wonder when I open my mouth to discharge them if I shall find myself in the position of *Punch's* cabby with the four drunken men inside mixed up beyond all recognition.]

To the Rev. J. LAYARD.

[*Kwei-yang Fu, November 6th*, 1874.—I have no

doubt you have long since heard of my mission to the extreme west of China, to the great province of Yunnan, on the confines of Burmah, in order to meet and conduct safely back to Shanghae three Indian officers sent by Lord Northbrook to investigate trade routes between the two countries. I have been now two months *en route*, and have experienced all sorts of vicissitudes. The first part of my journey was by boat, which mode of travelling, at first delightful, became at last very tedious, lasting in all about fifty days. We were perpetually ascending rapids and threading marvellous gorges, and my sight was at last completely satiated with the perpetual view of the most glorious scenery that ever made the human heart leap with wonder and delight. The province of Yunnan must be the region in all the world that was selected as the special play-ground for stupendous terrestrial convulsions. Perhaps my *ennui* was mainly owing to the fact that I was ill for many weeks. One disease after another attacked me with relentless rapidity; even dysentery came to add its terrors to my loneliness, and reduced me to a skeleton. All my pride of flesh and muscle speedily vanished beneath its dire influences; but, thank God, all this suffering was invaluable in curing me of a far greater disease. I told you that when I felt more deeply the glorious truths of salvation and the love of our Saviour, I would tell you; so now, in the midst of business and great pre-occupation, I gladly seize a few odd moments here and there to write and tell you of my happiness, for which you are justly entitled to my heartfelt thanks and deep love for the faithfulness with which you both explained and instilled into me the deep hidden truths of the gospel. Ever since we parted I have not been happy. I suppose the process of cleansing the Augean stables was going on, and required time, but certainly a very black dog sat on my back. America was insipid; friends were tedious; work was welcome, but proved heavy labour, and made me ill; yet, in the midst of my suffering in the boat, I was drawn nearer to God, and, at last, like Christian, the load rolled off, and I was another man. I hope you will not think me immediately full of conceit and vanity, and that I think myself an established Christian, but I hope when I get back, please God, to prove the armour which I have but put on in private, and don't yet know the strength and endurance of. The parable of the sower is ever before my eyes, and I have a horrid dread of the tares of society, but I think I am pretty safe this time. I often think of you both, and the thought comes involuntarily very often, for early associations are deeply engraven on my mind, and you have no idea how they crop up. You will probably smile, but it is a fact that I judge distance entirely by the dear old road from Swafield to North Walsham, and every Scotch fir on the roadside takes me back to the time when poor Jack and I searched for tiny shoots under the old oak with as much zeal as an archæologist for coins and buried remains. I long to tell you my adventures, but time forbids.]

November 6th.—Having on hand a great many things to do to-day, I have been much hampered by a number of visitors coming in one after the other to ask the same questions, and examine everything I have with me that is strange to them. However much it may have benefited my knowledge and study of the Chinese, and of their intricate language, it certainly taxed my patience to keep up a conversation so long, and my palate to have to promiscuously drink tea and wine, and smoke cigarettes with perpetual relays of visitors. But at any rate I feel some satisfaction in having enlightened their gross ignorance (although they were all of the literati class and expectant mandarins) with regard to our position in China, the rank of our representative at Pekin, and the goodwill which prevailed at the capital between the two nations. I called on the Governor of the Province at noon, by appointment, and was most civilly treated by him. A brisk old man, full of energy and intelligence, entered the reception hall after I had waited about a quarter of an hour for him. It was a large room, and two sides of it were panelled with glass windows through which I should think there were fully fifty faces peering in during my interview with the great man. There were lesser mandarins in full fig, and a crowd of household servants. We sat midway up the hall on opposite sides more than twenty feet apart. A visitor of high or equal rank, he would have conducted to the divan at the upper end of the room. My first object was to borrow money, which was readily granted, and the next morning a parcel of silver ingots amounting to Tls. 130, or about 40*l*., duly came to hand. I laid the case of the Ch'ên-yuan Fu outrage before him, begging for redress on behalf of the boatmen, and requesting him to have issued a proclamation forbidding the people to molest English officials and travellers in future. He promised to give directions to Wu Tao-Tai, the late prefect of Ch'ên-yuan, to settle the matter, and plunged into an animated explanation of the probable cause of the disturbance. He said that Roman missionaries were the only foreigners the people ever saw or came in contact with, and that as there had been a collision with them rather more than a year ago, when the mob destroyed a dispensary which the mission had established in the city, he thought it very probable that they mistook me for one of the same party returned to make another essay. On taking my leave, the great man, for such he is in very truth among his host of lesser officials, of whom there are several hundred in the capital, did me the honour of conducting me to my chair, which was twice as far as most mandarins of far lower rank would have condescended to move. I also called on the celebrated Tao-Ta Wu, to press the Ch'ên-yuan Fu matter, thinking it very necessary for the sake of future travellers or pioneers of commerce coming that way that the mobbing propensity of the people should be thoroughly checked. The Tao-Tai had a fine intellectual face and a benevolent eye. He said very little on the subject then, but on returning my call, some hours later, told me he had seen the Futai, and promised freely to carry out my wishes, and to have the boatman indemnified. My time was completely occupied all the rest of the day in making arrangements to lighten my baggage and to travel more quickly. Being behind time several days, I was anxious to get on as fast as possible, but I found it quite impossible to cut short my stay at the capital under two days, and I was further interrupted by incessant visitors, whose continual "coming" did not cease till midnight. My expenses from Ch'ên-yuan Fu were far greater than they would have been had I been able to arrange through my servants. But under the circumstances, I was completely in the hands of the magistrate, who hired carriers for me. I now determined to have nothing to do with carriers, but to put everything on horse-back, so that no delay might occur from short fatigue stages. My servant called my attention to certain strong baskets which were used here to carry loose packages, and we found that by discarding boxes, and separately packing their contents into these creels, the load of three ponies was reduced to two. By this lucky discovery I was able to effect a considerable saving. The hire of a pony carrying one hundred and sixty pounds was from 3 to 4 mace a day, or say 1s. 10d. to 2s. 6d. per day. That of a carrier, 2 mace, or 1s. 3d. per day. Two men carried the load of one pony.

To F. E. R.

[*November* 7th.—I have been fearfully busy, what with calling on mandarins, hiring ponies, and seeing to the proper packing and lading of boxes. I was most successful with the governor, a jolly old fellow, who received me with great civility and kindness. We sat on each side of a large hall, fully thirty or forty feet wide, and I should think there must have been fully fifty men, from lesser mandarins down to household servants, looking on through the glass which surrounded two sides of the apartment. These lookers on used to vex and disconcert me terribly, but practice has taught me to diregard them as much as the chairs and tables. I was in fine fettle and never faltered for a single word. The old gentleman lent me Tls. 130 and promised me to settle the Ch'ên-yuan business which I must now tell you of. Well, on arrival at that horrid place, I was mobbed—completely prevented from entering an inn or removing my luggage from the boat. I went straight to the magistrate's yamen, walking through the mob over which I was elevated head and shoulders higher. The mandarin, on hearing my complaint, began to laugh, and make light excuses for the mob, whereupon I rowed him well and showed him my credentials. This brought him to his senses, and he sent me in a chair with a strong escort to the inn. But the mob was determined and drove us back. I had to hit one fellow, and must have nearly broken his nose, for he skedaddled holding it in his hand most ruefully. I had to sleep in the yamen, and smuggled myself out of the city at daylight. The people on discovery of my departure actually had the ferocity to wreak their vengeance on the boatmen who brought me from Hankow, and destroyed all the upper part of their boat. I told the governor of all this, and have obtained a promise of compensation to the poor boatmen. I start on my eighteen days' journey to Yunnan Fu to-morrow morning. I am going to have the relief of riding, in lieu of being cramped up in a chair. I have had an incessant relay of inquisitive visitors pouring in, till I was quite tired of showing and explaining things, and my palate completely upset by promiscuously drinking tea and wine with fresh new-comers. They were all expectant mandarins of various rank, and dropped in quietly without regularly calling.]

November 7th.—The whole day was taken up in packing and fixing the baskets and boxes to the pack-saddles, which on the morrow would be lifted on to the ponies when they were ready to start. I should have mentioned that, at the instance of the governor, the magistrate, or Chih Hsien, had invited me to remove from the inn to an official dwelling, but the place was unfit to live in, and so I declined the honour. As he was in duty bound, this officer also sent me a fine haunch of mutton (goat) and a fowl.

He returned my call and was most inquisitive. I had to take out everything I possessed of foreign make to satisfy his wondering gaze; but in spite of opera-glasses, breech-loading gun, revolvers, flasks, and intricate despatch-box, the palm was carried off by Sheffield cutlery, and the magistrate amused himself like a child in cutting a sponge cake into pieces, which were speedily devoured by a half a dozen visitors in mufti. The table-knife had taken such a hold on his fancy, that this youthful official (he was only about thirty), disgraced himself by actually sending a messenger to ask for one of me, besides dropping many hints to my writer to the same effect. I refused his request on principle, veiled under the good plea of not being able to spare what I daily had in use. Much time was taken up in squaring accounts, for the exchanges in China are always intricate and varying at different places. Large cash were used in the country, but here in the city small cash of much less value were in vogue. I had also to do with lumps of silver, which required weighing and chopping into pieces. The Futai did me the honour to accept the present I sent him of cigarettes, liqueur, candles, and soap, sending in return a ham and some excellent tea called Pu-erh-ch'a, a celebrated product of Yunnan. He had also the politeness to send me a letter of introduction to his son, who is a mandarin in Yunnan Fu. Almost everything sold in the shops was brought from Ssu-ch'uan, particularly salt, silk, umbrellas, and earthenware, but I could not ascertain what was exported in return. The invariable answer was that Kwei-chou produced nothing; and depopulated as it is I can well believe there is no special industry in the province.

November 8th.—Started rather late, owing to difficulties connected with the baggage; and consequently did not arrive at our stage till after dark. Henceforth, we are to reach a city at the end of each stage, whether the distance be as short as fifty li, or as long as ninety li. We were now at Ching-chen Hsien, and the lateness of the hour deterred me from calling on the magistrate. We exchanged cards, however, and he sent me a present of a fowl and a duck. Two official messengers were also detached to escort me to the next city, as the Futai had directed. The military commandant had the civility to send a couple of soldiers to escort me as well; an act of great respect, for, as my writer informed me, " the Emperor's troops might not be lightly moved." I should have mentioned that the same compliment was paid me at Kwei-yang, where two soldiers were sent to accompany me wherever I went.

November 9th.—Travelled sixty-two li to Ching-ch'i Hsien, and called on the magistrate, who proved to be a somewhat jovial old man of sixty-two. He had a very pleasant face, a very husky voice, and a chronic laugh tacked on to his words. I had the pleasure of receiving him later, after dinner, when he showed a liking for sherry, and tried to smoke a long pipe of tobacco, after trying both cigar and cigarette. The road was very wet and slippery after a shower, and it was by no means easy to have faith in the invariable sure-footedness of one's pony in the rough places and frequent inclines. In fact, mine did fall, without hurting his rider, however, which is fortunately the usual case with these small animals. The country was rather more colonised and cultivated than on the east side of the capital, but still vast tracts of level arable land, bearing distinct signs of former tillage, were completely deserted and covered with long grass. The villages on the main road are of a most miserable description, composed of huts built of thick straw of the sorghum, and plastered with mud or piled up with the stones and débris of former prosperity. They were far apart and contained very few inhabitants, who were mostly immigrants from Ssŭ-ch'uan. In these villages, as on the previous route to the capital, food was spread on small tables at every door to attract passing coolies. But it was of a very inferior kind to that which was displayed to view on the eastern side of the capital. I could not find a decent room wherein to breakfast, and sat in the open air under the wondering gaze of the whole population. But everywhere the people were amenable and well behaved. It has been my habit to get out my writing materials whilst waiting for food, and the process always creates extreme astonishment. About midway of this day's route we crossed a very remarkable avenue of hills, extending in a straight line north and south for several miles, with a perfectly flat and narrow strip of fertile land between. Farther on, the general direction of the valleys was east and west. Wild flowers filled the roadsides, and the tea-plant, in full bloom like a camelia, grew wild all about the hedge rows, developed, untended, into a strong shrub eight or ten feet high.

November 10th.—On leaving Ching-ch'i Hsien next morning rather earlier than usual on account of the longer stage of eighty li, or twenty-six miles, lying before us, the chief military officer, who was only of the rank of a *Ch'ien-tsung*, or say a lieutenant, not only had the civility to send a couple of soldiers to escort me, but gave me the usual salute of three detonating crackers as I passed the city gates; and more than this he paid me all the honours of a *Ta-jên*, or a superior mandarin, by awaiting my arrival in full dress on the road, some two li beyond the gates. The ceremony took me by surprise, more especially as I was first made aware of his purpose by his card-bearer shouting out in loud tones (as he dropped on one knee in the road and held up his master's official card), that the *Ch'ien-tsung* had come out to pay his respects to his Excellency Mr. Ma. I dismounted and thanked the officer for his civility, but the brave soldier appeared to be so frightened by my condescension, that I remounted and passed on without more words. The whole route to-day passed through a fertile valley, perfectly level and some six to eight miles wide. It was only partially cultivated, for the country has not yet had time to recover from its twenty years of desolation. It was only last year that this main road became free from dangers and obstructions, and immigrants could come with safety to occupy the deserted wastes. The most remarkable feature of the province is its hills. I have above noticed the singular detached cones and pyramids, which dot the plain of Kwei-yang Fu (which by the way extends north and south), but on leaving Ching-ch'i Hsien a regular conclave of these huge tumuli meets the view of the traveller. I cannot call them mighty, as the highest does not appear to exceed three hundred feet. After passing through them we entered the fine valley above mentioned. It was bounded in its whole length along the eighty li we travelled to-day, by these same detached hills. They were not contiguous, nor in any way barred progress in between or round them in almost any direction; indeed long arms of the broad valley were seen to penetrate like estuaries through their midst. Far away in the southern boundary of the valley, where the hills seemed to be massed almost into a mountain range, the eye could still see similar separated peaks, which strengthened the presumption, that a very large belt of country was here both easily penetrable, and abounding in a complete network of small arable valleys. We reached the Prefectural city of An-hsün by six o'clock. The undulating downy ground to the east of the city, i.e., from the side we approached, was one vast graveyard extending over two or three thousand acres. I never saw such a large collection of funeral mounds. Either this must have been a favourite cemetery, or the population of An-hsün Fu must have been enormous. The city is certainly very full of houses, and presents an animated appearance on entering the gate. It is built in a deep hollow, so that the gates overlook its entire area. I was too tired to visit the local officials, and we merely exchanged cards and civilities. The inhabitants were as well behaved as those of the capital. This city was strong enough to resist the inroad of the Miaotze, who carried their ravages up to its very walls.

November 11*th.*—Left An-hsün at about 9 A.M. and passed through the same scenery surrounding the rich valley above-mentioned. Cultivation increased as we proceeded westward, and large tracts of fine rich soil were turned up to view by the plough. Villages were certainly more scarce, for we passed over fifteen li without seeing any, but small groups of two or three huts, far away off the main road, sheltered the new colonists. As we approached the city of Chên-ning Chow, sixty li from An-hsün, the hills north and south began to approach nearer, and to close in upon the valley. For one hundred and forty li we had followed a level track, and indeed from Kwei-yang to this point, a distance of nearly ninety miles, the construction of a railway, should commerce one day require it, would be as simple and inexpensive as in any other part of the empire. One thinks of Kwei-chou as an impenetrable mass of mountains, but it was most agreeable to find it possessed of many fine plains lying in the right direction. A nearer view of the conical hills brought to sight their rocky construction. Although vegetation climbed over their summits, yet the black craggy rock showed itself through the cloak. In most cases this weather-beaten sandstone broke out in even concentric circles from base to summit, giving the hill a fortified appearance, or at a distance a rich fluted look. But in a few instances a complete eruption of knotty crumpled boulders covered the whole surface like a disease. We passed several Miaotze women toiling along the road with very heavy loads for market, and shortly after came upon their picturesque retreats. These people perch their villages up on hills at a considerable height, and mostly choose out inviting spots where trees and shelter afford the best sites.

November 12th.—About fifteen li from Chên-ning Chow, we came to the end of the fine valley, but entered another smaller one after crossing an easy pass. The hills now began to unite, but while their bases were welded together, the summits still preserved their individuality in conical peaks rising out of the mass below. In ten li more the valleys came to an end, and the road wound in and out among low grass-covered hills; the rocky mountainous peaks having disappeared for the time being. We entered the village of Hwang-kwo-su, once a large town, over an old bridge of several arches, under which flowed a considerable body of water, after dashing down a series of small sloping falls. The village was half way, and I had my tiffin there. On leaving the place a grand sight met my view. There was the river, a couple of hundred yards below the bridge, leaping down a precipice of one hundred and forty feet in one of the prettiest falls I ever saw. The bank was wide, and the waters descended in two separate torrents, each of which would excite admiration by itself. The brown muddy look of the rock, over which the river flowed, added to the striking effect of the whole. From this point the road entered a mountainous pass, full of ups and downs. Far below was a deep ravine through which a stream flowed, but I could not see whether it was the same river I have just spoken of. Right out of the depths rose up a mighty wall of rock, topped as before by the comb-like row of peaks; while on our side a huge denuded rock, weather beaten and scored with streaks, leant over as if to peer into the canyon down below. It was a fine picture, and caused a refreshing thrill to pass over me as I looked on. Ten li farther, and we gradually descended into another plain and entered the town of ——,* where we took up our lodging at a new inn, which consisted of a wooden frame

---

* The name of this town is omitted in the MS.

work, thatched roof, and bamboo laths neatly plaited together forming divisions to the rooms. The walls were not yet built, nor plaster and ceiling added inside. Thick mats spread around and above served every purpose for temporary accommodation, and I must say I felt as warm as I wished with the thermometer at 55°. This is their way. They first build just the skeleton of a house, and then add on one necessary portion after another, according, as in course of time, they earn enough money to afford it. This inn will no doubt become complete in the course of some months, but by that time it will have lost all the charm of cleanliness derived from its fresh bamboo laths, new woodwork and inviting mats, which combined to make me feel very comfortable. The climate of Kwei-chou is very temperate in November, else I should have been miserable enough in these new tenements half open to the sky.

November 13*th*.—The damp white mist, which has surrounded us for a day and a half, was to-day condensed into the still more uncomfortable form of fine rain, and the thick vapour floated low above the ground. It made travelling both difficult and dangerous, for the stone-paved or rather stone-strewn track, was provokingly rough in itself, but to-day, for fully ten miles, we passed a mountainous barrier over which the road ascended and descended somewhat steep inclines. But even in the midst of this mountain mass, where the rocky cones were tossed and tumbled like a stormy sea, there was a succession of quiet valleys down below lying flat at the base of these abrupt boundaries. To this region there succeeded a milder track of undulating, grass-covered wastes, inclosed by moderate hills fit for pasture, which led down into another broad valley, through which we travelled on level ground for thirty li. to the city of Lang-tai, which is denominated a T'ing, an order of jurisdiction ranking a little higher than a Hsien or magisterial government. There are but few of them in the empire, compared with the regular departments of Fu, Chow, and Hsien. If a direct road were possible to Yunnan Fu, four or five days may be saved in the transit, but our route to-day proved how tortuous it will continue to be for the next five days, until we reach the plains of Yunnan. The road is almost deserted by commerce. For miles we have met no goods passing or repassing. Of travellers there are a few. Evidently little trade has risen as yet by this route between the two provinces. There *is* some, however, for on the *whole* way from the capital, I have noticed three or four consignments *en route*; native cloth and straw hats going west, and lead and tea to the capital, were distinguishable amongst them at a glance.

November 14*th*.—We left Lang-tai this morning with the promise of a short stage before us, which was a gratifying prospect, as it was raining still and a leaden sky gave no hope of change. The road

P

was extremely slippery, and in many parts almost dangerous either for riding, chairing, or walking. A fresh escort of two soldiers came in exchange for those from the last stage; I was thus forwarded on from place to place; but in every case I had to deliver the last passport and to make a request for the men. Everywhere, however, I have met with the greatest civility, deference, and even something approaching to obsequiousness. Lang-tai was full of houses, and struggling hard to recover from its long depression. At this place I first began to discover that there was a Kwei-chou dialect, which sufficiently diverged from the Pekin tongue to puzzle both me and those I addressed to entirely understand each other. From this I inferred that there must be a smaller admixture of Ssŭ-ch'uan men in these parts; an inference I might almost have drawn from an absence of the brisk geniality and readiness which marks the people of the latter province. For the Kwei-chou provincial is a dull heavy featured being, and hopelessly addicted to smoking Yunnan opium. Although our stage was short, it proved to be doubly tedious, as we entered a really mountainous region at last, and the road was full of steep inclines. After crossing a low ridge we skirted a fine valley for about two miles, at a great height above it, looking over a rich scene of cultivation and agricultural revival. After this we suddenly got locked in among the hills and rose higher and higher until we stopped to breathe at the very summit of a short rocky range, running N.W. and S.E., which fairly barred the way. My aneroid marked three thousand four hundred feet above the sea, or rather Shanghae (which is much the same thing), but I cannot trust its accuracy. A glorious sight was seen on the other side. We were on a level with the majority of peaks massed together right and left, and far before lay a small plain to which we had to descend by a very steep path. Masses of white mist floated below and for a time obscured the fine panorama. But we were up in clearer air, and it no longer rained. The descent was difficult and slow. At the half-way-down house, where the steepest parts came to an end, I again looked at my barometer and found we were one thousand four hundred feet below the splendid point of view we had just left, which seemed incredible. While scanning the mountains from above I estimated that the average height of the highest ranges was about four thousand feet. From the half-way village (of two huts) where we had to breakfast, the road wound down over a length of some two miles till we reached another plain little cultivated, but strangely enough, full of large villages; and shortly reached our halting place, which did not boast of a proper inn. I have to sleep in a mat shed with a pigsty alongside. But the barn-like structure is roomy and airy, and the temperature is high, or I should perish with cold. Being well guarded against pet Chinese "luxuries," by insect powder, clean mat, india-rubber sheet and air bed, I can lie down as calmly as a sybarite at home. The aneroid has fallen further to one thousand five hundred feet. To-morrow we are led to expect the hardest day's march of the road, and I anticipate a second ascent to the skies. I must not omit to state that within the first fifteen li from Lang-tai, we crossed a coal bed which cropped out abundantly on the surface. There were large blocks of solid coal bare to view, and the bank of the highway was a mass of coal dust, which the settlers simply scraped into their baskets and carried down to town for sale. We met several women bent on this errand with light loads, before reaching the source of their wealth. It may be worth mentioning that the rocky ranges which were grouped about the high ridge we crossed, one and all presented a grass-clad mild appearance towards the north and east, but on looking back at the towering summits from the valley, I noticed that vegetation stopped short within about a hundred feet of the top, facing south and west, and that a precipice of bare, black rock gave a sharply defined outline to the crest. White streaks also marked this rugged face, as though it had been irregularly whitewashed.

November 15th.—Mé-k'ou, our resting place last night, was only a village, and to-day's stage of thirty-five li has brought us to another village named H'ua-king. These places have not yet recovered their former size and importance on the main road.

A river flows past Mê-k'ou beside a dark pebble strand where the people of the place pick up bits of sandstone prettily streaked with quartz (for the latter has re-appeared in this region), which they cut and polish to sell to travellers. I gave 50 cash, or about 2d., for a piece which would have cost a shilling at Brighton, and incurred the moral censure of one of my chair-bearers, who could not get over such a show of extravagance for a long way, as I gathered from his remarks to the other men. This will serve to show how poor the Chinese are, and how far a few copper cash will go with them. A respectable gentleman only pays 100 cash for board and lodging per night at an inn; that is about 4d. I bought half a sheep at Ching-ch'i Hsien for a tael and a half, or 9s., which was at the rate of $3\frac{1}{2}d.$ per pound. It is sufficient to cumshaw an official messenger who has walked twenty miles in the rain for you with the handsome sum of 4d., which will make him *K'o-t'ou* with joy; a Chinaman would give him 2d. Coolies and bearers can eat and drink their fill for 3d. Many a gentleman is well off with Tls. 25 a year. Imagine an income of £8 6s. sufficing. My literatus will wrangle for 2 cash with the poor roadside purveyors. He will also go for any given time without a bath, sleep in the same room with filthy coolies, smoke their dirty pipes, and do an infinity of other unnecessary acts of condescension, which mark China as the true home of Democracy, and the place where Fraternity and Equality have taken root with advantage to the lower orders, but at the expense of a good deal to the more respectable classes. Yet, in ceremonious etiquette, this dirty pauper will claim equality with any one, and seem the polished gentleman.

As I anticipated, our road was full of rises to-day, and the aneroid marks three thousand two hundred and fifty feet. The temperature has consequently fallen several degrees, and I am lodged in a worse barn than the last miserable place. Not to speak of dirt and odours and the damp muddy floor, I have the cooking place on my left hand, sending its smoke from the centre of the floor throughout the barn, and the pack-horses stabled on my right, a little further removed by the blessing of an intervening compartment in which my servants sleep. We are boxed off by low partitions under a common roof. To return to the road. How the chair-bearers managed to pass over the most impossible quagmires strewed with jagged stones (displaced from the original pavement), and at an incline of over 40°, without even jerking me, was a marvel. I could only sit rigid and await a collapse which it seemed impossible to avoid. The viceroy of Yun-nan and Kwei-chou is on his way back from Pekin, and will have to pass over this wretched track. It is to be hoped, as I overheard a bearer remark, that his experience of sufferings will lead to a mending of matters. I underrated the size of yesterday's valley. On rounding a hill I saw that it extended a long way, and could afford ample occupation to the villagers. The whole plain was yellow with the rice stalks, and patterned out with good effect by the numerous meandering boundaries which banked up the paddy plots. A few acres were planted with the sugar-cane which had reached six or eight feet in height, and small attempts were made to cultivate cotton, which I likewise noticed in other places along our route to-day, but it was poor, and growing short. Two high ranges running east and west bounded our horizon, while the intermediate space was valley to the south, and a grass-covered uneven plateau to the north fit for pasturage. Cattle are scarce, but carefully bred. The local authorities forbid their slaughter yet. There were trees over the hills. Deep red, yellow, and orange tints of autumn showed up with beautiful effect amid the mass of green. The sun had appeared at last and dispelled the mists. So that altogether the scene was very refreshing, and the journey far less tedious.

November 16th.—The road to-day passed over a long stretch of wearisome hills covered with tall grass, without trees, without valleys, with only their endless rise and fall always hiding a view of the bold majestic peaks beyond. The river at Mê-k'ou, I should have stated, is the boundary of the wild-tribe settlements. They do not perch upon the hills this side of the stream, although their ravages were carried far beyond. Happily not a single bridge was destroyed in their sweeping rage, which spared neither monuments nor temples. Many fine stone structures span the frequent ravines and rivers which must obstruct a mountain road. By inquiries made through my writer, who required some work, I learned something of these Miao-tzŭ, and other wild tribes in the hills, together with the causes of their insurrection. There are two sets of social outcasts, the Miao-tzŭ, and the Chung-chia. The former, although they assimilate both in dress and general features to the Chinese, just as the Shans beyond Yunnan, described by Dr. Anderson, never belonged to the celestial race. They were the aborigines of this region at the time when the Han dynasty (B.C. 202 to A.D. 200) extended the empire westward, and colonised this province from Hu Nan. The Chung-chia are the descendants of those colonists. Both "nations" have several subdivisions distinguished by little peculiarities of dress, and are mostly called by names describing the same. I saw representatives of three or four sects, and could easily see the difference. For instance, there are the White Miao; the embroidered Red Miao; the Black Miao (who by the way wear earrings as well as black clothes; the men but one, the women both); the Light-blue Miao; the Flowered Miao (who wear sleeves only of coloured stuffs like chintzes or brocades); and oddest of all, the Duck's-beak Miao (who wear a thing like a duck's beak on the back). The women are the badge bearers, the men doing as they like in the matter. But the latter mostly dress like Chinamen in the universal blue. The Chung-chia have three classes. The Pu-la-tzŭ, among whom the women wear pigtails as well as the men; the Pu-i-tzŭ, whose women wear silver plates on the head for caps—*absit omen*—I hope the thirst for novelty elsewhere may not adopt the hint; and the Pu-lung-tzŭ, distinguished by the coiffure resembling a raven. They all wear the Chinese garments, but add a border of some other colour. These people exist in great numbers between An-hsün Fu and Mê-k'on, along the route we have followed. The Miao-tzŭ inhabit more generally the region between Ch'ên-yuan Fu and the capital. Judging by the state of the cities and the universal ruin, on that side and on this, I should say that the aborigines excelled the colonists in the fierceness of their onslaught. It was a combined movement, and the opportunity arose when the Mahommedans held Yunnan, and the Taiping rebellion overflowed Kiang Si and Hu Nan. The reason of this rising was not an idle one. The Chinese had oppressed both classes, socially as well as officially, and while the one said, "we are Chinese as well as you, and yet all honours, riches, and advantages are debarred us," the poor wretched Miao-tzŭ had to complain of scorn, contempt, and legal robbery in rents and taxes.

November 17th.—The night was cold in our barn,

or rather shed. On rising I found the temperature to be 48°; in the afternoon, however, it rose to 60°. I was told by villagers that they have snow now in winter. Their houses, built so open to the air, would lead one to an opposite conviction. But then these people never change their clothes night and day, and make up for the rest with cotton-quilts. The beds in the best inns are merely loose planks placed on log-wood tripods, and covered with dirty straw. Apparently the accumulated dust has never been disturbed, except where I happened to lie. Coal dust is in general use at the villages we pass through now, and to-day we crossed another bed of it, less distinctly marked on the surface. By compensation for yesterday's tameness, we were refreshed to-day along the whole route by the sight of smiling valleys full of life, and colour, and cultivation. They did not lie so flat as those seen above, but seemed to grasp the undulating hills of red sandy soil, and cultivation was carried up the familiar terraces to every available spot. Trees were plentifully scattered about, and added to the beauty of the scene. There were the sycamore, the plane tree, the poplar and the Spanish chestnut, a pretty smooth-leaved holly covered with red berries, and the universal pine. The further we go west the more we find of cultivation and population. The villages increase on the road and there is more small traffic; oranges from Yunnan and straw shoes come along; while drovers are met with flocks of sheep, flying eastward, some say, from the cold weather in Yunnan; others to feed their flocks on the grassy hills of which I have spoken, pasture being scarce in Yunnan. I cannot tell yet which is the true explanation. Baron Richthofen, in his able report to the Shanghae Chamber of Commerce, states that from the information he was able to obtain, Yunnan must be bitterly cold in winter. But I was repeatedly assured by natives of the province, who came to visit me at the capital, that the temperature was mild and warm. Kweichou must have a temperate climate, for the houses are not built to guard against cold, and among other signs I notice that the horse-chestnut has not yet dropped its faded blossoms. So far the average temperature we have experienced has been about 55°. The droves of sheep have been recently shorn, and numbers of young lambs accompany the flock. The very young and tender ones are carried in felt blankets on the backs of the drovers.

I came in time to witness a curious domestic scene in a village. A small child was being flogged by his father. Both parents were engaged in the operation; the one to ply the besom, and the other to meekly protect the little victim who dodged round her from one side to the other, catching a stroke at each move. The mother stood with her back to the executioner, and bore off the child as soon as she dared, pushing it forward gently with both hands; for the Chinese never drag young children along by the arm. The group was decidedly interesting, more especially as the scene was enacted in the street. Some people do these things in private.

November 18*th*.—We stopped last night at the town of Yang-shun, in clean but rather cramped lodgings. The traveller has to look out sharp for mandarins and others in company, for if they should arrive first and occupy the only good inn, his plight is rather hopeless. This was somewhat our case at Yang-shun, for a mandarin in charge of the repairs to the official resting house had already established himself in the best inn. The inhabitants appeared to be extremely poor, for I saw scarcely an individual whose clothes were not patched with native "buff," and their hovels are fearfully filthy. But they have a habit of spending their money on opium and even costly ornaments, such as jade for mouth-pieces to pipes. The barber of the town had given Tls. 2 for a piece of green jade for this purpose, a monstrous extravagance, in his condition. But he was decidedly better off than the rest, probably owing to the fact that shaving the head is a recurrent necessity to all. A similar example of childish extravagance occurred in the early part of my journey. One of my boatmen had spent Tls. 3 on a singing bird which appeared to be the sole object of his affections. After hours of tracking, perhaps in the rain, he would rush to the cage as eagerly as the rest to their meals. Yet the price was more than he could earn in a month in his hard calling.

The road passed through a number of valleys full

of rice, and watered by small streams running in a
north-easterly direction. The distance to the *Chow*
city of Pu-an was only forty li, which had to be accomplished in one stretch, as it was impossible to find a
place fit to prepare breakfast in at the villages on
the road. This was owing to the fact of our having
quitted the main road in order to give the bearers
and animals a day's rest in the city. This, however,
was not granted after all, as I discovered that the
men had deceived me in losing a day by making one
short march. Another reason, which would have
sufficed, was the absence of any accommodation in
the city, and being lodged in the yamen I was
anxious to put the inmates to as little inconvenience
as possible. The mandarin was away, and at first
there was no admittance; a strong disposition being
shown by the servants to treat me with contempt.
I was closely surrounded by a large crowd, which
behaved well, but pressed uncomfortably. I was talking to an old man through the window of my chair,
and on remonstrating against the rudeness of the
people, he remarked that they had never seen such a
thing as a glove before, and must be excused. I
found my gloves everywhere the object of intense
excitement. Under these circumstances there was
no alternative but to enter the precincts of the
yamen in my chair and request to see the *Shih-yeh*,
a gentleman who fills the post of *fidus Achates* to the
magistrate in every city, and is often tutor to his
sons. In the present instance the *Shih-yeh* proved

to be a very sensible man. So soon as he had recovered from the trepidation caused by my bold intrusion, he was good enough to find quarters for me and all my incumbrances in the yamen. The main road would have taken us to a place called ——————,* seven li to the northward of Pu-an Chow.

November 19*th*.—On leaving early this morning we met hundreds of men and ponies carrying coal into the city. It was mostly in dust, but a small quantity was in lumps of a useful size. Further on we saw the mine or narrow shaft from whence it was all procured. The shaft was driven at a downward incline, contrary to the usual practice in China. I don't know how they get rid of the water. About a mile from Pu-an, we began to ascend the last great barrier on our road. It was called the Yunnan pass, and exceeded all the others in length. But the incline was easy, and the summit moderately high (three thousand three hundred feet). There was no steep descent on the other side, the road passing over a high plateau of very poor land. Before reaching the crest of the pass I looked back on a lovely scene. The fine valley was decked out with autumn tints and harvest gold. The high hills all round were strewn with large patches of red soil in among the trees, and the city with its crowded roofs and triumphal arches lay in a cradle below. The last half of the stage was barren ground; rocky,

* Name omitted in the MS.

rough low hills on both sides, and coarse grass growing among boulders in the middle. Towards the end, however, we came across a beautiful valley in which all the harvest operations were over, and instead of yellow the sombre colour of rich earth relieved the eye. It had a comfortable look, as though the land had put on its winter clothing. The stage had been a long one, the bearers, thoroughly tired out, dropped the chair with a well-feigned slip, and so compelled me to walk a long way in the closing darkness over an atrocious path. When at length I reached the inn, it was full of smoke, and could not be cleared until the cooking was over.

November 20*th*.—We were now fifteen li from the boundary line of Yunnan and Kwei-chou. The excitement of crossing the border and entering the famous province which filled us at starting was rather damped by the morning rain, but by noon the sun shone out almost uncomfortably and dispelled the mists. The road sloped down easily over a red sand waste towards the frontier town, which was distinguished by an arch at each end of its single street. The first thing that attracted my attention was a cart. Here was the very baggage cart of Pekin employed in agriculture, and drawn by oxen or buffaloes. The view towards Yunnan was disappointing. There did not seem to be any termination of the undulating rock-covered hills, which extended as far as the eye could see. But the road was level, and the hardened red sand made it firm, and easy to travel on. Large pits and gullies exposed the red sand to a depth of fully forty feet. We met quantities of salt on its way to Kwei-chou, in symmetrical blocks of a spherico-triangular shape, and covered with mandarin "chops."* There were also a good many men employed in carrying gypsum to the same destination. It is used in the preparation of bean curd, a favourite article of food. A short stage brought us to the first city of Yunnan, lying in our way, the magisterial city of P'ing-i Hsien, where I was received with marked incivility by the mandarin (a Kiang Su man named Hsia). It was a kind of rudeness which a Chinaman can so easily show without going far out of the way, and consists in using expressions applicable to an inferior, and omitting forms of etiquette which are held indispensable. He seemed to be suspicious of the local passport, and examined the seal critically. I was able to cut all this short by reference to the Tsung-li Yamên despatches, and the letter of the Kwei-yang Fu-tai, which he owned to having received. He carried out his instructions, however, and sent two men as escort.

November 21*st*.—Our road to-day was beautifully level over the broad battened red sand. Still, barren wastes continued on all sides, well peppered with rocks and stones. One or two dry gullies abounded

* [Written characters indicating the places between which the salt was travelling or the barriers it had passed.]

in quartz. The rocks were all rotten and disintegrated, just as they appeared in many places on the way, and more especially round about Pu-an Chow. At eight li from P'ing-i Hsien there is a remarkable cave on the left of the road. Its mouth had been filled up with a temple, which the Mahommedans destroyed, but the huge space of the cavern is still full of hideous figures of demons and deities perched up on ledges, or bound to the bristling roof. There were small stalactites hanging from the vault. The decrepit priest said the cave had been penetrated to the distance of three or four li, but no gigantic bones or such-like deposits had been found. The upper part of the cavern was grey sandstone; below this I tested limestone, and red sandstone lay at the base. Before reaching our resting-place, a town called Pai-shui, there intervened one fine plain at last through which a narrow stream flowed in a general northerly direction. The harvest was just over, and beans were shooting up between the stubble. In every village a lively scene met our view. One and all were engaged in either stacking the straw or wielding the flail. In Hu Nan and Kwei-chou they have a curious habit of hanging the straw on trees instead of stacking it on the ground. They select a tall young fir, or any tree which is free of leaves for fifteen or twenty feet, and suspend the bunch from a point in its trunk. The tree looks as if it wore a crinoline drawn up rather high. The plain was full of flocks of storks.

November 22*nd.*—The road to-day for half the stage passed over another plateau of waste uncultivable land on which there was little grass even, but a great quantity of rocks and stones. We noticed lumps of iron lying about in an almost pure quality. My writer ferreted out a story about some one having discovered lead incorporated with it; and that a number of his associates found it sufficiently remunerative for a short time to extract it on the spot in a rough way, but that they soon had reason to abandon so incomplete and rude a project. The soil everywhere on this plateau was very rich in variety. Underneath the all-pervading red there were calcareous deposits. Numbers of large boulders of pure chalk (?) lay about. There were several banks of clay of various colours, especially green and purple. The whole field was painted. But the region was nothing but a rough desert of undulating ground surrounded with hills. The latter half of the stage, however, beyond the half-way village of Hai-tzŭ P'u, improved in scenery and verdure. Wherever the rice harvest was being gathered in, the road was full of buffalo carts conveying the grain to the village. The people are not particular about choosing a clean threshing-floor, and as often as not scatter the very street with grain and straw; and the street of a Chinese village is better left undescribed. But certainly the mud and dirt were dry, and the buffaloes shied at my chair, and the pack-horses shied at the carts, causing a stampede, which excruciated my feelings over the possible fate of my filter and my wine. Each day I received the report of my servant with an inward groan. Glass and crockery went their way long ago, and yesterday, two precious bottles of brandy closed the list. On nearing the end of our journey, the plateau suddenly came to an end, and a very fine plain burst on our view. It stretched away to the south and widened as it went. The city of Chan-i Chow lay opposite us on the other side of the valley, about two miles off. The bearers, with the goal in view, redoubled their speed and almost ran me into the city. I sent my card to the mandarin; but here again the same sort of incivility was offered. No card was returned, and no answer could be obtained to a civil request that the escort might be sent early, since we had to start at daylight. As the mandarin probably knew little or nothing about all this, I sent my writer with the treaty to enlighten this all powerful janitor and factotum on my position. The result was that he rated them soundly (for the writer had been very prone to clothe himself with a little official pride on account of being attached to a small mission), and his lecture had the desired effect, for the magistrate's card arrived by-and-by with an answer to my request.

November 23rd.—After waiting in vain for an escort I started without it, and had proceeded a long way before anyone came from the yamen. At length a stupid old man turned up, who proved very

useless. He was dressed in the garb of a common
coolie, and I strongly suspect had been hired out of
the street for the purpose. His warrant only contained
one name. So that instead of sending two or
more men, as all previous officials had readily done,
they had taken the liberty at the yamen to change
the number stated in the warrant, and so reduced
me to the certainty of having only one man sent for
the rest of the route; for they copy one another
faithfully. But we are near the capital, the road is
good and the people are civil, so I do not pay much
attention to this want of courtesy. On starting from
Chan-i we at first followed its splendid valley due
south for a mile or two, and then abruptly broke out
of it at right angles, to ascend a series of small but
uncomfortable passes which led up to another dreary
plateau, like those we have already passed. The
valley was well cultivated with rice, and the harvest
being over, the numerous flooded fields gave the
appearance of a vast lake to the plain as seen from
above. Numerous flocks of storks found a good
feeding ground thereon. But a good deal of this
space was really a swamp, and not yet put to use.
There were high causeways running in all directions,
but many had fallen to pieces in different
places. Their existence seemed to indicate the occurrence
of floods. We reached the city of Ma-lung
Chow in good time, and found a very fair lodging at
the kung-kuan. I sent a civil note to the mandarin
announcing my arrival and errand, and regretting

my inability to call, on account of having injured
my foot. To this a verbal answer was sent, and as
to the matter of an escort, the example set by the
previous magistrate was of course followed, except
that a youth was sent to take care of me; but he
was a decided improvement on the old man.

November 24th.—Left Ma-lung Chow before sunrise
in order to complete eighty li in good time. The
country improved in appearance by the addition of
trees, which, though stunted, grew abundantly on
the hills and plain, relieving the desertlike monotony
of the red soil which still continued. At the halfway
village of Pai-tzû Pu, a Roman priest came up to me
suddenly as I was seated at one of the public tables,
having tiffin, and commencing in Chinese, continued
in French, that he was also travelling to the capital,
and was delighted to meet a foreigner. We sat
down together. But my reverend friend had so poor
a larder that I was obliged to supplement his bit of
cold fowl with half my beefsteak, and he was so
delighted to see bread, that before he had finished
his repast I had no more to offer him. However, I
made the cook serve up an omelet for him, and a cup
of cocoa, which was welcomed. As is very common
among missionaries, there was a rumour in his community of hostile feelings having been exhibited
against foreigners in the north lately, and the
rumour was tinged with a halo of imaginary massacre. The cry of wolf is so often raised that foreign
residents will speedily become indifferent to the

reality some day. I also learned from this gentleman that there had been a disturbance at Yungch'ang Fu, which, if true, would cause me serious difficulty in passing through, but further inquiry proved that something much less imposing had occurred somewhere else, and that the matter had been long since settled.

November 25th.—We slept last night at the town of I-lung Ssŭ, and having another long stage of seventy-five li before us, left at daylight. Our fresh escort again consisted of a dirty-looking lad, who could be of no use whatever. The country was full of trees and underwood. Our road, always wide and level, passed through many lanes and hedge-rows. The wind, as usual every day, blew uncomfortably from the south-west, parching the skin of our faces and producing disorders of the throat. I noticed that it sprang up about 9 A.M., the earlier hours being still and undisturbed. Houses everywhere wore a neat and comfortable look. They were detached and roomy, built of sun-dried mud bricks and well tiled. But we no longer saw the open exposure to the air which distinguished those of Kwei-chou. Wind and cold were carefully shut out. On nearing Yang-lin, which was a town now, but must have been a city once, the road skirted a large lake covered in many parts by tall reeds. It was an immense expanse of water, and is said to afford quantities of fish. Soon after this a magnificent plain burst on our view, well studded with new villages, but swarming with ruins of old ones. We struck across the valley at right angles and entered the town of Yang-lin, where there were inns enough to accommodate several parties arriving in company with us.

November 26*th.*—On leaving Yang-lin the ruins caused by the war were sadly prominent. The area covered by houses was evidently very large, and from its splendid site, and quick revival, I should think this must have been an important city. The distance to the capital was one hundred and five li, on a very level road, so that it might be accomplished in one day; but as I wished to be well lodged in order to be able to complete my arrangements easily, I preferred to stop short of the capital, and sent my messenger on ahead to secure a good house. He was also charged with letters to the bank and the yamen, reporting my arrival. We stopped at the town of Pan-ch'iao. It has several inns, but they are exceedingly bad. My room was choked up with smoke, but the excessive annoyance of this nuisance was no novelty by this time, for my eyes and throat have suffered not a little from its almost nightly repetition. Along the whole route I have had to struggle against wrong information. Distances and routes vary, apparently according to the ideas of different persons, and the result is that I have been misled to the extent of losing ten days. Instead of twenty-five days being sufficient to accomplish the journey from Ch'ên-yuan Fu to Yunnan Fu, I have only managed to reach the threshold of the latter city in thirty days; and this after every effort to hurry my conductors. One more vexatious "fact" was accidentally learnt to-day in conversation, at the tiffin stage, with a very polite military mandarin who was travelling in the opposite direction. He had been to Yung-ch'ang Fu, and showed me stage by stage on the map that it took twenty stages to reach that city. Now I had been assured at Kwei-yang Fu, by men of the official class who had also been over the road, that there were only eleven stages. This discrepancy fills me with much anxiety as to the possibility of arriving at the rendezvous in good time.

November 27th.—Started early and reached the city before noon. My servant met me at the gates and conducted me to a very good official inn. The road was crowded with people passing to and fro. Carts conveying firewood, mingled with ponies carrying charcoal, jostled coolies coming out with loads of salt slung at the ends of their useful bamboo. The short suburb was full of saddlery shops, and the stalls displayed nicknacks, opium, lamps, and ornaments. One solitary clock was the only representative of foreign ware which met my gaze. The people were not curious or troublesome, and I entered the city unescorted, without the slightest difficulty. There was nothing showy in the approach. Ruins surrounded the walls and dotted the magnificent plain stretching far away. The city is on level ground, and therefore not picturesque. A few very neat and original examples of roofing near the gates showed the best points of Chinese architecture.

November 28th.—Yesterday I had just had time to establish myself at the inn and unpack all my baggage in order to rearrange it, when a couple of messengers came from the Chih Hsien, inviting me to remove into the official quarters, which had been prepared, and by way of stopping all objection on my part, they urged that the acting viceroy had directed these arrangements, and that the magistrate had sent a couple of men to meet me in the suburbs, but that they had missed me altogether. We moved accordingly into the temple where quarters were assigned to us, and found everything very clean and convenient; comfort, however, was marred by the absence of a paper covering to the windows and door. Thirty feet of open woodwork letting in the night air at a temperature below 50°, made us feel extremely chilly; and the only means of warming the room was a small brazier of glowing charcoal. This deficiency, however, was corrected by the paper-hangers in the morning. A splendid double repast of choicest Chinese dishes was also sent down by the magistrate for me and my servants. Eight large wooden trays containing fifty-six bowls of different dishes and sweetmeats, all ready for the cook's hands, met my view on entering the room, and four cooks from the yamen were ready to operate. But as I had already dined, I requested them to come on the morrow and prepare the banquet at eleven. Accordingly this morning I invited my writer to help me to do justice to the rich viands, and we set to work with chopsticks and a keen relish. I never enjoyed a better dinner. A crowd of harpies in the kitchen fell upon the abundant remainder, and soon reduced it to nothing. After this I proceeded in my chair to call on the magistrate, who received me very well, and pleased me so thoroughly in his appearance, bearing, and straightforward manner, that I no longer cared to see the governor, and entrusted all I wanted to him. He said if I particularly wished it, the governor would appoint a place to meet me, but that he was very busy, and the revenue commissioner was engaged in handing over his charge to a successor; so that if I had no objection he, the Hsien, would attend to my wants, and convey messages to and from these high officials. I readily assented, and delivered the yamen letter into his hands. My first object was to communicate with Colonel Browne in case his party should arrive first, and to request the acting viceroy to send instructions post haste to the Yung-ch'ang Fu officials, to give him every assistance. And secondly, I asked for an escort for myself and a letter to all the mandarins *en route*, explaining my position and object. The magistrate, whose name is Pien, readily promised to convey my requests to the viceroy, and so with warm thanks for his civility I concluded a very agreeable visit. I then went to the bank and drew out as much as I immediately required. Chinese money matters are hedged about with complications; not only do the intrinsic and artificial values of the sycee silver vary at every new place you arrive at, but the weights in vogue are as different as possible.

To his Parents.

[*Yunnan Fu, November 29th,* 1874.—Once more I am able to put my head out of the bag and tell you how I prosper. I have had a long trudge over the hills of Kwei-chou, and am stopping for a couple of days at this renowned city. The whole party required rest, but, independently of that, I had a great deal to do. Having yet to travel eighteen stages to the border city of Yung Chang, four, and perhaps five more, to Momien, and then to return to this city, I naturally wish to carry only enough for the trip, and lighten expense as much as possible by leaving behind the rest. Everything has been opened and the contents distributed. I had nine pack-horses, and four saddled in my train coming here, and a chair with four bearers for myself. The chair was indispensable, for three reasons: first, because of dignity, being a mandarin, I could not travel without one; secondly, from the necessity of visiting the local officials whenever I reached a city; thirdly, for occupation, as I can read comfortably when seated in a chair. The idleness of passing a whole day in the saddle, for a number of days on march, is very oppressive. I ride for recreation or change of position now and then. The road was rough for many stages, and, over the mountains, we had to mount to the skies and dive to the valleys. Many a vexatious time a traveller has to be patient in China, but it is harrowing to be carried over a towering, rocky range, when a detour would ensure an easy opening. However, I quite enjoyed the journey; everywhere the people were charming, and the mandarins extremely civil, so that I had quite a triumphal progress. Small exceptions to the rule only served as a sauce piquante for the general banquet of novelty. I have often longed for a pea-shooter, and imagined what fun it would be to pepper those peering faces. It is annoying to have to eat your dinner under the silent gaze of eyes, fixed to innumerable holes and crannies in the rickety walls and windows. Sometimes I hurl a slipper suddenly, and create a panic, followed by a patter of hurrying footsteps, but a calm succeeds after the storm, and, one by one, the eyes steal back to the holes, until, perfectly worried under such a satanic gaze, I cause another stampede. I had thought I possessed a quiet retreat for once, in an upper room, when all of a sudden, a whispering filled the air; I hurried on my pyjamahs to search round the room, and found that the whole family next door had been enjoying reserved seats for a private view, until the excitement of some female member had loosened her tongue and revealed the cunning ambuscade to me. The greatest trial was to undergo a continual course of "curing." I was well smoked more than once; you can imagine the misery of every day, for three weeks, sleeping in a dirty room smothered with smoke, and the disappointment, at the end of a day's journey, to have no place to rest or write comfortably in. The very last stage was the worst of all, owing to passengers in and out of the capital arriving in shoals and filling the inns. On the road, I used to look out for fellow-travellers, and prestall them by sending my servant on ahead to bespeak the best place he could find. The misery of the last stage was, however, a good foil to the luxury we have enjoyed yesterday and to-day. The magistrate, under orders from the viceroy, prepared our lodging for us, and sent down a magnificent Chinese repast, which I did full justice to. They found me quarters in an official temple, and had arranged everything very nicely, except that the open trellis of woodwork of the window had not been papered up, and with the thermometer below 40°, this was a disturbing element in my comfort. The magistrate sent me two relays of presents; meal, poultry, rice, fruit, sugar-cane, firewood, and oil, in addition to the magnificent dinner presented to me and my servants. I start to-morrow for Sa-li-ju, thirteen days north-west; thence, almost due south, five days over mountains to Yung Chang. It is wearisome work, day by day rising at daylight and dressing in the cold, on a damp mud floor; jogging all day, and not much to look forward to at night, except my glorious bed, which is thoroughly good. I have an air mattress, lots of blankets, and india-

rubber sheet, and insect powder, to guard against
pet Chinese luxuries. I have been wonderfully well,
thank God, though just now I am lame. There is so
much to do that it is difficult to keep my mind to one
thing. I have to calculate; send messages; engage
men and horses; draw money from the bank; and
each thing has to be done at the right time. The
whole day is mapped out and arranged, one part
depends on another, and if I neglect a thing at the
right moment, something else will be deranged by-
and-by. I have Bombazine with me again, and he
is an excellent boy. All my glass, and the cups,
were smashed a few days before getting here, and
five precious bottles of wine; however, I hug my
filter with anxious care, and brandy goes a long way
to guard against the effects of bad water. I found
a letter awaiting me at the bank from Mr. Hughes,
saying that fresh orders had arrived for me to go
back and proceed to Rangoon by sea; but, though
he sent messengers post haste to catch me, I was
already beyond their reach. They pursued me for
fifty miles above Ch'ang-tê without success. It was
a pity I did not know earlier, for I should have enjoyed the journey the other way round. However,
this trip has been invaluable to me in fifty ways, and,
while I lay ill in the boat, my eyes were opened to
many things in the gospel which I did not understand, and my faith as a Christian was confirmed, or
rather, made into a real thing instead of a desire.
I wonder what has been the sequel of all these

telegrams, and whether I shall be delayed longer in this *ultima Thule* in consequence. It is a fine province, and I am very happy. At any rate, I could not be back here until the end of January, and I very much doubt if my mission will end before May. At the capital of Kwei-chou, whence I am sorry to say I had no time to write to you, having been disturbed by a crowd of visitors who wasted a whole day for me, I visited the governor, and altogether made a good impression. I also called privately in the evening on the French bishop. He received me with two of his priests. They were all dressed as Chinese, and we conversed in the same tongue; in fact, I really believe the old bishop had forgotten his own tongue. It was odd for four Europeans to be conversing in Chinese. The bishop lives in a yamen, has a green chair, and is called a Ta-jin, or great man, all attributes of a first-class mandarin. The assumption of this lofty character also disgusts many Celestials. I am now seated on the divan in the centre compartment of my room, with a brazier of glowing charcoal at my feet. On each side hang curtains of some parti-coloured canvas like huge flags, dividing off my bed in one compartment, and my waiter and boy in the other. They papered up the windows yesterday and all is snug. A message from the governor, requesting me to wait one day more, has just arrived; this is to give time for my escort to prepare. I am to be accompanied by two military officers; letters have been sent on to every place to prepare. The magistrate even wanted to provide horses and carriers, but this I evaded. They have shown me all sorts of kindness and honours, which rather takes me aback. I am always ready for a brush, if they want it, and eager to meet a hostile policy, but I never knew how to thank gracefully or liked receiving; such overwhelming courtesies abash me. Even birthday presents annoyed me sometimes, because it was one of the troubles of my life how to say "Thank you," when I felt it. I expect to find it bitterly cold by-and-by, but I am well provided; unfortunately, my throat is a very weak point, and always inviting some complaint. One invaluable possession I daily bring into requisition is a white knitted comforter with purple ends, which a kind mother's care sent in my last box, and which has saved me from much. . . . I have seen some beautiful views, but nothing extraordinary, except two large caves and a really grand waterfall. The country has been in rebellion so long that nothing but ruins and rank grass is to be met with for miles. The high road is often a horrible goat-path, not so good as an English village lane in the best parts. The people are immigrants, and everything dates from last year. The aborigines are still to be met with on the road, and don't look the brutes to have created all that havoc around; but they were goaded to it by many years of oppression. Dinner is coming, and I have yet letters to write. I think of you all often, and hope to meet again some day. I like to be well occupied, and this is a grand mission; besides, I expect to have accumulated pay by the time I get back. Often a sigh of separation comes and fills me with sadness when I think of you all. How I long for an embrace! What a heap of news I shall have to learn when I emerge. I may be able to write from Talifu, the famous city of the west, which the Mahommedans so lately held as their capital.]

November 29*th*.—The magistrate returned my call this morning and said that the governor was extremely busy just now, but would be ready to see me when I came back from Yung-ch'ang Fu. He had deputed a couple of mandarins to escort me the whole way, and was about to send a flying despatch to Yung-ch'ang Fu, which would arrive in four days at that city, and my letter to Colonel Browne would be forwarded by the same opportunity. The magistrate further undertook to supply me with the necessary horses and carriers for my journey, and I had more than once to decline putting him to any such charges. After a long amicable visit he left, begging me to rest assured that all would be well. In the course of the afternoon I received a message from the governor requesting me to wait another day to allow time for the escort to get ready. I was obliged to acquiesce, although time was very precious. It is impossible to get things done promptly in China. I have not been able to go about yet, but by report I find everything is exceedingly dear in this city. Considering how lately it has been reoccupied, and

R

the expense which has been incurred by every shopkeeper in opening his business, it cannot be wondered at that prices range high. Food also is dear, and porterage adds greatly to expenses. The fine plain which stretches away into the far distance lies fallow for want of hands to cultivate it, and numberless ruins of villages mark the devastation of the late war.

November 30th.—I was led to expect a visit from the escorting mandarins to-day, in order that we might become acquainted, but as no one came, and nothing further was heard of arrangements for starting to-morrow, I called on the magistrate late in the day to take my congé and impress it upon him that I was to start next morning. The fact seemed to wake him up as if he had not realised it, for he had neglected to inform the deputed officials of my haste. His mind was full of the coming magnate, and he had to leave the city the next morning to meet and escort him into the city. The revenue commissioner ranks next to the governor, and all the mandarins have to go out to welcome him. The result of my reminder was a hurried visit very late in the evening from one of the officers who was to accompany us. He had not been told to get ready, and consequently was the bearer of a second message requesting me to wait yet another day. After some argument I was obliged again to submit, more especially as an opposite course would put my visitor to great inconvenience, and, as he was a vigorous and intelligent man, it was important to secure his goodwill for the journey. Another person came to see me about the same time, who had been to Bhamô, and was able to say a good deal about the road to Yung-ch'ang Fu, which will be of use to me. He had some official capacity in his expedition to Bhamô, and was well acquainted with Mr. Cooper, our political agent at the town, whose card he produced. A lithograph portrait of the King of Burmah (after a sketch by Colonel Yule) was in his possession, and he seemed extremely delighted to have such a treasure. The viceroy was to see it when he had an audience. He told me that the tribes inhabiting the country between Bhamô and Yunnan were dreadful robbers, and that travellers incurred heavy mulcts at every town on the road.

December 1st.—This morning I had a visit from the other official who was to accompany us. He was a middle-aged man with a very dark visage, well tanned by military service and exposure. This grim warrior has an agreeable manner and a kindly disposition, and I felt well satisfied with both my conductors. They are named Chow and Yang, respectively. Both of them, civilian and soldier, were engaged in the campaigns against the Mahommedans, and the taking of Ta-li Fu, and they described the rebels as fighting with great ferocity; even the wounded lying on the field being actuated with a hatred that fought to the last without seeking quarter.

December 2nd.—After the usual delay of a start, when at length everything was ready, and the packhorses had received their loads, down came a message from Mr. Chow, begging me to wait a little for him; accordingly I despatched my baggage and servants ahead, and waited behind a full hour until it was so late that I was obliged to start, leaving a message to indicate our rendezvous for tiffin. The road passed across the valley towards the hills. Peasants were hard at work irrigating the fields with water-troughs and paddles worked by the hands. The framework was from eight to ten feet long, and portable from place to place, while one man's exertions kept the paddles revolving with rapidity, by means of bars fitted to two cranks, and held one in each hand. Several strings of animals came along the road, loaded with salt for the capital, and irritated the chair-bearers greatly by their erratic motion, which continually threatened a collision with the chair. "*Chao-hu shêng-k'ou*," "look to your animals," was the frequent cry of the bearers, followed by thwacks, which raised the ire of the apathetic muleteers and drew on a storm of choice abuse. Mules, donkeys, and ponies were mixed up together in each gang, and a couple of mules invariably led the way, decorated in the most fantastic manner about the head with red rosettes and tassels surmounted with a bunch of long feathers like a Red Indian chief. I was surprised to see in one instance that the leading animals were adorned with pendants of rich brown fur, fit for a lady's boa. At twenty li we stopped for tiffin, and Chow *ta-loa-yeh* came up with us, Yang *lao-yeh* having already arrived. Chinese officials have certain progressive designations in common parlance, such as Lao-yeh, " Honourable ; " Ta-loa-yeh, " Right Honourable ; " and Ta-jin, " Excellency," which fitly mark their rank, and afford a graceful mode of address, which has no equivalent in translation. I have been promoted *nolens volens* to the highest of these grades, and treated with extraordinary respect, both by my servants and chair-bearers, and by the accompanying mandarins. I presume the former act on the principle that the higher they lift me the more honour they reflect on themselves. After all these delays it was hopeless to think of going seventy li, more especially as the bearers cannot fall into their stride for a day or two, and require more rest at the beginning of a journey. We consequently came to a full stop comparatively early in the afternoon at the top of a small pass between thirty and forty li from the capital, called Pi-chi K'ou, where there was scarcely room for so large a party.

There was only one decent inn to be found, which consisted of a single large chamber, a small corner of which was boxed off with clean woodwork for superior guests. Two gaunt buffaloes were stabled in close proximity on a floor of slush; the kitchen filled a third corner, and Messrs. Chow, Yang, and three or four of our servants found their roosts along the other sides. Chow filled up the time by smoking opium. There is something attractive in the process of taking opium, which must compensate a Chinaman for a great deal of discomfort. His bedding, which merely consists of a couple of quilts, is neatly arranged by his servant, part as couch and part as pillow, and he throws himself down to play with his pipe, and tray full of inviting nicknacks (treasures in themselves), careless of surrounding circumstances. And each whiff costs him some pleasant exertion, for fully ten minutes elapse before the pinch of opium is reduced to the proper consistency by being twisted and twirled about at the end of a short spit in the opium lamp. I had a long conversation at night with the two officers on the subject of railways, and modern inventions. They praised up the English with a flattery that I was obliged to rebuke. But their appreciation of our moderation in war was genuine, and the name of Queen Victoria was mentioned in terms of respect and admiration. They knew the history of Her Majesty's accession and reign, and the exalted character of our sovereign reflected most favourably on the estimation in which they held the nation, and its representatives in China.

December 3rd.—We only accomplished forty li to-day, stopping at An-ning Chow. Since the war brought ruin on every town, there has not been sufficient time for resuscitation, and consequently travellers cannot move beyond stated distances where inns are to be found. To-morrow we shall have to go seventy li before a resting place can be met with, a distance which was beyond our reach to-day, and we have to remain content with the short stage. The country to-day showed signs of past cultivation, but now lies utterly deserted. A large quantity of young trees grew on the hill sides, and we were not far from a range of mountains. The hedgerows and surrounding ground abounded with brambles, and the cactus appeared in thick bushes. The road was still full of carriers occupied with nothing else but salt. Even oxen were in requisition, saddled with packs like the ponies, and they lumbered along over the roughly-paved track with great difficulty. The coolies here do not use the bamboo much. They carry a truck on the back, which is hooked over the shoulders and curves forward above the head. Upon this they fix their load, and a very heavy one it often appears to be. Numbers of women with stout bare legs carried tremendous bundles of fuel in baskets fastened in a similar way over their shoulders. Many instances of the goitre complaint have now begun to appear among the peasants. The Chinese attribute the existence of this malady, so common among mountaineers, to some deleterious quality of the salt in general use, and I was amused one day by my servant seriously warning me not to eat it. At An-ning Chow, I was paid extraordinary honours by the local authorities. The viceroy has most certainly kept his word with regard to notifying the mandarins *en route* of my approach, for the sub-prefect and deputy went out to meet me in full dress, and actually knelt when I left my chair to acknowledge the compliment. Few words passed, as they begged me to be seated and shouted out " to the yamen." I arrived before my hosts, and seemed to be installed, as though I were a Chinese superior, master of the establishment, for the mandarins sent in their cards, and in their own yamen humbly asked if I would see them. Throughout the interview they observed the rigid etiquette of inferiors, while I was forced to play the part of a real mandarin of authority, much to my inward amusement. It was a poor house, for a new official residence had not yet been built; I was put into the best room, one which the viceroy himself had occupied. It was just eight feet by six. Our host further honoured us by having a big dinner prepared, to which I sat down in company with my two good protectors and the writer. I saw no more of the sub-prefect till next morning, when he came out to pay his respects before we departed. The city walls were completely destroyed, and nothing had been done yet to rebuild them. A couple of hundred houses constitute the city at present.

December 4th.— Having a long stage before us, we started early. The thermometer marked 46°, and a thick white mist filled the air, until the sun rose high enough to dispel it; and the rest of the day was almost uncomfortably hot. The road was rough and deeply indented by mule tracks. Hundreds of animals met us, employed in carrying salt. The narrowness of the track, and the undulating nature of the ground, made it extremely difficult to pass them without a collision. The chair-bearers did not hesitate to strike the muleteers as well as their beasts, and I was surprised at the meekness with which the blows were received. The Chinese lower orders are apt to be high-handed when they serve officials, but I forbade my men to touch the drivers again, however provoking their stupidity, lest they should lay at the door of the foreigner the cause of such rough treatment. The greater part of the way was waste, uncultivated land covered with hardy shrubs and stunted trees. But now and then a valley appeared which was partially retilled, and one or two villages, re-established among ruins, stood prettily embowered among trees. The semi-civilised border tribes seem to trade occasionally in the province, for we passed a group to-day with their ponies carrying salt. They seldom come below Ta-li Fu. But these, probably finding employment for their animals, thought it worth while to go further. They wore coloured, embroidered garments, and presented other peculiarities which I had not time to notice in passing. While halting to rest at a tea-shop, my men began to discuss the manners and customs of these "barbarians." They do not pass the night in the villages, but camp out on the hills, and the chief accomplishment they possess, according to my interlocutors, is to bring down birds on the wing with their arrows in such a manner as to make them fall close beside them. On arriving at the town of Lao-ya Kuan, we had to put up at a wonderful specimen of an inn. There was plenty of accommodation for animals and drivers, but only one or two small rooms for guests. I found one good room, however, and took possession thereof. We met at this place a messenger sent from the next city by the magistrate to attend to our wants and provide anything that was required. It appears that the orders of the viceroy have been stringent and liberal. Each official along the road has been instructed to supply horses and bearers if necessary. It so happens that my writer sustained some injury to-day by a severe fall from his pony, and my conductors have ordered the magistrate's messenger to procure a mountain chair and two bearers for him to-morrow. They all tell me it is my duty to make some requisitions, or else both I and my retinue will "lose face," as they term it.

December 5th.— On rising I was informed that the magistrate had sent down his cook as well, and that breakfast was provided for the whole party. And a very good breakfast it proved to be. There was one excellent circular dish containing duck, fowl and pork, with vegetables swimming in a substratum of broth very much after the manner of an *à la braise* pan. The road to-day has outdone everything hitherto encountered in utter badness. In addition to its natural imperfections, I believe the retreating Mahommedans purposely destroyed the pavement in order to throw difficulties in the way of the imperial troops. It is far from being an easy task to describe the incredible obstacles which are suffered to remain unheeded on this track. In the first place there is scarcely any level ground in the whole length of this tedious stage of seventy-five li to Lu-fêng Hsien. It is full of steep passes, the chief of which rises to three thousand five hundred feet (by my aneroid), and the track by which it is surmounted is simply a chaos of deep ruts and broken stones, offering the acme of dangerous footing to animals as well as carriers. Chair-bearers have to be supplemented by six or eight coolies dragging a rope passed round the chair, and even with this aid it is difficult to conceive how they retain their footing at the rate they press up the incline. Often it appears to be only a feat of balancing skill which saves a dangerous fall, and many are the knocks sustained by the traveller from the collisions between his chair and projecting stones. In many places the steep path has a horizontal slope as well, and to complicate the danger, pack animals passing both ways have to be avoided. At one point in this wretched highway I was saved from an imminent collapse by the strength and marvellous stability of the four bearers. There was a stampede of loose animals trying to press by us in a narrow place just as a string of loaded mules arrived from the opposite direction. The result of which was that the rope-pullers got entangled and thrown over, dragging the chair aside in their fall. The usual babel of altercation followed, and the ragged tracker, who was most hurt by the fall, seized the head drover, without resistance on his part, neither of them indeed showing any signs of exasperation whatever. It was curious to see a big strapping man like the drover, who wore good clothes, quietly submitting to be clawed and detained by a miserable starveling in rags. But it was the dread of officialdom which affected him, for he knelt down in his confusion to my official messenger, who quickly released him, and the coolie only got laughed at by his companions for his pains. On arriving at Lu-fêng Hsien, I was greeted outside the city by the magistrate's card-bearer, who knelt according to custom, holding up his master's card, and politely informed me that the official travelling quarters were ready for my reception. Messrs. Chow and Yang invariably pass on ahead to prepare everything before my arrival, and I found them at the door as usual, ready to receive me. We were soon comfortably installed in two side rooms, and dinner was served from the magistrate's kitchen in the centre compartment. Having sent my card with polite excuses for not visiting the magistrate at so late an hour, I was pleased to receive a visit from him later without ceremony. He was a Ssŭ Ch'uan man, Hsiao by name, and like all his fellow provincials exceedingly intelligent and agreeable. The city was still in ruins and only contained a small number of houses.

December 6th.—We started, after doing justice to the magistrate's breakfast, at an early hour, in a thick white mist (which the officials one and all so much dread), and the thermometer at 46°. The stage was the longest we have yet accomplished, being ninety li, and much of it over steep passes. The mountains were thickly covered with pine. All the villages were in ruins, and the valleys, of which we crossed three or four, are sparsely inhabited. One very heavy pass, involving several li of a severe incline, though fortunately without many bad places on the road, intervenes in the long march, and by a steep descent leads to the town of Shê-tzŭ, where there is an inn, and a dilapidated official rest, or Kung-kuan. Messrs. Chow and Yang thought the inn preferable, but I was obliged to alter their choice, and select the Kung-kuan for my bed. The place was quite empty, and I was obliged to request the Pa-tsung, or ensign who had charge of the town, to supply me with tables and chairs, which he readily did. My servants spread their quilts on straw, and we got through the night fairly well, considering it was bitterly cold. It is surprising how the Chinese neglect good property. This Kung-kuan, and all others, were repaired and cleaned only last year for the governor; but as soon as he had passed, not a soul was left in charge, and the paper ceiling has all but come down, while the walls have become begrimed with dirt and smoke from impromptu fires lighted by vagabonds on the floor. Yet it was preferable to the inn. Messrs. Chow and Yang thought they had offended me by having chosen the latter, but I soon reassured them over some mulled claret. Chow is a young man, and as affected as some women are; full of mannerism, and pointing his conversation with histrionic movements of eyes, lips and brow. Yang, on the other hand, is an honest, blunt soldier, hale and hearty under the weight of sixty-five years, with a deep voice and kindly eye. His face is so dark that he looks like a mechanic, while blackened teeth and rough hands bear out the impression. He takes great care of me, and exerts himself far more than the other. I remarked with satisfaction to-day that the road of the salt carriers branched away from ours. I hope to add some remarks about the salt trade when I have made further inquiries. On entering and leaving Sai-tsŭ, I was saluted by half a dozen of the Pa-tsung's soldiers, who prostrated themselves to perform the k'o-t'ou, and shouted out the usual formula of welcome, or good speed.

December 7th.—The temperature was 42° at starting, but before very long the sun shone out strong, and by sunset the thermometer had risen 20°. The difficulty of dressing in accordance with the weather becomes a hardship under such circumstances. The road was still full of difficult passes and deserted villages, and one could not help deploring the existence of such barriers to the advance of commerce. If only an easy road lay ready between Yunnan Fu and Bhamô, a perfect flood of British goods would be swallowed up at once for the Kwei-chou and Ssŭ Ch'uan markets. The merchants of the latter province would naturally prefer to buy at Yunnan, and float their goods down the Yang-tzŭ, to the risk and expense of the difficult ascent from Hankow up the I-ch'ang gorge. Native cloth is so dear in Kwei-chou and Yunnan, that the people cannot afford to buy it, and their ragged appearance is due not so much to poverty as to the price of cloth being beyond their means. There would be an immense sale if only Manchester goods could be cheaply conveyed. Matches have not penetrated so far, and the people envy me the possession of them. Watches are wanted badly by the rich classes. And there is a great eagerness to know the price of most of my foreign productions. Cutlery and ordinary crockery excite admiration, and almost anything foreign would speedily entice buyers, if I may judge by the high appreciation and unfeigned coveting displayed by the few who examined my possessions. The country on this side of Yunnan Fu is sadly deserted. We lunched to-day on the brow of a hill in the open air. A woman held a stall on the spot, and sold rice and other food. We lighted bush fires, and ate in picnic style, seated on logs of timber brought up for building purposes, and undergoing preparation then and there in the hands of carpenters. The latter use similar tools to those employed by our workmen, but they apply the axe in many operations where saw and plane would ensure more finished work. Kuang-t'ung Hsien, our destination, lay in a fine valley which sadly wanted inhabitants to recultivate its broad acres. I was exceedingly well received by the magistrate, who was a young Kwei-chou man, and before leaving we became great friends. His jurisdiction was a very poor one for want of men and habitations, nor was the yamen a fit house for his own residence. Yet everything in it showed taste and liberality, and although he had but three habitable rooms, he managed to make me and my three "gentlemen" (viz., writer and two Wei-yuans) thoroughly comfortable. He gave us an excellent dinner, and equally good breakfast. This part of his hospitality was, however, due to the acting viceroy's orders, which, I am privately informed, instruct every official *en route* to expend six taels on my entertainment and requirements. The rope-pullers and extra coolies are all supplied by the local authorities, and, I am sorry to say, at little expense, for there is a class of men and boys who are constantly called out for this mandarin service, and receive scarcely sufficient remuneration to buy them rice. I created extraordinary surprise and admiration in the breasts of my six diminutive trackers by the present of 100 cash each, or in this local currency the equivalent of $3\frac{1}{2}d$. They never get a cash from mandarins after toiling like slaves over the high passes. I shall have to add some remarks on their condition.

December 8th.—The temperature was exceptionally high this morning (58°), and the sun raised it to 66° by 2 P.M. The whole day has been clear and warm, in spite of a southerly wind. We left Kuang-t'ung highly pleased with our reception. It is amusing how all my servants share the honours paid to me, and plume themselves in the reflected rays. They even tell me so, and acknowledge my bounty with thanks, as if I commanded all this attention of my own inception. The magistrate both welcomed and dismissed us with the usual salute of three loud crackers. The road was far better to-day, and only two insignificant passes had to be crossed; but there were still some impracticable spots with footing only fit for mules. From a tourist's point of view the scenery was rather pretty. Young trees covered the hills and shaded the road in many of its windings. There were more villages and peasants, and we crossed several good valleys. The last of these in the long stage was of a wide extent, and full of ruins. The houses here are built partly of sun-dried mud bricks in large squares, and partly of massive walls of the same material piled up like similar structures in "concrete" elsewhere. These walls evidently resisted destruction, for they stand in silent attestation of ruin all around, and frequently deceive one with the appearance of extant villages. I lunched at a town called Yao-chau, which lies in a fine valley watered by a good-sized stream, and contains some inns. The road followed the banks of this river for the latter half of the stage almost up to the prefectural city of Ch'u-hsiung, where we stopped. Some peasants were engaged in floating timber down the stream. It was all cut into small lengths, and myriads of these covered the face of the river, part in swift motion with the main current, and part lazily floating down the sluggish flow, while a quantity remained jambed in an immovable mass. The wood-cutters running along the banks with poles seemed to have no easy task in hand to keep their straggling property together. The villagers appeared to be better off and more comfortably clad in the Ch'u-hsiung district. Those of them who hailed from Yung-ch'ang Fu, or T'êng-yueh Chow, on the borders, showed a decided predilection for colour and embroidery about their persons. Several individuals wore scarlet jackets of a ribbed cloth which, I am told, is a product of T'êng-yueh Chow, and I noticed how many of the wayfarers who met us on the road were becomingly decked with waist-bands or cummerbunds of pale pink or yellow. This taste for colour is no doubt derived from the example of their nomadic neighbours on the borders of Yunnan, and presents a very agreeable contrast to the uniform dark blue which otherwise prevails throughout China as the national dress. A shopman who was clothed in the red jacket above mentioned told me that the price of the material at T'êng-yueh was Tls. 2.5 per ten feet (Chinese), and on my asking the width, he held out his hands three or four feet apart, saying it was of a good broad measure.

On descending the last pass the city of Ch'u-hsiung came in full view at some distance across the splendid valley, situated under the hills toward the southern boundary of the plain. Once on level ground and with the goal in view, my chair-bearers and rope-pullers set off at a run, with encouraging shouts and frolicsome laughter, until they ran against a bank and fairly upset me on my side. After this catastrophe a becoming gravity suddenly replaced their mirth, mingled with fear for having so offended the Ta-jin. But I had suffered too many falls to care about one more, and soon after we met the magistrate's messenger, who, as usual, came to bid me welcome from the yamen. The city walls enclosed an almost houseless waste. Only the high street, together with a few houses which had crystallised in its neighbourhood, had as yet arisen out of the ashes. The prefect was living in a temple converted temporarily into his yamen, and the Hsien occupied side quarters in the same building. I called on both, although the lateness of the hour required torches. Neither received me. This apparent incivility, from an English point of view, was really a mark of respect; for in Chinese etiquette the refusal is meant to convey a sense of inferiority, and unworthiness to accept the honour of a visit. On my return to the inn, which had been cleared out and prepared for my reception in the want of any official building for the purpose, the prefect, who was unwell, sent his card, and the magistrate called in person just as I and my bear-leaders were sitting down to the dinner provided by him. After the necessary bowing and preliminary civilities we resumed our chopsticks at the request of our host, who sat down alongside and kept up a sparkling conversation about Shanghae and the splendid steamers on the river. He thought the roast mutton served on board these palaces at dinner-time was excellent, and after exhausting his eulogy of foreign manufactures, gracefully withdrew and left us to finish our meal. He was a tall, clean, well-dressed man, with an almost European face and engaging manners. Ssŭ Ch'uan again deserved my thorough appreciation of her sons.

December 9th.—We started early this morning in order to accomplish a very long stage. The proper resting-place was in a village, but as the road was said to be level we determined to break into the next day's march in order to reach the city of Chên-nan Chow, and so avoid the discomforts of a country lodging. The men were persuaded to go the extra thirty li, and no doubt the good things of a yamen added their enticement to make them undergo ninety-five li. In so long a march the phases of country naturally varied considerably. The road was certainly good, not however without exceptions, and the bearers were able to keep up a fast pace throughout.

After passing through the rich valley of Ch'u-hsiung Fu, we crossed a series of low easy passes, always leading to a valley, with the surrounding hills prettily covered with young pine trees. The country was less and less inhabited as we proceeded, and the people more miserably clothed; often wide flats appeared given up to rank grass, and occasionally the road crossed a desert of brambles and wild bushes growing on a hard bed of clay. There was a quantity of pure white clay fit for porcelain, and different coloured mounds of lias gave a strange aspect to the ground. Coal cropped out at one spot, and a shaft was actually being worked higher up on the hill. Buffalo carts reappeared on the plains, and a river frequently had to be crossed over good stone bridges. In the earlier part of the stage a good deal of building was being carried on by rich proprietors, and I noticed one example of the way they construct the massive earth walls so characteristic of the district round about. The mud was thrown in between planks of wood, and battened down with clubs. Each layer became hardened in the sun, and the wall had the appearance of being built in strata of about a foot thick. An amusing incident occurred on leaving Ch'u-hsiung Fu. Just as we passed the door of the yamen, a miserable looking dog which had lost almost the last shreds of his coat through mange placed itself at the head of my procession, and persistently escorted us for sixty li. He rested where we rested, and never failed to pick out my chair from among the others as the special object of his care. I set the whole crowd of Chinamen in a roar of laughter by suggesting that this must be the Chih Hsien's especial messenger sent to escort me. On reaching Chên-nan Chow we were very comfortably installed in the yamen, which was in a better condition than most. The sub-prefect was away in the country, but he returned at night, and came in to see me after dinner. He was a quiet, agreeable man of somewhat over fifty, and a native of Shan-Tung. His cook must have followed him from the north, judging by the superiority of his culinary skill over all the other cooks who had regaled us hitherto. There was a good deal of traffic on the road, but it consisted of the cheapest and most ordinary objects of daily use, such as pottery, calibashes, hats and straw shoes. The High Street in the cities was always full of stalls, most of which displayed native cloth for sale in small quantities.

To F. E. R.

[*At the city of Chên-nan Chow, half-way between the capital and the great city of Ta-Li Fu, lately the Mahommedan head-quarters, December* 10*th*, 1874.— It is melancholy to see these fine valleys given up to rank grass, and the ruined villages and plainly distinguishable fields lying in silent attestation of former prosperity. Every day I come to what was a busy city, but now only containing a few new houses inside walls which surround a wide space of ruins, swept empty of many hundred habitations. But the people are returning gradually, and the blue smoke can be seen curling up here and there against the back ground of pine-clad hills. It must take some few years to repeople the country, rich as it is, at the slow rate of Chinese enterprise. I am travelling in clover comparatively; quite a royal progress, thanks to the hospitality of the viceroy, and the very high and proper sense of his obligations towards a British official which he entertains. I wrote a very meagre letter from Yunnan Fu, as I was unexpectedly pressed to catch an outgoing courier. I was indebted to the great civility of the banker for the opportunity of sending my mail so safely. We bought a letter of credit at Hankow on the Yunnan bank, and my first visit, after the chief magistrate, was to my banker. He proved to be a charming old man, and I had several conversations with him in our visits to and fro. The money I drew out was in lumps of silver, and every payment I make entails all the trouble of carefully weighing out the sum, and involves a somewhat easy but troublesome calculation to adjust the difference between Hankow and Yunnan "touch," or value of silver. Of course I have to keep a native scale by me. It is a pretty little instrument in ivory, on the steelyard principle. I think I told you how civil they were to me at the capital, and the attention has been redoubled on the road. The viceroy not only deputed two mandarins to accompany me, but sent a mandate along the route, which has made all the local authorities treat me with marked respect. I am called Ta-jin, or excellency, and such of the mandarins whose acquaintance with the outside world has been contained within a very narrow horizon, or whose sense of duty and bump of humility have been largely developed, treat me with a deference which often goes the length of kneeling to me. Some come outside the walls in full dress to meet me, according to their native etiquette, others send their cardbearers, and all provide me with quarters and sumptuous repasts. These latter vary according to the poverty of the city, or the badness of the *cuisine*. They study my apathy to pork, and compose the very savoury dishes of mutton, duck, fowl, fish, etc. Imagine my astonishment at finding one day that under the latter designation I was actually eating the octopus. Indeed, the devil-fish is a common article of food among the richer classes, and he possesses a rank flavour which I can well understand the Chinese palate enjoying. Fancy how the multitudes who visited the poor wretch at the Brighton Aquarium, that was swallowed by a dog-fish, and commemorated in *Punch*, would shudder to hear of his daily immolation on the altar of Chinese "gourmandise." Rest assured,—*Je m'éloigne du reste de cet égard*—and though I am scarcely yet a safe connoisseur of Celestial cookery, yet you may believe me when I tell you that much of it is excellent, and as I invite my two guardians and my writer to sit down with me to the superabundant feasts, in order to pick up *les nuances* of their impossible lingo, I am really becoming a fair critic of their culinary art.

I wrote this first sheet this morning at the city where we slept last night, but since then we have progressed another stage to a country town, where, having arrived early, and being comfortably quartered in the official resting-house, I have been able to write my journal, take my servants' accounts, and still find time to continue my home letters. The mandarin had the civility to send his cook here, as others have done before when we slept in villages, to prepare our dinner to-night and to regale us tomorrow morning with a good breakfast. We have five stages before us to Ta-Li Fu the renowned city of the rebels. Four of these pass through a mountainous district devoid of cities, wherein we shall be thrown on our own resources for food. The mandarin at Chên-nan Chow gave me a black goat, which will no doubt have to support us on the way. But I have tins of soup and meat with me to guard against a dearth of food. I have been on excellent terms with all the mandarins *en route*, and by being daily thrown into the very midst of their private life, have learned more in this trip than I could have done at the ports in any number of years. Three or four stages back I became immense friends with one of these local mandates, and you may judge how much

I liked him by my having presented him with a bottle of claret out of my precious slender stock. He gave me a small silver chatelaine of Ta-Li Fu work, which is worth having as a specimen of their metallurgy. I have been now nine days travelling from the capital, whence I could not get away before the 2nd inst. Twice the viceroy sent me a message to wait yet another day to allow my escorting mandarins time to get ready. The idea of doing things quickly is unintelligible to them, and were I a Chinaman, I should have wasted ten days instead of four getting ready. Although fretting at the delay, I felt comfortable with regard to the Indian officers arriving before me, as the viceroy at my instance sent off a quick courier to the local authorities on the borders, ordering them to look after the expedition till my arrival. At length my escort was ready, and we started with a numerous retinue. My writer and three servants all mounted, and myself and the mandarins in chairs. Then there were *my* luggage animals and *their* carriers to swell the train. With all the delays of starting we only travelled about ten miles the first day, and slept in a fearful inn at the top of the pass. It contained a single spacious chamber. I occupied one corner in a horse-box sort of room, which separated me from two gaunt buffaloes, stabled on a bed of slush; the kitchen, which spread its smoke pleasantly over our lungs, took up another corner, while Messrs. Chow and Yang, whom I have described elsewhere, together with three or four servants, rested on pallets along the other two sides.

Both take great care of me, and I like them well enough. The road is dreadfully rough, and passes over high mountain barriers, which try the strength of the chair-bearers greatly. They have to be supplemented by six or eight rope trackers, who are harnessed to the chair and help to haul it up. You can hardly imagine what incomparably bad roads they have to traverse. It is a perfect marvel how they manage to carry a heavy chair along. I was lamed, and therefore could not relieve them by walking, though mandarin dignity would forbid so *infra dig.* a proceeding, and verily, so would the roads, for I could defy any European to *walk* on such a track. It is a very chaos of deep ruts and jagged pointed stones, either mounting to the sky or driving towards a valley, not to speak of narrow banks, precipices, and horizontal slopes. Often it seemed but an effort of balancing skill which saved a sudden collapse. I tried to sit calmly and to see whether I could sustain a philosophic smile under the gravest of these circumstances, as I plainly saw it imminent, and while it was actually occurring— but each time I found either my leg involuntarily drawing itself up or my eyebrows screwed tight, or some other extremely unphilosophical index of apprehension. I did not escape many a collision and complete collapse. To add to the complications of the road there were long strings of mules and ponies meeting us laden with blocks of salt, and loose animals pressing by in the opposite direction. At one very bad point there was a stampede, and the trackers getting involved got turned over and dragged along, endangering the safety of the chair, but the bearers, with amazing presence of mind, kept their balance throughout. I fully expected a roll in the mud, and was thankful to have escaped a fall. So we go on from day to day, and I must say it is getting to be a tedious operation. I have now been thirty-eight days on the tramp, and have sixteen more before me, and after that there will be nearly as many again *de retour*. I shall have seen a vast deal of China by the time I have floated back to Hankow, on the swift bosom of the Yangtsze, through the rich province of Ssŭ Ch'uan. It is now too late to write more, as I have to rise at daylight for a long stage. It is unpleasant to have to dress every morning with the thermometer at 42°. I am writing with a blanket round my legs, and am obliged to breathe on my hands *de temps en temps*.]

December 10th.—Having cut out thirty li of to-day's stage, and the country ahead being thinly populated, we could not go beyond the regular resting place, which was now only thirty-five li distant. Accordingly the whole party gladly availed themselves of half a day's rest in comfortable quarters. I wrote my letters till 1 P.M., and then, after a short interview with our worthy host, took my departure for the town of Sha-ch'iao. The sub-prefect gave us a good breakfast, and sent on his cook and servant to prepare dinner for us at the next stage, where there was no yamen. He was also good enough to present me with a live goat, which is destined to feed us during the next four stages, traversing a mountainous district wherein no city is to be met with, and we shall, I presume, be thrown on our own resources at small country towns. The road to-day crossed one or two hills, and then descended into a beautiful valley well cultivated and containing many villages. The town of Sha-ch'iao came in view about two miles away and covered a large extent of ground. On entering it we observed that the place had suffered less in the war than its neighbours, and can now compare favourably with the walled cities in size and population. I could not judge fairly of the latter, however, as it was market day and the main street was thronged with country folk. We were lodged in a remarkably good kung-kuan, which showed signs of having been a temple once. With a clear sky and hot sun, the temperature was uncomfortably high all day. There was a strong breeze blowing from the north towards sunset, but we fortunately escaped its attendant dust by a speedy arrival at our resting place.

December 11*th*.—We had to rise early this morning as ninety-five li lay between us and the next resting place, a town called Pû-p'êng by the natives, but which is entered in the Chinese map as Lien-p'êng. The first thirty li of the way skirted the well cultivated valley of Sha-ch'iao, where we rested last night, and the road thus far was level and really good. Then followed twenty li of steep climbing up a narrow ravine, which was full of trees and shrubs, and contained a brook of clear mountain water tumbling down at a great velocity. It was a beautiful piece of natural scenery, but the dangers of the rough and tortuous track by which we had to thread our way marred the pleasure which it excited. It was disturbing to be hung over a precipice at an angle of about 30°, while the bearers were turning a sharp corner, and to feel the slips which they could scarcely avoid on the loose red sand which thinly covered the rock underfoot. It was one long ascent every inch of the way until we reached a village at the summit, which was the halfway rest. It was a poor place and could not afford a decent lodging for a European traveller. He must go forty-five li further for that. The remainder of the road was tolerably good. It first descended a ravine slightly, and then followed a high level overhanging a deep precipice well veiled with trees. This debouched at length on to an arid uncultivable plateau of red sandstone, undulating, and sparsely covered with shrubs and a few stunted trees. Along this desert we were on a level with the tops of a mass of hills stretching away before us as far as the eye could see. A little cultivation was carried on in terraces, but otherwise it seemed to be a red sand waste far and wide. I was surprised to see quite a large town in the midst of this wild plateau, and still more to find that it contained a yamen, in which we were soon very comfortably settled and fed by the hospitality of the prefect of Yao-chow, in whose jurisdiction the town lay, and who had actually sent down his servants a distance of one hundred and eighty li, or two days' journey, from the city to provide for us. Such incomparable civility proves how thoroughly the viceroy is to be relied on. His career has been marked by "thoroughness." I listen daily to stories of his remarkable campaigns against the Miaotsze in Kwei-chou, and the Mahommedans in Yunnan, which the old soldier Yang loves to dilate upon after dinner. But as his accent is provokingly provincial, I unfortunately cannot keep pace with his rapid utterance, but I hope to know all about this hero before returning to Yunnan Fu, where I have been promised the honour of an interview. The Ta-li Fu people are troublesome and dangerous. I was told so by the Chên-nan magistrate, and it was for this reason that the viceroy sent two mandarins with me. We are four stages from that city, and I am to remain a whole day at the previous stage, while Chow and Yang go ahead to ensure arrangements for my comfort and safety.

The journal is not continued beyond this date.

To his Parents.

[*Chao Chow, December* 15*th*, 1874.—I posted my last letter to you at Yunnan Fu, the capital of this province, in which I conveyed I fear a very imperfect account of my journey of twenty days from Kwei Yang. In the capital of the adjoining province of Kwei-chou, I intrusted the packet in which that letter was enclosed among others to the hands of my banker, a charming old man, with whom I had occasion to interchange several visits, and who was just sending off one of his periodical couriers to Hankow, the head-quarters of his business. He delivered to me also a letter from the consul of that port which, as you may imagine, I very eagerly opened, but there was nothing in it except a hurried intimation that they had tried to catch me and send me by sea to Rangoon. Naturally this upset me a little, for I may have incurred a wigging for not waiting for further orders when I was still on the Yangtsze; but calm reflection has set my mind entirely at rest. I had Mr. Wade's orders to proceed without delay, and my start had already involved several hundreds of dollars. The telegram said "Interpreter had better postpone departure till he hears from Mr. Wade." Well, I could not postpone my departure, having already taken it, but I could afford to wait long enough for orders to catch me, and this I did until it was too late for me to have any choice in the matter; I must either proceed or give up the land journey. But the clearest inference was that, as no further orders reached me and time enough had elapsed for them to arrive, Mr. Wade must have telegraphed back: Impossible; interpreter has started; large expenditure incurred; must stick to original plan. This is what I should have done, I said to myself; and then I thought, supposing this to be the case, what a fearful mess I should make of the whole affair by waiting longer. However, as it happened, Mr. Wade did countermand my journey, and the despatch arrived six days later than it ought to have done. I am, of course, in ignorance how my decision is interpreted at head-quarters. I may be blamed and I may be excused, but, in any case, I care very little. My journey has been eminently successful, and I can show that, without my preparing the way for the expedition, we should have met with extreme difficulty in travelling to the capital from the borders. Mandarins are very capricious, and I have learned by experience that they will shirk responsibility when there is any danger of an *émeute*. But having gained the care of the acting viceroy at the capital, who happened to be a very "thorough" man, and whose career is a very remarkable one, I have obtained such powerful aid that the mandarins are bound to tremble and obey. Not only did he send stringent orders along the route to all the local authorities to pay me every attention, and even to spend a certain sum on my entertainment and requirements, but he further deputed two mandarins to accompany me the whole way. My progress accordingly during the last fortnight has been quite princely. The city magistrates come out beyond the gates to meet me, and even bend the knee. Everywhere

T

official quarters are provided and a sumptuous repast spread for us. In one instance, about three stages back, a sub-prefect actually had the civility to send his servants and cooks about forty miles to the small country towns within his jurisdiction through which the road passed and where we had to rest. I am afraid I can only give you a "bird's-eye" view of my journey, full of incidents though it has been. I am at this moment writing at an inn within ten miles of the famous city of Ta-Li Fu; I ought to have been within its walls to-night, but the local authorities fear the turbulent disposition of the people, and two mandarins sent to meet me here, and with whom I have had a long discussion to-day, tried hard to dissuade me from proceeding there. They succeeded so far that I was obliged perforce of limited time to relinquish my visit to day, but I firmly insisted on the necessity of seeing the chief mandarin to-morrow and they were obliged to yield. But I am anticipating. I was at the capital when I last wrote, and I had to remain, wasting three more days after posting the letter I wrote you, requested by the viceroy to allow that time for my escorting mandarins to get ready. The Chinese cannot do things in a hurry. They require several days for the simplest act. Being behind time, I naturally fretted at the delay, although I was comfortably quartered (comparatively) and received great attention. My two conductors managed to steal a few more hours over and above the extra days of delay, and kept me waiting so long that I had to be content with only half a stage on the first day. It was a sorry place we slept in, but opium compensates Mr. Chow for any amount of discomfort. There is no doubt something exceedingly attractive to a Chinaman in this indulgence. I have often envied them the pleasure it affords. The fifty little instruments required in the process are treasures analogous to the well coloured pipe of the European or his favourite walking-stick. This sheet should be dated the 16th, as I have marched another stage since I began it, but I am tired, and it is midnight, so I fear I must close, but hope to snatch an hour to-morrow, early, to finish.

December 17th.—And I am not disappointed in my hopes. *Me voilà!* wrapped up in rugs and still shivering as I write, for the wind pours in through the open eaves just above my head; the window is paperless, and the whole passage, containing the four or five dormitories occupied by me and my suite, is an open funnel creating a draught. But in a few minutes I shall have a good hot cup of coffee, which my boy is getting ready in an Etna. The thermometer marks 45° and it is 7 A.M. At ten I shall start off in my chair for Ta-Li Fu, to visit the Tartar general, the Tao-Tai, the prefect, who ranks with me by treaty, and the magistrate, who was here yesterday, and proved to be a man from Pekin, whose familiar accent is delightful to me after the exertion of conversing with natives of Yunnan, Kwei-chou, Ssû-chuan, and other provinces whose accent is

T 2

invariably mingled with their native brogue. The magistrate is a Tartar, and I like him. He will give me a luncheon in his own yamen, after which we shall proceed to visit the big-wigs. I have to make an experiment of the real disposition of the people, whose turbulence the authorities so much dread, to break the ice for the coming expedition, and to familiarise the mandarins with the presence of a British official. They tried to keep me out of Ta Li Fu, but I gained the day in diplomacy so far; for I felt the great importance of establishing a precedent which will open the doors to future visitors. Whether they will try again to-day to stop my ingress, I cannot say; I have many troubles to contend against, and the greatest is the unwillingness of my muleteers to carry me on; but I shall soon settle *their* hash when I see the authorities.

Here then I will resume my trip and leave the sequel of to-day's adventures for to-night. At the second stage, which was the city of Chen Ning Chow, the sub-prefect and his deputy, together with a large suite, came out to pay me the honours of a Ta-jin or superior mandarin. They knelt on one knee, when I descended from my chair to acknowledge the compliment so unexpected and hitherto so unexperienced by me. "To the yamen, to the yamen!" was shouted out, and I shortly found myself seated in princely dignity on the high seat, while the master of the house begged an interview and preserved a most respectful decorum in my presence. A Chinese dinner was served, and I again made a favourable impression by my use of the chopsticks. Next morning a breakfast was served, the baggage despatched ahead, the yamen servant tipped with the munificent sum of 1500 cash, representing to us three or four shillings, but to them a "cumshaw" worthy of thanks on bended knee, and so we jogged on to the next stage, received with civility and hospitably well lodged and fed. The degree of respect shown varies according to the temperament of the local rulers. Some were obsequious, others reserved, but most of them met me with high-bred courtesy worthy of praise, and such as befits a welcome from man to man. I must say I feel uncomfortable whenever *too* deep a sense of humility overcomes the mandarin with whom I have to do.

8 P.M. *Veni, vidi, vici.* I have just returned, darkness and a high cold wind having set in long before reaching the inn. In order to save every precious minute while my boy is serving dinner, I resume my "breathless" pen—to lay it down again, for here comes dinner—and now having finished, I have lost an hour in entertaining a local official who dropped in to see me and remained a monstrous long time. But I must say he was exceedingly intelligent and agreeable. Well, I proceeded to the city this morning, attended by an officer in full uniform and an escort of soldiers, and at two or three stations *en route* the guard turned out and gave me the usual

three-gun salute. I visited the mandarin in turn and had a most successful interview with all, but especially with the Tartar general, who treated me with extreme civility, very much in the style of a polished English gentleman receiving a younger man. I was perfectly delighted with his reception. He complimented me over and over again on my knowledge of Chinese, and so far got over his first apprehensions about the people that, in direct opposition to his own hints of the day before against entering the city, he said he hoped on my return I would spend a few days with him, adding that it was perfectly natural that travellers should wish to see something of new lands. "I should naturally wish to see everything, if I visited your country," said he, "and I shall have a house ready for you and your honoured officials when you return." Such a *bouleversement* of my anticipations as to my reception by the great man put me in high spirits. They tried to keep me at arm's length at the little town of Hsia Chwang, where the road branches off to Yung Chang, ten miles from Ta-Li Fu, but I made such a point of paying my respects to the local authorities that they could not refuse the flattering request. It appears that the magistrate went back with such a complimentary account of me that the mandarins were positively anxious to see me!

I feel not a little elated at my success; instead of running away at the ominous warnings poured into my ears, I have established the very best relations with both officials and people, opened Ta Li Fu, and vanquished the dragon which guarded its gates! More than one foreigner has been driven away in attempting to gain admission. My baggage animals have been secured and all is now ready for a start to-morrow on my last stage of seven days. I hope to arrive first at Yung Chang Fu after all.

There are rumours among the Chinese of the approach of foreigners from Burmah, and I trust it is a true bill. I have so much to do and so much to write that I cannot give you much more. You can review each step of my way when my journal is printed. The other day, in the middle of our stage, a splendid lake burst upon my delighted gaze. Full of water-fowl, I could not resist such a temptation to fill my larder. Careless of distance, time, and everything else, I hired a punt, and had a glorious chase after wild duck and geese. I had only seen the ducks and they were wild, but on a sudden a wonderful sight transfixed my eyes on the opposite shore. A gun-shot far away raised a perfect legion of wild geese, whose wild cries, and even the very sough of their myriad wings, were borne on the air. I was quite bewildered by the dazzling interlacement of their flight under the bright rays of a hot sun; but soon an orderly line was formed out of the rout, and the long array came on and on right over my head, near enough to add a couple of fine fat birds to my larder. Fortunately, my boy only brought eight cartridges, which made me relinquish a chase which had caused me to forget how many miles lay between me and my next resting-place, and how dangerously hot the sun was striking on my head. The punt was a toy for littleness, and I had to sit very cautiously while Bombazine propelled the cranky thing. I have marked this delightful lake for a day's shooting on my return, and if I can bag a good number of these beautiful ducks you may look for the softest and prettiest muffs you ever saw. On hurrying after my retinue which had passed on and left me to my luck, and on nearing the half-way village, I was surprised to see a mandarin and about a dozen graduates drawn up to do me honour. I hastily donned my gold lace cap, and soon the whole row saluted me with folded hands raised to the eyes. A room was prepared all ready and a repast served which I had to eat in the presence of the dozen silent graduates who occupied a bench at the back. At every complimentary expression the whole array rose up and bowed like so many rooks in a masquerade. It was by chance I had to fill so unique a *rôle* (as elsewhere explained). Not one of them had set eyes upon a foreigner before, and my strict observance of etiquette and knowledge of their customs made so favourable an impression that they one and all expressed their appreciation of the foreigner to my writer after I left. All these meetings effect an infinity of good in establishing an amicable feeling between us and the Chinese, and I am proud to think that I have drawn a successful trail across a large extent of country. I am not boasting, and really don't care two pins about myself in the matter, but for the good sound impressions I have laboured to produce, being zealous for my country's advantage, and I am filled with elation.]

To F. E. R.

[*December* 18*th. Near Ta-Li Fu.*—Since I last added a line to this letter, we have progressed several stages, and I have set foot in the celebrated city of Ta-Li. I am so pressed for time that I can only give you a couple of pictures of my journey. They are very agreeable ones. About three stages back we passed a fine lake covered with water-fowl, and as it was still early, I determined to have an hour's shooting. The rest of my party, mandarins, writer, animals and carriers, all passed on ahead, while I hired a diminutive punt, and Bombazine propelled it with a bamboo over the lake. After a long chase, I managed to bag a brace of beautiful ducks with coloured plumage, when all of a sudden a perfect myriad of wild geese rose near the opposite shore, and came flying over my head near enough to leave two fine fat victims to my gun. The sun was hot, and I only had eight cartridges, so I was obliged to relinquish the exciting sport and hurry after my caravan. On approaching the tiffin place, I observed a mandarin and body of graduates drawn up to receive me. I stopped my chair, and donned the gold lace cap according to Chinese etiquette, and received a most respectful salutation from the party, together with the usual three gun salutes. On leaving my chair they ushered me into a room, properly prepared with divan and seats. A lunch was served, and I sat in company with my custodes, writer and mandarin, while the band of students sat on a bench in the rear like mutes at a funeral, watching our gastronomic efforts. I had to carry on the conversation, and at every compliment the mutes got up and bowed with distressing precision. However, my writer informed me with a glowing smile that, on my departure, they one and all expressed flattering opinions about the foreigner. These good people had come four or five miles out of a neighbouring city, which the road did not enter, in order to pay due honours to a high mandarin who was expected that day. But as he happened to take a different route, and they heard of my approach, I was substituted for the big wig. Hence the bows and the crackers, the tiffin and the mutes all fell to my lot by this odd chance. On reaching the city of Chao Chow, which is one stage short of Ta-Li Fu, my mandarins begged me to rest a day, while one of them went on ahead to prepare the local authorities for my arrival. They represented with grave faces that the city populace was unruly and pugnacious, and that I might come to grief, unless they concerted measures for my proper escort, and proclamations were first issued to the people, describing my position and errand. As these ominous words echoed the viceroy's previous statements, and I had been seriously warned about the turbulent Ta Li Fu people, there was no alternative but to acquiesce. I did so the more readily as we were in a neat new kung kwan, or official travelling quarters, and above all there were marshes hard by full of duck. So next morning, early I took Bombazine and "Leila," my two servants, and we trotted off on three ponies with a yamen runner for guide. But, oh! the misery of my mount; in order to lessen the uneasiness of riding *à la Chinois* I had bought a saddle at Kwei Yang Fu for about 15s., but it was so loosely girthed, and the stirrups were composed of string and straw, while the bridle was only a piece of string, that I found it perfect misery to balance myself, especially as the saddle is high and narrow. However, we reached the marshes, and after plunging into paddy beds, and squatting on banks, I succeeded in adding a wild duck and brace of teal to my larder. The sun was quite hot, and visions of a plunge and swim in the Ta-Li Fu lake impelled me to remount and canter away some five miles farther to the delightful spot. Just as we reached the north-west corner of the Chao Chow valley, a glorious view burst on our sight through an opening in the hills leading to the Ta-Li Fu plain. There lay the city twenty miles away by road, but seeming so close over the calm blue waters of its splendid lake, that half-an-hour might take me there. A back bone of black rocky heights guards its rear, bathed in colour by the lights and shades of a bright sun's rays playing over its slopes. We rode into a large village. I was anxious to test the temperament of the country folk. Far from ill-will being shown, we were courteously welcomed and fed, without being able to prevail on our kind hosts to accept a single cash. I cannot describe the pleasing scene now. They got a boat for me, and I chased the wild duck in vain over the magnificent lake which extends for forty miles one way, and ten in breadth, cradled in glorious mountains. Ta-Li Fu with its white walls and white pagodas glistened in the sun over against us. I rode back to Chao Chow well pleased with the day's excursion, and set myself to writing journal and letters. Next day we started full of anticipations about the famous city. But what was my surprise to find on reaching the half-way town that the Yung Châng Fu road branched off from there, and that the city lay ten miles away off the track. They took advantage of this to try and persuade me not to enter Ta-Li Fu as they were so apprehensive of the people. I was not going to be baulked of so long wished-for a pleasure, and had quite a diplomatic battle with a civil and military mandarin sent down by the Tao-Tai and Tartar general to keep me at arm's length. They had hired an inn for me, and prepared a breakfast to delay me, and I was perforce obliged to remain that night at Hsia Kwan. But I gained my point, and sent the magistrate and captain back with a message that I was bound to pay my respects to the high authorities, and intended to proceed to the city next day for the purpose. I felt it all-important to break the ice, and open Ta-Li Fu for a visit for the expedition. Missionaries had lately been driven back from the gates, and it seemed as though the Ta Li Fu people would have none of us inside their city. Well they could not resist my demand, and next day I started with mingled feelings of delight and curiosity, escorted by the self-same captain who so strenuously opposed my entrance yesterday, and with him a troop of soldiers. Four train-band men kept by my chair. Well, the result was, that I had quite a triumphant day's work. The people treated me with respect and courtesy, calling me Ta Jin. I went first to the Hsien, or magistrate, who was a Tartar and spoke the pure accent of Pekin. We were great friends already, indeed, my interview with him at Hsia Kwan had brought about the favourable sequel, for I told him I did not fear the people; I could speak to them and soon make friends; and when he went back the high authorities received his report with a great deal of curiosity, and ended by writing down to invite me in. I went in turn to the prefect, who treated me with a very friendly air, mingled with nervousness, for we were equals by treaty; then to the Tao-Tai, who was my superior, and he showed it in his manner, although

etiquette was strictly observed. I knew his style
beforehand, for I had made my inquiries too, and
knew exactly how to treat him. He had been most
curious of all to know all about me, and privately
expressed high appreciation of my qualities, especially
my being able to eat with chopsticks. I went from
him to his far greater superior the Tartar general.
I found myself in the presence of a perfect gentleman, who showed an enlightened understanding. He
was an enormously big man for a Chinaman, and I felt
quite small beside him. He insisted on my sitting
in the place of honour beside him on the divan (a
courtesy the Tao-Tai, a young man, had been afraid
to extend for fear of damage to his dignity), and
asked me innumerable questions about England and
Burmah. He said, on my return, he would invite us
to stay in the city a few days, at which I inwardly
exulted. You may imagine how thoroughly pleased
I was at the result of my campaign. Ta-Li Fu
understands me, and I have succeeded in brushing
away their prejudices. On leaving the general's
yamen, I was set down in the main street, while my
bearers went to find two or three fresh men. The
crowd came round me at once, and this dragon which
was set at me to keep me away proved quite a tame
animal. I leaned forward smoking a cigar, and
chatted most agreeably with the most respectable
members of the formidable body. We parted with
bows and the mostly courtly adieux. I feel quite
proud of the success of my diplomacy. . . . I had

hoped to get off to-day by noon, but Chinese dilatoriness now makes it quite out of the question. I shall accordingly hope to spend an hour or two on the lake sketching if I can, and shooting if the birds are accommodating. Starting to-morrow, I shall not reach Yung Châng before the 26th.]

To F. E. R.

[*Yung Châng Fu, December 28th*, 1874.—We left Ta Li Fu on the 18th. The road has been glorious in scenery, and, though passing over high mountain regions with many steep ascents and declivities, there was nothing so bad to encounter as those horrid passes further back. I cannot in this letter give you an account of much, for I am off again to-morrow and have to engage baggage animals, receive mandarin visits, and make my official report during the day, far too short for so much expenditure of thought and action. Not a breath of the approach of the expedition can be caught anywhere, so I expect to arrive at our rendezvous first. The city of Têng Yueh Chow lies only four stages away, and having spent Christmas on the road, I hope at least to eat a New Year's dinner at the end of my journey. I could have reached this place on Christmas night, but for the alarm of the mandarins at a daring robbery on the road, which they magnified into brigandage, and begged me to rest a day while their troops scoured the hills. I was at a pretty little town called Sha Yang, comfortably quartered in the yamen of the petty mandarin who ruled the valley. His house was small enough, having only three habitable rooms, and the centre one of these, as in all yamens, was the reception hall where visitors were both "divaned" and fed. The red cushions and miniature table gave place to my bed, while my three gentlemen conductors and the mandarin reclined in the rooms on either side. They chatted like magpies, and disturbed my rest far into the night. I ordered my cook to make the "thunderingest" Christmas dinner he could think of with the few materials at our command, and he succeeded well enough. A tin of mock turtle and another of boiled veal, a roast duck, and boiled fowl, with curry, and pancakes soused in melted sugar, and a sponge cake, really made a fine feast, and as we sat down, six in number, to devour it, there was not much left at the end, in spite of the ludicrous attempts of most of my guests to manage knives and forks for the first time. Mrs. Hughes had very kindly given me a large fat bottle full of mincemeat, so that even in these far distant regions, I was not doomed to break through the superstition of mince pies. . . . Five days more at Teng Yueh I will commence another letter. Just room for one incident. At three or four stages back we came on a rough, long, neglected valley, where villages had scarcely existed above a few months, and the new settlers were burning the long grass off the ancient boundaries of the fallow fields. Mountains all round sent down their grassy slopes to where our path wound easily on with the resting town in view. All of a sudden my servants roused my attention, as I sat in my chair with one eye on a book and the other on the scenery, to some animals up on the hills which everyone took for deer. Immediately I got my gun, and began cautiously to make my way through the wild grass. But imagine my excitement on discovering that my deer belonged to the feline tribe. I was actually stalking three leopards, as I supposed at first, and they were rapidly trotting down with the wind right in my teeth. Just then a shout from my attendants below showed that they had discovered the fact too, and I saw the intrepid Lin with a young and lusty chair-bearer rushing up the hill armed with sticks. The animals raised their noble heads above the grass in attention, and then ran off a few hundred yards behind a knoll. I was puzzled. They were not leopards. Excited by such an adventure I made my way up, half enveloped in tall grass, until the tracks and lair of wild animals brought me to a sense of my dangerous position. Lin was checked by the same warnings, but I called him up and we reached the knoll. The animals had evidently paused a while, for we saw them hurrying off at no great distance, and the streaks now clearly visible showed how rashly we had pressed upon tigers, armed with sticks and two feeble shot cartridges in a fowling-piece. . . . My journal is taking the alarming proportions of a volume.]

To his Parents.

[*Yung Chang Fu, December* 28*th*, 1874.—Here we are again, this side up with care. I have had a fine journey over magnificent mountains since I wrote last to you from Ta-Li Fu ten days ago. Christmas had to be passed on the road, and I made the most I could of the glorious day. My writer is a Christian, and he thoroughly joined with me in celebrating the day.

We were at a pretty little town called Sha-yang, and hospitably received in the yamen of the little mandarin who ruled the valley. I had intended to start by moonlight and run the one hundred and twenty li which separated us from this city in order to have a Christmas spread in comfort, but curiously enough a dispatch from the general at Teng Yueh, my next destination, arrived overnight to say that brigands were abroad, and ordering the local officer to scour the hills and take every care of a British officer named Mā who was expected to arrive. So, at the earnest request of the latter, I spent Christmas in peace and quiet, instead of hurrying over a long rough stage. I ordered my cook to make the biggest dinner he could command, and invited my three gentlemen and the two civil and military mandarins to try an English spread. It was amusing to see the difficulties they suffered under in trying to use a knife and fork. We had mock turtle and veal from Crosse and Blackwell, roast duck and boiled fowl from the market, curry and two puddings, besides fish, which I had forgotten in its proper place. As Chinese have dessert and wine mingled with polite speeches *first*, before proceeding to heavier meat, and rise up the moment they have finished the last dish, the reversal of this order of things naturally depressed their spirits, and we progressed in mournful silence, till my writer, with a twinkle in his eye, proposed my health, and all became merry. Each thought it incumbent to make a speech, and I seized the opportunity to impart lofty ideas of amity and national goodwill. I can only afford time for one more roadway incident in which I might easily have run into extreme danger. It was in a newly re-peopled valley where the long grass was being burnt off the ancient acres to bring their long-deserted boundaries to light again, and the big eagles and mountain beasts had not yet learnt to understand the change. My servant recalled me from my book in the chair with a shout of "deer! deer!" and getting out with all haste I seized my gun and waded through the long grass up the slope towards the exciting game, absurdly trusting to a light breech-loader charged with No. 4 shot. The animals came down with far too great rapidity for browsing deer, and at one hundred and fifty yards or so, I thought they must be leopards. Just then a shout from the intrepid Lin made them raise their noble heads above the grass and I knew they could not be leopards. A rush by Lin and one of my chair-bearers armed with sticks far on my left frightened the beasts out of my line, and the three trotted off with the slouching gait of the tribe behind a knoll some three hundred yards to my right. Entirely forgetful of my feeble weapon I pressed on in pursuit till the peculiar tracks and the actual lair of wild beasts in the long grass made me pause to look well round. The men below shouted cautions which only reached the ears of Lin, but he overcame his momentary alarm and dashed after me. We gained the knoll, and there were three fine tigers trotting off at no great distance, plainly distinguished by the streaks which I had hitherto failed to discover. This would be a fine joke against me at Shanghae. The idea of a man stalking tigers with No. 4 shot under the impression that they were small deer! It nearly rivals the absurdity of a brother officer at Amoy, who pursued a tiger into a deserted joss-house, and charging his gun with consular buttons, fired at the beast through a window. A roar and a crash found him in a ditch and the animal rolling down a precipice with the fragments of a stone window-casing after him. I am at Yung Chang Fu and start to-morrow for Teng Yueh Chow, four stages from this, and the end of my long journey. I can hear no news yet of the approach of the expedition and may have to wait at the latter city two or three weeks. It is by all accounts a great place for treasures. Country people bring precious stones in their hands and part with them for a song. I shall not believe this, however, till I prove it. How long it must be before I can hope for a line. This continual jogging and contending with Chinese diplomacy and obstinacy is getting somewhat tedious—but I am well and jolly.]

To F. E. R.

[*Teng Yueh Chow. January 4th*, 1875.—The Indian mission does not start till the middle of this month, and they wish me to join them at Bhamô. I sat up till 3 A.M. the night before last, meditating my proper course, maturing my plans, and writing my despatches to communicate them to Colonel Browne at Bhamô. At 4 A.M. I sent off a messenger with the packet. . . Yesterday I visited the mandarins, and arranged all sorts of business. To-day I engage baggage animals, and write my letters amid many interruptions from visitors and business. To-morrow I start again *en avant* for Bhamô. My messenger is to return and meet me on the savage borders with instructions where to meet the party. I cannot explain all the ins and outs, but it requires a good deal of planning to ensure co-operation at a distance. I am perfectly delighted at going farther, and seeing something of these wild regions ahead. . . I sent my last letter six days ago from the city of Yung Chang. Four stages brought us on here, but I spent New Year's Day *en route* at a lovely spot in the mountains. It was the only spot in all the long journey which came up at all to my panting desire for something wild and grand, worthy of Nature's finest efforts. An accidental difficulty in procuring carriers detained me there, much to my delight, and I determined to rummage the forest which crowned the mighty hilltops. On our way up the steep pass which leads to this nest in the mountain forest we had a grand view of the valley below the night before. Having started too late, the long stage had buried us in darkness before we could reach this eyrie rest. We proceeded accordingly for the last two weary hours by torchlight. It was like going up an interminable staircase, and I was obliged to dismount. Our torches were ten feet long, made by simply binding sheaves of dry reeds together, and we only had just enough to carry us up. The last spark died out as we wakened the echoes and the sleeping village with shouts for assistance. One of my men foolishly set a light to the parched-up grass as we were coming up, and it blazed away like a train of gunpowder, involving, I fear, many a young tree in its ruthless rush. The valley below was glittering far and wide with similar illuminations, where returning agriculture was burning away the tall grass which had hidden the fields for two years of anarchy. The rivers and gorges in this part of the country are crossed by elegant suspension bridges, and sometimes one of these may be seen like a thing of beauty left alone in the midst of a silent rugged waste. I started for my holiday in the woods with Bombazine and a boy to carry a small basket of provisions. We plunged into a woodcutter's path, and soon came to its end, after which we forced a way for ourselves, buried up to the shoulders in fern brake. All of a sudden an infernal noise fell on our ears, and came nearer and nearer, till about fifty yards off it sounded quite appalling. I could not for the life of me make out what animal it could possibly be. Bombazine, in his terror, thought it must be a tiger, although it was as much like a feline roar as a trumpet to a whole brass band. It was more like a howl. Whatever it was, the beast which owned this singular voice seemed to be in a rage about something, for we distinctly heard it striking the ground with a heavy tread. But none of us caught a sight of the mystery, although we followed it for some distance. I believe it was one of the horned tribe. After this little episode we lit a gipsy fire and made ourselves some lunch. The woods were as silent as ourselves for the rest of our ramble, and all we got to reward us was a fine orchid perched in the branches of a tree. This precious specimen fell a victim to our goat in the evening, whose voracity seizes on anything carelessly left about. But Nanny suffered for two days for this piece of folly. It was quite amusing to see how tenderly my chair-bearers and servants nursed him, and carried the favourite in a basket. He was a gift from a mandarin nearly a month ago to feed us on the way, but I saved him from such a fate, and he will, I hope, still continue to trot along with us on the long trudge home. We intend to give him something to do when we reach Ssŭ Chūan, and can buy a monkey, and give it a ride. . . Bhamô is seven stages from this, but whereas I follow this nearest route to join the expedition, we shall pursue a wider track in returning of which I know nothing yet. . . The mandarins here are delightfully civil, and my business with them has exceeded my best hopes. The Yung Chang ones were brutes, and gave me trouble.]

To his Parents.

[*Teng Yueh Chow. January 5th*, 1875.—Here I am at the very end of China, and at the goal I sought; but I am going farther. I had not arrived half an hour the night before last, when a packet was put into my hands, from the political agent at Bhamô, announcing that the expedition was not yet started, and that I was to join it at Bhamô, if possible, soon after the 1st of January. As there are seven stages between, and a savage territory, I was obliged well to consider my plans, and it was 3 A.M. of the same night before I had resolved, written, sealed, directed my packet, and prepared my messenger. The latter, after receiving my instructions, had a three hours' nap, and called me at four, to receive my final blessing ere he started off with my packet, for I was determined to see him depart with my own eyes. I was "in the arms of Murphy" again in five minutes. Yesterday I arranged business with the mandarins; to-day I write letters and engage baggage animals; to-morrow I start again for the savage borders, four stages off, to await my return messenger. If, as I hope, they have not started from that end, I go on, if otherwise, I drop back to await their arrival at the conjunction point of the three main routes. The expedition is to follow a wide detour, I suppose they wish to survey a railway route. This letter will, I hope, go viâ Burmah, and outstrip the last three sent from Yunnan, Ta-Li, and Yung Chang, on November 29th, December 18th, and December 29th (all these have been received), which will drag their slow length along ever so many provinces before they reach the mail steamer at Shanghae. I am at the ancient city of Momien, as the hieroglyphics at the top will explain. It is in ruins, for only last year this remaining stronghold of the Mahommedans became a scene of slaughter, and by falling into Imperial hands again, an end was put to the fifteen years' kingdom of Tu Wen Hsin. I visited the Tartar general at Ta-Li Fu in the palace of this late worthy and much-to-be-respected rebel. I have no time, I am sorry to say, for a good long letter, but it is a great comfort to be able to gladden your anxious hearts with even a scrap from these buried wilds, and to be able to avail myself of the shortest route through Burmah. You have done the same for me with three delightful letters, which reached me in a large packet from Hankow, almost immediately after the one from Bhamô, dated July 28th, and two of August 11th.

I might have got through sheets by this time, but for interruptions. The brigadier commanding the centre division of the army paid me a long visit, and brought his little boy with him. It is customary in

China to give presents to children in such cases, and as I am all but cleared out of everything, I was obliged to give the little fellow a pair of tortoise-shell sleeve links, which seemed to delight him much. I like these military men. They are devoid of the stuck-up pride of the literary mandarins. I called on the general yesterday, and had a very civil reception. His name is Chiang, and he is much famed for a daring military feat which brought about the fall of Ta-Li Fu. I was very curious to see the intrepid man who scaled the rocky heights behind the great city, and dropped down in its rear. He has a calm sphinx-like countenance, and a charming smile. Yet this man slew thousands of Mahommedans on that day without quarter. It was his birthday, and he was giving a fête to the people. A "sing song" was progressing in front of the audience daïs, and I had my interview in the presence of two or three hundred citizens, who thronged the courtyard.]

To his Parents.

[*Territory of Nan Tien, Town of Manwyne, January 11th.*—I have travelled four stages farther since I wrote the first sheet of this letter, through a beautiful valley inhabited by a people called Payi, who are a mixture of Chinese settled here five hundred years ago, and the Shans, or Laotians, who cover the whole country between Burmah, Siam, Cambodia, and China. Their dress and habits have afforded me intense interest and curiosity. Divided into little principalities, three of which we have visited on our way, they are governed by native chiefs under Chinese supervision. In every case I have, of course, been the guest of the chief, and, owing to their sociable disposition, I have a good deal of intimacy with their families. The women are not shy, like the Chinese, nor do they fear to talk with a stranger. Their dress is marvellous. I could not keep my eyes off the strange and picturesque figures which met me at every turn. The marvel consists mainly in their turbans, which outrival the busby of a Grenadier. They rise in concentric folds backwards from the forehead, and attain a diameter of fully a foot at the same height above the head. The head cannot be seen in the hollow behind, where large silver buttons attach the hair, which is plaited into the folds. A neat little dark blue jacket, fastened at the throat with a broad silver buckle, and short petticoats tightly folded to the figure of the same dark material, is relieved by a phylactery of red, blue, white, and embroidered panels. It has a neat homely look. They wear also embroidered shoes, and wrap their ankles and shins in blue embroidered cloth. I spent the whole afternoon surrounded by the male members of the family; they examined all my things, and I learned a good many sentences of their language which they wrote down for me. They write like us, from left to right, and the characters have almost a Roman look. The men are light, active, well-made fellows. They wear blue cloth round the shins, and expose the knees in a fashion which, at a little distance, looked uncommonly like the Highland dress. Sometimes dressed in pure white with a red girdle, their heads covered with a straw hat like a Leghorn, and carrying a long sword in the belt, they enliven the road with their picturesque attire. The earrings of the women are made of silver in profuse variety, and other ornaments of silver adorn both sexes.

January 12*th*.—I am still waiting my messenger, who ought to arrive to-night. I was quite tired out yesterday, and felt in no mood for writing a good letter, and the above hurried account of these interesting people is very unsatisfactory, but you will understand how much I have to do. I was only able to snatch an hour in the afternoon for a stroll through the market. It was frequented by a number of queer little semi-savages from the mountains; most of them were women, and they certainly had a most repulsive scowl on their faces. Colour, cowries and silver ornaments distinguished their attire, and they moved about with a shuffling trot, throwing hurried glances right and left. The men carried javelins, but dressed much like Chinamen. These curious creatures inhabit the country lying between this and Bhamô, and the two stages ahead of us are infested by their dangerous presence. I am protected by the Chinese Government, and so have nothing to fear.

A furious ex-brigand, called Li Hsieh Tai, who

attacked our last expedition in 1867, has been rewarded lately for his services against the rebels with a military command over all this country. He is here, and I felt much curiosity to see how he would receive me. To my surprise, he prostrated himself, and paid me the highest honours. I had a most successful interview. He sent for a few notable townsmen and the chieftain of the savages, and introduced me with the greatest respect. We sat in a small room, badly lighted, quite a conclave, and carried on a regular battery of mutual buttering.

Li told them I had come protected by an Imperial edict, and that they had better take care of me. This morning I went out with my gun to get some exercise, and having bagged half a dozen wild duck, I have just sent a brace to the commander as a present. I took two of my servants, and we had great sport. The river was half a mile wide and full of sand-banks, on which the duck rested. The first difficulty was to find a boat; and after searching up and down stream we were fortunate enough to find a diminutive punt under the bank without an owner, of which we calmly took possession. But we could not manage it against the stream with the slender paddle that was attached to it. A native, however, offered to paddle us over, and so, with a present of a few cash, we soon found means to be landed on a sand-bank. Kicking off gaiters and boots, I waded about after the duck, and managed to bag a good many. We returned through the motley market with our spoil, and excited quite a sensation. Cries of Ah-a-ah in the peculiar high-pitched tones of this people greeted me; and they held up their thumbs to express their admiration for such prowess. I have bought one of the jackets worn by the little wild women, but cannot find a petticoat to complete the attire. The villages in this lovely plain are all embowered in groves of feathery bamboos and plantains. The latter are ripe even now, and I can buy any quantity for a couple of copper cash apiece. The weather is as temperate as we could wish. On the third stage to Teng-yueh we rested at a little village nestled high up in a forest-clad mountain. It had been a long stage, and full of magnificent scenery. After threading a long gorge with a torrent dashing below, we entered a wide plain covered with a jungle of two years' growth, and crossed the Nuikong river by a suspension bridge. . . .

I have not time to give more of our numerous incidents. You must kindly wait till the official journal is complete. It has already attained to three volumes of foolscap. I don't remember whether I have mentioned our goat before. Miles away back a mandarin gave it me for food, and I saved it from the butcher's knife, and he has trotted along ever since, repaying us with much diversion.]

To F. E. R.

[*Manwyne, January* 13*th*, 1875.—Since writing my last letter of January 4th from Teng-yueh or Momien, a frontier Chinese city, I have travelled on five stages through a most interesting country, of which I must give you a hasty sketch. But first I must tell you that all my plans succeeded without a hitch. My messenger arrived at Bhamô just in time, and has returned with despatches requesting me to proceed. They sent a Burmese guard of forty men under two officials to escort me back. . . . They are footsore and want to rest two days. . . . Yesterday they arrived at about 4 P.M. and came into my room, squatting down silently to smoke in the most undignified manner. They spoke neither Chinese nor English, and so I took them all over to the Chinese commander, who is a famous man named Li Hsieh Tai, once a brigand, now a Chinese general, in reward for services against the Mahommedan rebels. Arrived at his yamen we had quite a conclave. There were savage chieftains from the mountains, with whom the general was negotiating a treaty, and notable townsmen interested in the proceedings, besides a crowd of idlers who cannot be got rid of at official interviews in China. We sat round in a large circle, the Burmese squatting on their haunches. A long discussion was carried on through an interpreter, which ended in my finding it impossible to get them to move sooner, and had to submit to the delay. To-day, however, I have visited Li early and induced him to give me a guard to-morrow morning, so that I may hurry on and leave my baggage and servants to the care of the Burmese for the following day. I cannot yet feel certain, however, that I shall not be foiled after all. There are wheels within wheels innumerable, and intrigues going on which require my most careful watchfulness. The Burmese want to thwart our expedition; and Li himself some seven years ago attacked our last expedition and may not be entirely free from enmity. But I have a very powerful engine in the will and expressed commands of the great Viceroy at Yunnan, who has been an almost unexpected friend and ally throughout.

Our journey to this interesting town has lain through a lovely valley full of villages embowered in groves of plantain and bamboo. High mountain ranges towered right and left. The people are subject to China, but are governed by their native hereditary chiefs. They are sociable and amiable, while their striking costumes quite delight the eye with their novelty. The women wear the most marvellous turbans of black crape. When I first saw them, I could not help staring right and left at such magnificent beings as their majestic head-dress made them appear. A Grenadier Guardsman would pale beside one of these. This wonderful covering rises in concentric folds (each partly visible) to a height of fully twelve inches, and, narrow at the forehead, expands to more than a foot in width at the top. Dark blue jacket, ditto petticoat, red cuffs. Red, white, blue, and embroidered border. Red shoes. I was of course a guest of the local chiefs, wherever we spent the night. At the first stage, Nan-tien, the brother of the head man put us all up in the outhouses of his courtyard. It was a sorry lodging, but experience has not made me critical, and my utmost demand is now for a sound roof and a heap of good straw. The next two stages will possibly abound in neither, and we shall either camp in the primeval forest among tigers, or worse still, have to put up in the loathsome villages of the wild tribes.

January 14*th*.— . . After expending much energy in trying to "double" on my dusky guard by persuading the redoubtable Li to give me a few men for to-day, I am brought to a full stop by rain. The climbing road is impassable in wet, and the Celestial won't attempt anything in a shower. The family of my host came round and examined all my things. We got very sociable, and I profited by the occasion to study their language a little. I got one young scion of the reigning house, who was a pleasant young fellow, to write me down several sentences in their own characters, and we subjoined sounds and meaning in Chinese and English. One or two of the majestic females were moved by curiosity to come and look at my photograph book, and the dresses worn by the ladies created quite an enthusiasm amongst them. Ah-ah! they exclaimed, and laughed with delight. They were homely, amiable creatures, in spite of their black teeth and betel-nut stains. I quite regretted leaving the family, although we hoped to meet again. Now, however, I fear the expedition is to take a long unexplored round

which will bring us out in a different direction. We
exchanged presents. I gave our host a sword-stick
and his amiable spouse a fine pair of scissors. They
gave me a piece of amber, which is a prized orna-
ment here, and a black cane pipe-stem, which will
make me a very handsome walking stick. I only
saw two young maidens, and they looked very in-
nocent and really pretty. Neither black teeth, busby,
nor coiffure had as yet transformed their naïve
simplicity into majestic matronly dignity and, in
most cases, ugliness. The chief paid me a visit with
his two fresh-looking nice boys, whose handsome faces
paid too great a compliment to their ugly parent. He
was, however, very fond and affectionate to them, and
displayed many homely virtues. His manner was
restless and odd. Jerking out questions without
waiting for a reply, he would seize on something
novel among my things and examine it with a surprised look and then suddenly return to his dignity
again. . . . 9.30. A.M.—I intend to seek exercise with
my gun. I come and go without meeting with the
slightest rudeness among this charming people; and
they address me with the greatest respect. The streets
are narrow and horribly dirty. I am obliged to make
my servant carry me over the puddles. The river
teems with duck, and I calmly appropriate any
tenantless punt I can ferret out lying under the
banks. The other day I had great sport with
Bombazine and a boy named Soo-ah. Kicking off
gaiters and boots, I waded after the duck on the

sand-banks, and they drew me across deeper channels in my frail canoe which we could not manage with the slender paddle attached. We tried once to navigate in this novel manner to the opposite bank, but the deepening water began to wet their short jackets and the current drove us back. I shot half a dozen fine "yellow ducks," as they call them here, and on our way back through the motley market, which is daily held outside the town in a meadow, we created quite a sensation, and the crowd suspended their business to come and look at my astonishing gun and the game.

Bhamô, January 17th.—Now I am over the savage hills and have wrung the hands of fellow countrymen again. It was so delightful to come down from the hills to the Burmese plain and see the semi-Indian civilisation all around. . . . Col. Browne and a string of distinguished officers gave me a hearty welcome, with congratulations on my splendid journey. I am the first European who has traversed the trade-route of the future. No time for more now. We shall not start for a week yet.]

To his Parents.

[*Bhamô, January* 17*th*, 1875.—You will, no doubt, be surprised to find me in so advanced a position, but here I am safe and sound. They sent me a Burmese guard of forty men, who conducted me through the savage Kakhyen hills. When we debouched on to wide flat Burmese plains covered with jungle and forest, on the 15th, just as the evening sun was bathing the wide expanse in colour, and the new life and semi-Indian manners and customs of the Burmese burst upon us, as we rapidly trotted through their picturesque and homely villages, a sense of relief and pleasure came over me and my Chinese companions alike. We slept in a Burmese bamboo cabin perched on piles, and next day floated down the river to Bhamô. It was one of the most delightful periods of my life to come in sight of the British flag again, and to be congratulated on my splendid journey by the Indian officers. I look forward with intense pleasure to spending hours in such intelligent company. We have an officer with a guard of fine Sikhs and hosts of baggage animals, and countless stores. The steamer is going soon and I am pressed for time, and can only add a sort of latest intelligence. We shall go a long round, I expect, and I very much doubt if May will put an end to my long travels. I am the picture of health, people will tell me, which is about as annoying as to be called "amiable." You may imagine how full of delight I am at the happy results of my journey and the glowing prospect ahead.]

To F. E. R.

[*Sawaddy, January* 24*th,* 1875.—Since my arrival I have had six days' rest in the hospitable house of Captain and Mrs. Cooke, and yesterday we rode down here, a ten mile ride, to make our final preparations for the great journey, which is an entirely fresh excitement for the rest of the party, but a somewhat weary continuation for me. Colonel Browne, Mr. Fforde, and I, are the only members of the party down here; the naturalist, Dr. Anderson, being detained at Bhamô by the illness of the remaining member of the party, Mr. Elias, who fills the post of astronomer and topographer. We hope to have him among us again by the time we reach Mansey, our first stage from this. We shall be detained here two or three days whilst our enormous baggage of over two hundred boxes is "fixed up," as the Yankees say. The enormous difficulties which stood in the way of the last expedition in 1867 have been guarded against on the present occasion, and Colonel Browne seems to do just what he likes with Burmans and Kakhyens. My arrival from the China side created a wonderful sensation among the Bhamô population, and has done wonders in smoothing matters on this side. They would not believe that we had any officials in China, and my arrival from that side considerably surprised them. I am called the "Pekin man," i.e. the Pekin mandarin, and the local official, who rejoices in the name of Woon, was quite anxious to see me. His principal occupation seems to be to sit cross-legged in state in his open verandah (which like all Burmese houses is raised several feet above the ground on stakes), and listen to what is called a pwai. This is a national song accompanied by slow movements of the arms, performed by women. He has only to order a pwai and twenty or thirty women come together dressed in their most brilliant clothes, and wearing all the jewelry they possess, which is more or less a sign that they belong either to a rich or a fond husband. It is a pretty sight, but a dreadfully tedious affair to sit through. . . . The floor of these houses is made of split rattan, so that in walking across it you have, at first, an unpleasant sensation of expecting to go through, and the whole place rattles as you proceed. The women stand in rows in the courtyard below, which is covered in with a broad flat shed, and lazy townspeople stand round to watch the entertainment. The Woon has a whole crowd of petty officials squatted in the background, and we filled up the centre. My writer, whom we now call "Goggles," from his enormous heavy brass-rimmed, window-like spectacles, has also assumed a position of importance among us, and the old Woon was delighted to ask him up to the entertainment. Fortunately, we could come and go as we liked, and I stretched my legs outside as soon as the squatting became tedious. Married and single, old and young, alike took part in the pwai. Some were young and pretty, but most were quite the reverse. I had a very novel journey of two days across the mountains which lie between the Shan Valleys on the China side and the wide plains of Burmah. They are inhabited by the wild Kakhyen tribes, and my rabble guard of forty Burmese was no idle precaution on the part of Captain Cooke. We passed through eight or nine of their curious villages, and experienced one or two amusing examples of their bold impudence. My servant Lin was menaced by one of these semi-savage brutes with a large stone, which he raised to strike him with; and another drew his dâh, a rough weapon sheathed on one side, which they all carry, and made a daring attempt to rob one of my men of his bag. Their long thatched cabins of rattan peeping out of the still forest here and there had a strange exciting interest for us, and the little scowling, vicious-looking women eyed us with the unchanged countenance of savages.

We had a strange lodging that night in the hills. We merely travelled on till the sinking sun warned us to halt, and on reaching an open clearing the brave captain of the dusky tattooed army slid off his pony and pointed me to a low hovel of twigs and dry leaves which some recent occupants had left for the next comers. There were three or four ready made, and I enjoyed the look of amazement on "Goggles'" face when I told him to look sharp and appropriate one for himself before the Burmese anticipated him. We crept in on all fours, and spread our beds, adding fresh twigs outside to keep off the heavy dew. The "forty thieves" set to work to build themselves huts, and before long a whole cordon of camp fires surrounded the gipsy-like lodgings. We were astir again by daylight, pursuing our difficult track through dense forest and tangled vegetation, which required both hands to protect the eyes, and both feet drawn up to avoid projecting rocks, whilst one's pony slid down a slippery path ten feet at a time. The transition from China to Burmah with a bit of savagery between was most striking. We descended on the second day after a long tedious march to the jungle plains of Burmah, and trotted off with delighted feelings some six miles on the pleasant level to the first Burmese village, where the brave captain put us up in his bamboo stake house. The scene was novel indeed. Here were women going about freely in the very slight dress of the Burmans, displaying a shocking amount of their persons to view. The third day took us to Bhamô in a clumsy boat, and I arrived early in the afternoon at the Political Resident's house. Since then Colonel Browne has made a start, and we are living *al fresco* in an open shed surrounded by a strange medley of nationalities. The wild Kakhyens are in treaty with us, and some two hundred boxes of treasure and presents is being made over to them rapidly for carriage. Just outside the village some hundreds of these rough brutes are encamped, and the bullocks they have brought down for carrying our enormous baggage roam all over the wild jungle for food. We make excursions in the surrounding forests with our guns, in search of peacocks, tigers, wild elephants, and a host of wonderful game which abounds in the vicinity. Yesterday Mr. Fforde and I had a long ramble. Each had a boy guide and a tall sepoy in attendance, and of course very soon lost sight of each other in the jungle. I walked over acres of marsh, sinking over knees among the reeds, and crept into the forest through thorny openings made by wild boars or other savage monsters. Footprints of large tigers and innumerable beasts abounded, but the forest was as still as death, and neither of us saw anything at all.

January 28*th*.—We have all collected now and are under orders to start to-morrow morning. . . . Our quarters are exceedingly simple and open to the night air. I am sitting on the floor writing on my tin desk.]

To F. E. R.

[*Bhamô.—February* 5*th*, 1875.—The expedition is not off yet, on account of those troublesome hillmen with whom it is so difficult to treat. My last letter was from Sawaddy, on January 28th, after we had spent a whole week encamping in the jungle village, surrounded by the wild Kakhyen hordes. It was a fruitless attempt to get off by that route, and after the daily pretexts for further delay, trumped up by their ugly avaricious old chief (he with the big hole in his ear filled with coils of gold ribbon), Colonel Browne broke up his camp and resolved to go the way I came, which is thirty miles farther north of the Sawaddy passes. So we all returned in detachments, and sent all our baggage, with the fine old Sikhs, and the whole army of attendants, on in boats to a village called Tsikaw, which lies at the foot of the other route some fifteen miles from this. Some members of our expedition have already gone up to settle themselves in their new quarters, and Colonel Browne and I are to ride up to-morrow. The road to Sawaddy was bad enough to break our girths and stirrups, but here we shall have to swim our animals over three large streams, and ride over goat tracks under the cliffs. We were in the midst of a very novel scene at Sawaddy. . . . In order to put the picture before you more vividly, I must try and make you imagine a vast plain here profusely covered with forest and jungle, sometimes of underwood, sometimes of thick grass, standing fifteen feet high, such as buries the track to Sawaddy out of sight. You must not think of smiling fields, or picture to yourself farms and busy cultivation. It is as wild as wild can be, with but few villages between large places like Bhamô, Magoung, or Mandalay. This, to me, delicious burst of nature, is overlooked by a long narrow range of high forest-clad hills to the east, which it is our ambition to cross. . . We were very nearly off by the Sawaddy route. The whole of the baggage, with the exception of the boxes which held the silver, was going over to the savages, and when complications began to arise, I certainly thought we were in for a row. But Colonel Browne cut short further parley by telling them he would go another way, and rode up to Bhamô to make new arrangements. Dr. Anderson and I accompanied him, and we had no easy ride. There was a nasty creek to cross with a steep sandbank on the other side, surmountable only through a narrow trench scarcely affording room to dismount at its base. The water was from two to three feet deep at its side. I attempted to ride up, and my pony gave a bound out of the water to rush up the bank, but not only did my knees catch in the narrowing sides, but the animal could not maintain its footing, and we simply slid back into the water in a most ridiculous plight. I then managed to spring off on the wrong side, and ran up, leading my pony, who plunged so much that the stupid beast knocked me down and knelt on me, but we got up at last in a pretty state of ruin. Having reached Bhamô and made all arrangements, we dropped down to Sawaddy again by night in a boat. Captain Cooke was to start next day for Tsikaw to see the savage chiefs. . . I rode into Bhamô again next morning with old Goggles in company, for I wanted him to write some Chinese despatches. We had great fun, anticipating Goggles' difficulties at the creek, and the whole party had the cruelty to walk out to see the fun. But I had a man to assist the old chap, and he got up beautifully. We then started off without a guide, and of course lost our way in the jungle. Following what seemed a broad track, we soon found it narrow into nothing. After trying back three times and wasting forty minutes, I at last hit upon the right way, and we got into Bhamô pretty hot.

February 6th.—We are just about to start off for

Tsikaw... We shall be five days probably before finally starting over the hills, and then I shall be retracing my steps.]

To his Brother.

[*Tsikaw, Burmah, February* 10*th*, 1875.—A very welcome letter of yours, dated I don't know when in the now distant past, reached me at the ancient city of Momien among a whole heap of correspondence forwarded after me by the consul at Hankow. I have been wanting to write to you, old boy, for a long time, but as each rare opportunity occurred I was compelled to write long official yarns, which left me little time for home. You have, however, I hope, heard from time to time of my progress. I was continually on the tramp for four months and a half, and eventually got as far as Bhamô, being the first European who has yet succeeded in coming through. They thought I was lost, and Lord Northbrook telegraphed for another man, the result is Clement Allen came round by sea and dropped into our camp one night as we were at dinner in the open air. So now there are two interpreters instead of one. We have wasted a lot of time trying in vain to get off, and from all I have seen of the dirty brigands who live in the range of mountains that bar our way to China, we shall be lucky to get off in a fortnight more. Meantime we sit jawing in the midst of a stinking crowd of savages. We annihilate time by shooting excursions in the surrounding jungle, and living *al fresco* in open bamboo huts raised on piles, which are necessary for this country to guard against floods, reptiles, *et hoc genus omne*. We are supposed in a couple of days to take our part in a disgusting ceremony with the savages of swearing eternal friendship and concluding a treaty. They will slaughter a bullock before us, and the blood must be drunk all round after the chiefs have dipped their spears into the revolting bowl. They are a rum lot to deal with, and we have only as yet succeeded in paying away a lot of money, and being robbed of nearly all our liquor. There are three routes through these brigand-infested hills. Two have been already explored by the Sladen expedition of 1867, and we tried to go by the remaining Sawaddy line. We lived *al fresco* for a week in a village of that name on the Irawady, and gave over our boxes to the Kakhyens for carriage, after which all sorts of troubles arose, and they coolly helped themselves to the contents of our baggage. We ultimately got it back by surrounding the dirty thieves with a Burmese rabble of a " brave army," and removed our camp up here twenty-five miles farther north to cross by the route I followed in coming over. It is in the hands of different clans. As most of us have little to do but amuse ourselves, you may be sure we take fine excursions into forest and jungle, marsh and lake, wherever there is game at hand. Sawaddy was surrounded by a wonderful jungle, and the forest at the back abounded in wild game. One morning, in the pursuit of peacocks, I came across tracks of tigers and wild boar, deer, and other things. Fforde and I started, with sepoys to guard us, but soon separated, after wading knee deep in green marshes; the way into the forest often led through a narrow *tunnel* made by some wild beast through the thorny jungle.

Sunday, February 14th.—We are not off yet, although there are signs of an approaching start. Inaction in a camp is fatal to high spirits and good humour, though this is not the case with us, for we meet over our late dinner with many a laugh and joke, but my Chinamen have broken out into irritable fits, and four of them tried to break each other's heads the other day. I have a good deal of influence over them, and brought them to their senses again after a sound lecture. . . I tell you what, old boy, I don't find writing by any means a pleasant occupation, squatted on the floor with a box for a table, and a perfect plague of flies settling over my face and hands. We have been stringing beads all the morning to captivate the savages, and those other fellows are at it still; but as the whole mass was put in basins of water first, my hands are like a washerwoman's after fishing them out. I hope to goodness we shall get off soon, for although snipe and deer abound in the fields and jungle around us, and we have a jolly swim every evening in the river, it is anything but comfortable living long in a rattan shed, open to wind and weather, getting every day more musty inside and out from the accumulation of refuse and unavoidable dirt. The doctor's museum does not contribute towards sweetening the air, and a host of natives of various race and complexion take kindly to grubbing. I often think of you when we are in a particularly nice fix out riding, and wonder what you would do, eh, old centaur? Would not your long legs have stuck in the mud at some of the choicest mud-larks we have occasionally come in for! I smashed my bridle and girths the other day in crossing a river. There was a steep bank rising out of deepish water, and a narrow cutting up it. My pony got restive and plunged up the slope with a sudden bound out of the water, and when we got half-way up my knees got jambed against the sides, and the poor beast could not keep his footing, so the result was a slide down backwards into the river again. On coming over here we had to swim our animals across three rivers. It was a fine sight to see five or six ponies swimming on each side of the canoe and the syces holding up their heads by the bridles. We have an Arab and a huge Australian, which are intended as presents; the latter kicked up no end of a row in the water, rearing, and attempting to take passage in the canoe. Colonel Browne gave me the prettiest pony of the lot, but he shies badly. Out for a ride in the jungle the other day, a dark deep ditch barred the way, and while the others leapt over and galloped away I spent about ten minutes trying to get my beast over, putting him at it again and again with terrific results. It is not pleasant being left behind in the gloaming with tigers kicking about. We have a fine body-guard of fifteen Sikhs. They go in for athletic sports, and as for swimming they are perfect fishes. I never saw anything of the sort finer than the way they plunged into the river the other day; with a run of thirty or forty yards, they sprang off the high bank, feet foremost, and disappeared in the rushing current fifteen or sixteen feet out. Allen and I go in every evening and attract a big crowd of Kakhyens and Burmans, who live on the banks above us, and seemed considerably astonished at our little feats of swimming. We swam across one night, the river is not above a hundred yards wide, but the current carries you down a long way. I got giddy, and came to an anchor in my depth till a canoe came to pick me up. Here come a lot of these filthy savages; some of them speak Chinese, so I get along splendidly with them. One of the Pawmynes (or deputy chiefs) has taken a fancy to me (I hope it is not too strong), and promised to get me some of their dresses and ornaments. No time to write more, but shall be able to write again from Momien.

To F. E. R.

[*Tsikaw, fifteen miles from Bhamô.—February 9th*, 1875.—I have been out all the morning after snipe with the colonel. We have been tramping through mud and slush and sinking over knees in treacherous marshes. At one place we got entangled in high elephant grass, and had to cut our way out of it. The four stalwart Sikhs who accompanied us hacked away with their short swords and bent down the thick grass to pave a way for us. We are encamped on the banks of a small tributary of the Irawady called the Tapeng, which flows by with a tremendously strong current. It is about one hundred yards wide, and we try to swim across occasionally, but the stream of course carries us down a long way before we reach the sandy stretch on the opposite bank. The sun shines hot all day, and the refreshing coolness of the water in the evening is delicious. There is a large village of Burmese and Chinese here, and we live in a deserted kyoung or priest's house, just outside their stockade. The Kakhyens have not yet infested us, but as it was arranged in the preliminary parleys the other day with their chiefs, who go by the titles of Tsanbwas, and Pawmynes, that the bull sacrifice, by which horrid ceremony these dirty ruffians conclude a treaty, shall take place in a couple of days more, I shall expect to see their filthy hordes encamping round next week. The only result of our week's stay at Sawaddy, was, that the dirty thieves broached all our liquor boxes, and provision stores, about which few questions were asked, and we are now reduced to the necessity of writing down for fresh stores which may not catch us after all. However, I do not believe we shall get away for ten days yet. These brigands know too

Y

well how to trump up excuses and squeeze money out of us. We shall be accompanied through the hills by a Burmese brave army, whose rabble ranks surround us now with a cordon of huts—no unnecessary precaution in this tiger-teeming jungle. I am going to make a trip to-morrow to a certain forest in which the gorgeous peacocks perch about as numerous as magpies. We are more comfortable up here than we were at Sawaddy, and the air and water are superior to Bhamô.

February 10*th*.—We have put off the peacocks. A flock of geese settled this morning on the sands opposite, and Dr. Anderson and I dropped down from above in a canoe till the unsuspecting birds came within range, and then blazed away. I bagged nine. He missed, but two wounded birds were seen to separate themselves from the flock and settle in the creeks away above the sandy stretch. We went in pursuit, and had a veritable wild goose chase. It was a frightful sell after all our trouble to lose our game just as we had stalked it down by the provoking report of a savage's gun hard by. The birds had settled on a small island in such a position that we could not approach within shot without wading through the river for more than one hundred yards behind a bank of reeds. It was the greatest fun in the world. . .

February 12*th*.—We are still here, but there is a slight prospect of our getting off in three or four days. The sacrifice is to be dispensed with out of respect to the Burmese repugnance for taking life. The Kakhyens are flocking in now in numbers, and bring us presents of vegetables and a fermented drink like beer which they call "sherroo." We let them ascend to our rattan floor (raised on stakes) and apart from the novelty and indeed fun of chaffing them and trying to buy their various curiosities, it is by no means a savoury infliction. The shocks of an electric machine produce a constant flow of merriment, and we roar with laughter at the grimaces and contortions of our savage guests while under its treatment. The women are getting bold by this time and come in considerable numbers, bringing us their simple offerings of friendship. They are the queerest creatures imaginable, and dirty beyond all description. Yet we humour them, and there is no small degree of coyness about them, which makes them interesting in spite of their redstained lips and unwashed legs. They wear the most marvellous girdles of loose rings of rattan, split to the thickness of a thread, and a belt covered with cowries. The ears are pierced with big holes, in which they insert silver tubes six inches long and adorned with tufts of red cloth. We have been trying to-day to tempt them to sell these strange ornaments for dazzling bead-necklaces, but to no purpose. One creature permitted me even to draw a tube out of her ear, but my attempts at bargaining only produced good humoured laughter from the men, and giggles from the women. A Kakhyen has a horror of water, and this evening we excited immense amusement and screaming exclamations of surprise by diving into the river and swimming about performing all sorts of tricks on each other. The river is too swift to admit of our stemming its current, so we dive in above and swim down to a landing, and then run back most unceremoniously along the bank to repeat the operation.

Yesterday we went a long expedition with Dr. Anderson fifteen miles across the opposite jungle and bang into the Kakhyen hills. We met several of these uncouth marauders, but I suppose they would think twice before attacking Europeans armed with double barrelled guns, more especially as we were not encumbered with attractive plunder. A glorious sight certainly rewarded us for the weary tramp, for we saw our Tapeng leaving the deep hills by one of the most lovely gorges I ever saw, and I have seen many. We were too hot to risk a most tempting bath in such a climate. Excursions like this are of course of daily occurrence, and we live a regular gipsy life.

Monday, February 15*th*.—I really believe we are off in earnest to-day. It looks very like it. The cramped Zayat is full of people packing up and carrying off our personal luggage, while a whole host outside are rapidly attaching the vast baggage to pack saddles. There is a look of business about them which augurs well for our progress. The Woon has taken hostages from the Kakhyen chiefs.

and we shall in all probability go through their hills without much delay. . .

We were awakened last night by a hideous yell which appeared to our sleepy senses to overwhelm us in the midst of a very pandemonium. It proceeded, however, from the throats of our friends, and not from bloodthirsty savages in a night raid. The brave army of two or three hundred Burmans gave tongue with terrific effect. If their bite were only equal to their bark, we might laugh at our Kakhyen marauders. The cause of the outcry was an unfortunate buffalo which dashed into our camp with a gash across its sacrificial throat, followed by a savage band with drawn dâhs. The incident passed off without disturbing our equanimity long.

Here the story, as told by Mr. Margary himself, breaks off. What followed during the next five days has been shortly told in the opening sketch, and may be found more at length in Dr. Anderson's 'Mandalay to Momien.' To his kindly and sympathetic notice of his young comrade the doctor adds, page 451: "He may be said to have bequeathed it as a public duty—made more imperative by its being the most fitting tribute to his worth—to establish in those border lands the right of Englishmen to travel unmolested." And, "for the present, above and beyond the task of avenging his murder on the guilty, of whatever rank they may be, his name will be most fitly honoured by a party of his countrymen formally asserting their right to traverse, in honour and safety, the route between Burmah and China, which he was the first Englishman to explore, and which should be maintained as his most durable monument."

Already an investigation into the circumstances of his murder, and the attack on the mission, is being held in Yunnan, in the presence of Mr. Grosvenor and his staff representing England. It seems more than probable that it will be avenged amply enough, more amply indeed than he would have desired. But whether, and how soon, his countrymen will be able to travel in honour and safety the route which he was the first to explore, will depend upon the faithfulness with which they copy his example. As soon as Englishmen shall be able, as he did, to find " the people everywhere charming, and the mandarins extremely civil" (134)—in spite of all the serious and petty vexations, discomforts, and discourtesies, which met him day after day, and which he had to brush aside with a firm hand, but without losing temper— the route will open out, and become as safe to them as it proved to him on his lonely westward journey. For his short story, if read aright, and in spite of its violent ending, adds yet another testimony that a little genuine liking and sympathy for them, combined with firmness, will go further and do more with races of a different civilization from our own than treaties, gunboats, and grape-shot, without it. If the route is ever to be a durable and worthy monument of the man, it must be opened and used in his spirit, by fair means, and for beneficent ends. If a reluctant consent is only forced from the Chinese by threats of war, and the route becomes the highway for the opium traffic, it may enrich the spinners of Lancashire, and the planters of Bengal, but it will never be a true or satisfactory memorial of Augustus Raymond Margary.

CONCLUDING CHAPTER.

By Sir Rutherford Alcock, K.C.B.

I HAVE been requested to furnish a few notes that may serve to complete the record of an expedition brought to such an abrupt and untimely end, by the murder of the author of the journal and letters now given to the public. As the Minister at Pekin when Mr. Margary first joined the consular service, where his assiduity in the study of the Chinese language at the Legation brought him frequently under my favourable notice, it was natural that I should follow with interest his subsequent career, which so fully realised the promise of his student days at the capital. It is, perhaps, no less natural that I should now be appealed to by his friends and the publishers, to complete, as far as possible, the interesting narrative which will be found in the preceding pages.

It is too early yet to form any definitive judgment as to the causes of the hostility the expedition encountered on the Chinese borders. It would be equally premature to anticipate the results of Mr.

Grosvenor's mission. Whether he has succeeded in obtaining trustworthy evidence as to who were the responsible parties, and instigators of the attack upon Colonel Browne's party, of which, as Sir Thomas Wade has justly said, the murder at Manwyne was but one of the incidents, we do not yet know. With whom the responsibility properly rests for both hostile acts, either as planners or perpetrators, cannot profitably be considered until such authentic account of the inquiry as only the Government will be in a position to furnish, with all its details, is accessible.

As to the origin of the expedition, Sir Thomas Wade has told us that "the Government of India having signified a desire to send a small mission into Yunnan, a passport was obtained by the British Legation from the Chinese Government to enable four officers and gentlemen with their followers to cross the frontier from the Burmese side, and that Mr. Margary was sent with a separate passport to meet the above mission under the leadership of Colonel Browne." Why the Indian Government came to such a decision, and chose the particular time selected for renewing an enterprise which had led to no very satisfactory result under Major Sladen, are questions of considerable interest. We learn from a narrative of both expeditions lately published by Dr. Anderson,[*] that some years

[*] 'A Narrative of the Two Expeditions to Western China of 1868 and 1875, under Colonel Edward B. Sladen and Colonel

previous to the date of that expedition in 1868, the attention of British merchants at home and in India had been directed to the prospect of an overland trade with Western China, and most "especially did this interest the commercial community of Rangoon, the capital of British Burmah, and the port of the great water highway of the Irawaddy, boasting a trade the annual value of which had increased in fifteen years to 2,500,000*l*. The avoidance of the long and dangerous voyage by the Straits and Indian Archipelago, and a direct interchange of our manufactures for the products of the rich provinces of Yunnan and Sz-chuen, might well seem to be advantages which would richly repay almost any efforts to accomplish this purpose." But the official answer to both questions has been given in a despatch from the Government of India to the Marquis of Salisbury dated the 5th of March 1875, written after news had been received of the disasters which had befallen the Yunnan expedition. In this is embodied "a statement of the origin and progress of the expedition undertaken by the Government of India in furtherance of the wishes of Her Majesty's Government that efforts should be made to explore trade routes between British Burmah and Western China." The despatch proceeds, "Your Lordship is aware that the Government of India have never been

---

Horace Browne.' By John Anderson, M.D.—London: Macmillan & Co., 1876.

disposed to entertain sanguine expectations of the advantages to be derived from the schemes which have, from time to time, been proposed for the exploration of the routes from Burmah to the Western Provinces of China." To which is added the fact that they became aware, from a despatch of Her Majesty's Minister at Pekin of the 24th of July, 1873, "that in Mr. Wade's opinion there was no prospect of trade across the borders of Yunnan." The statement continues in the following terms: "While the matter still engaged our consideration, we received the despatch from the Secretary of State, No. 45, dated 23rd April, 1874, in which we were informed that recent reports from the Chief Commissioner of British Burmah and the Chinese frontier had convinced your Lordship of the importance of instituting an examination of the country between British Burmah and the Chinese frontier, and the Secretary for State for Foreign Affairs had been invited to instruct Her Majesty's Representative in China to co-operate, should he be aware of no objection to such a course, in aiding the proposed expedition to Talifu and other arrangements connected with the same purpose." It was clearly therefore the act of the Secretary of State for India—moved no doubt by the successive memorials of the Associated Chambers of Commerce in this country, as well as in India and China.

To a mercantile nation, the simple fact that there

was a possibility of a great shortening of distance, and a diminution of danger in the transport of goods, would be quite enough to justify strenuous efforts to secure such results. And as to the particular route, the further fact that the Burmese annals testify to this having during several centuries been the passage from China to Burmah for "invading armies or for peaceful caravans," would naturally direct those efforts in this direction. Perhaps, as not wholly foreign to this predilection, the very terms used in the treaty of peace that was signed at Bhamô in 1769, may have had their influence. It was there stipulated that the "gold and silver road" between the two countries should be reopened. But the truth is that long before, as well as subsequent to that date, a good deal of attention had been devoted to the development of a trade by this route, in which British and Anglo-Indian merchants might reasonably hope to participate largely with mutual advantage. Not to speak of references to this in the last century by Colonel Symes, the East India Company's Envoy to Ava in 1795, there has been a continuous series of notices all tending to direct public attention to the value of such a line of communication across Burmah into China. Wilcox and Crawford in 1826, and the Bengal Government's map, published in 1827, containing the best procurable information about the Burmo-Chinese frontier, all point to the same end. Colonel Burney, our resident in Ava in

1830, Pemberton later, and Hannay, all made contributions pointing to Yunnan and the north-eastern boundaries of our Indian Empire, as naturally indicated for commercial interchange. In 1862 the Government of India, in prospect of a treaty being negotiated with the king of Burmah, instructed the British Commissioner, Sir. A. Phayre, to keep in view the advisability of a stipulation for reopening the caravan route from Western China by the town of Bhamô, and the concession of facilities to British merchants to reside at that place or to travel to Yunnan;—and for Chinese from Yunnan to have free access to British territory, including Assam by Upper Burmah and the Irawaddy. Dr. Williams also, when resident at the court of Mandalay, proceeded to Bhamô, a journey of twenty-two days, to test the practicability of a route in this direction through Burmah to Western China. In a word, the opening of a practicable trade route has, for a long series of years, been a favourite project with Indian residents in Burmah, and merchants, whether located there or at our centres of trade in England. Even the French, who by their late conquests and annexations in Anam and Ton-Quin, have established themselves in the Indo-Chinese peninsula, are seeking very perseveringly to create a commerce and facilities of access into Yunnan by means of a direct route from their own possessions. And they appear to have found the best and shortest route in this direction by the

Sankoi river. Unfortunately for the development of any large trade the mouth of this river is on the eastern instead of the western side of the peninsula, and can only therefore offer facilities to vessels having already incurred the delay and expenses of a voyage through the Straits and up the Chinese Sea—a long and more or less dangerous navigation, which would be avoided by any route starting either from the coast in the Gulf of Bengal, or Rangoon.

Enough evidence is furnished by all these various reports and explorations to show that European travellers and traders had very early believed in the importance of this field for commercial enterprise, and the desirability of establishing lines of communication between India and the western provinces of China, either through our north-eastern frontiers in Assam, Tibet, or Burmah. Nor has there been wanting foreign aid to stimulate the Indian government to active efforts to secure if possible this end, for in 1848 Baron Otto des Granges published a survey of the "Countries between Bengal and China, showing the great commercial and political importance of Bhâmo, and the practicability of a direct trade overland between Calcutta and China."

In the meantime the Mahommedan rising in Yunnan, by which the greater part of the province was lost to the Chinese for some seventeen years, went far to destroy all trade between China and Burmah: Dr. Anderson tells us that the trade, which in 1855 represented half a million sterling per annum, had almost entirely ceased when General Fytche, then Chief Commissioner, anxiously pressed upon the Government of India the importance of ascertaining the cause of this cessation, and whether it was attributable to the Mahommedan insurrection, or as alleged by some, to Burmese policy? He also urged the opportuneness under the treaty of 1862 of thoroughly examining " the possibility and probable results " of reopening the Bhamô trade route.

How far the time selected was really opportune in the midst of an insurrection which extended over the whole province, and a civil war raging close to the frontiers of Burmah and China, may be considered very questionable. If the chief objects of the expedition were, to use the words of General Fytche, "to discover the cause of the cessation of the trade formerly existing by these routes, the exact position held by the Kakhyens, Shans, and Panthays (the latter being the Mahommedan insurgents) with reference to that traffic, and their disposition or otherwise to resuscitate it, also to examine the physical conditions of these routes," it cannot be doubted that we were engaging in an enterprise that must necessarily involve official relations with the men in open rebellion with our ally at Pekin, and could not fail to be regarded with suspicion and dislike by the Chinese Government. That this was one of the most prominent results of Major Sladen's expedition in 1868, and that it has had some sinister connection with the tragic termination of the second, seems distinctly traceable, in the journal and letters included in this volume, as well as by all the information which has since been obtained. Of course it is impossible to say what may be the precise extent of these influences, unless the Grosvenor mission supply us with fresh facts. But the charges so freely made against Lee-see-tai, as the immediate instigator, if not the actual leader of the Chinese force which attacked Colonel Browne's party, pointed to his previous relations, as the Chinese commander on the border when Major Sladen crossed it under the protection of the Panthay chiefs, and resided for a term in their camp at Momien. It is indeed clearly shown that this visit, and the friendly relations established by Major Sladen with the Mussulman chiefs of the rebellion, had a more decisive and disastrous influence on the fate of the insurgents, than either they or Major Sladen could have well anticipated. It is true that the chiefs, and the Sultan, as he was styled, were not without hope of securing some powerful support by means of relations to be established with the British for commercial objects only. But they could little have foreseen that the fact of such relations being contemplated, and the possibility of foreign aid being obtained by the insurgents, should have so alarmed the Chinese Government as to lead them to make a supreme effort to stamp out the rebellion. Certain it is that such effort was successfully made; and it dates from the

z

arrival of Major Sladen's party at Momein, and the subsequent despatch of the Sultan's son Hassan to Europe on a mission to the British Government, seeking for help. But for these events, it seems more than probable that this insurrection, like so many others in China, might have been allowed to smoulder on for many years longer, without any adequate effort being made by the Chinese Government to put it down. It is impossible to doubt, that if the appearance of an expedition headed by a British officer on the Chinese border, and the establishment of friendly relations with the insurgent chiefs, could so deeply move the Imperial authorities and government, and excite so much alarm as to lead to the concentration of all their forces for the destruction of the rebels, the expedition itself is not likely to have been forgotten. It is equally improbable that the hostile feeling it created should have wholly disappeared in the breasts of the Imperial soldiers and authorities engaged at the time in a death-struggle with the insurgents.

Dr. Anderson, in his account of the two expeditions, to both of which he was attached, cannot avoid referring to the untoward connection between the first and the second. In speaking of the intermediate events and relations with the Panthays, he says:

"It was a necessary, but regretable consequence of the reception given to the first expedition by the Governor of Momien, that we maintained friendly relations with successive Residents. It appeared desirable, with a view to maintain the security of the trade route, to keep on friendly, though strictly neutral, terms with the holders of the commanding position of Momien. It is, doubtless, easy to look back, and be wise after the event; but rightly or wrongly, the intercourse once begun could not well be abandoned; at all events, it was judged prudent to maintain it. It certainly created in the minds of the Chinese at Bhamô a distinct impression that the interests of there possible commercial rivals and of their actual foes were identified. The Kakhyen chiefs of the southern route even complained that since they and the Shans had become friends of the English, the Bhamô Chinese were no longer amicably disposed towards them. The presents sent by the Residents from time to time were doubtless magnified by popular imagination, and neither side found it easy to believe that the sole object was the assurance of safe and commodious transit. Thus at least it may be conjectured, from the study of the course of subsequent events, as well as from the manifestations of feeling on the part of both Panthays and Chinese."

Again, we are told further on, that " the conflicting accounts and reports which were brought in, and which enable us in some degree to trace the progress of events in Yunnan, which led to the complete overthrow of the Mahommedan power, all combined to show that from the time of the visit to Momien, the Chinese Government would seem to have aroused itself to the necessity of recovering the almost lost province." The distinction here sought to be drawn between relations that should be "friendly" with a province in active rebellion, "and yet strictly neutral" is much too fine and subtile for the Chinese intellect. Both in the popular and the official mind, such a plea would make no appreciable difference in their estimate of the proceeding—and its object. That it was giving strength and encouragement to their enemies, and therefore disloyal in a friendly nation, was the only conclusion they could be expected to draw. Still less was it likely they would form any more favourable opinion, seeing that they had a very similar experience of our opening friendly relations, for commercial objects, with another insurgent chief in Turkestan, Yakob Beg, who had already wrested a large territory from their rule, and was seeking in Russia and England, his northern and southern neighbours, both support and alliances. Sir Douglas Forsyth's expedition to Yarkand in 1870, and the subsequent convention or treaty entered into with Yacob, another Mahommedan rebel, must have greatly tended to confirm the deep distrust of the Chinese in our good faith on either border.

If I insist upon this in some detail it is not with a view of attaching blame to the chief actors, or the responsible authors of both expeditions, but to show the importance in reference to the future, of observing a certain logical sequence in the events—and the necessity of not overlooking the relation in which they stand to each other. The second expedition, in which Mr. Margary lost his life, was the heir of the first, and reaped the fruit of the seeds sown in 1868 at Momien. Major Sladen's expedition, so fatal to the Mahommedan cause in Yunnan, was scarcely less prejudicial to the success of the second expedition led by Colonel Browne. And if any future efforts in this direction are to be made with better success, we must address ourselves to the consideration, how the misgivings and animosities which have contributed so largely to the failure of the two now on record, may best be removed? It is true, that in the last of these missions we are held to have had the full sanction of both the governments concerned; the Burmese on the one side, and the Chinese on the other. But a question has been raised how far this is true? And certainly the Blue Book recently issued on the 'Indian Expedition to Western China,' is not as conclusive on this head as might be desired. That passports were given at Pekin, on the application of the British minister for Mr. Margary to proceed to, and for the officers to come from Burmah, is beyond doubt. But there is a distinct disclaimer on the part of the Prince of Kung, in the subsequent correspondence with Sir Thomas Wade, of any information as to the ulterior object both of Mr. Margary's journey and the Indian mission. That this object was to establish a caravan route into Western China from Burmah; to assert a permanent right of access for British traders, and establish a trade in Yunnan, by sending goods across the border overland, was of course known to all foreigners. But was this explained, or any attempt made to explain the real purpose of the mission, to the Tsungli yamen? and did they in effect understand what was the object proposed? In the absence of more precise information than the Blue Book supplies, it is impossible to say; but Lord Northbrook in proposing a mission to Ta-Li Fu himself telegraphed to the India Office: " Agreement of Chinese Government an essential preliminary." And the Earl of Derby had pointed out to the Marquis of Salisbury that "Her Majesty's Government had no right to appoint consuls at any places in China, except the Treaty-ports, and that there were grave difficulties in the way of establishing consulates or British communities in the far interior of China where British protection could not be extended to them in case of danger, which, in the present state of the Chinese Empire, is in some shape, constantly threatening foreigners, and which the Government of Pekin, even if well disposed to do so, can often only imperfectly guard against." While a year antecedent to this Sir Thomas Wade had written: " As to the prospect of trade across the border of Yunnan, I regret to say there is none. The western and south-western frontiers are as jealously guarded as ever." Yet the expedition started, and Mr. Margary was despatched to meet it with a passport from the British minister countersigned (sealed) by the Chinese Foreign Office. So far they obviously had cognizance of the two parties being engaged to meet in China, and that from Burmah passing over the border. But how much more did they know? The Tsungli yamen, in a memorandum of the 22nd of March 1875, states that "the original understanding with reference to the Indian expedition was that the purpose in view was travel. *Nothing was said of any other objects*; and the province, in fact, is not one of those comprising ports open to trade." If this be true, the Chinese Government has certainly some ground for complaint. And what is still more important perhaps, in one sense at least, the expedition had no fair chance of succeeding in its real object, since that must have essentially depended upon the willingness of the Chinese authorities, not only to make a very large concession, to which they had always evinced the greatest repugnance, but a fundamental change in their relations with other Treaty Powers, as well as ourselves.

To this negation of the Tsungli yamen there is no rejoinder in the Blue Book. The answer actually sent by the British minister appears to be given *in extenso* in the Blue Book, under date March 25, 1875, in an official despatch addressed to the Prince of Kung. In this Mr. Wade observes that when he applied last summer for the passports, the yamen was informed of the official character of this mission, and adds, "I stated that the passports were applied for, in the terms of Article IX. of the treaty, as for persons touring, not travelling for purposes of trade."

And in the preceding paragraph he gives, what probably was intended to convey at the time referred to, all the information which was thought necessary, to the following effect: "The Government of India desiring to possess itself of information that might prove useful to the traders of the province of British Burmah, between whom and the province of Yunnan there is in times of peace a considerable traffic, resolved to send a mission headed by an officer, who would be accompanied by three or four gentlemen. They were to make a tour through the province and report upon the conditions of trade." Whether such an announcement as this was all that was required— or whether other and more precise information as to the ulterior object of the mission may not have actually been given—are questions which cannot be satisfactorily answered without further information. But this much may be very confidently affirmed, that there was no reasonable prospect of any satisfactory result, by any intercourse or negotiation with the provincial authorities, of establishing a trade, or obtaining commercial concessions and facilities of any kind, without the full concurrence and authority of the Central Government. It is possible, however, that in sending the expedition, it was hoped such preliminary information might be obtained as would pave the way for some ulterior concession or trading facilities, which would be so much gained, without, in the meantime, committing either government to any more formal act or policy. But the event seems to show, if this were the case, that the chances of success had been miscalculated, and the *damnosa hæreditas* of the first expedition, and our subsequent missions to Yarkand, had not been sufficiently weighed. We must not complain that our reputation in the East takes its complexion from our conquests and progress in India, the history of which, in broad outline at least, is perfectly well-known in China, if not over all Asia. How we began by asking for a privilege to trade, and ended by annexing provinces after disastrous wars is no secret. Whatever explanations or defence we may have to offer, as to the causes of this irrepressible advance from trading factories to Empire, we can scarcely expect any Eastern sovereign or people to attach much credit to them. We must be content to trade and to negotiate, weighted with this heavy burden of distrust and suspicion.

It seems impossible to maintain that the mere consent of the Tsungli yamen to affix the Foreign Office seal to the passports issued by Sir Thomas Wade, conveyed any "agreement of the Chinese Government with the objects of the mission" either as to the opening of a trade route from Burmah, or the establishment of a British official at Ta-Li Fu, or at "inland centres to watch proceedings, and on occasion to remonstrate with the local authorities;"—as the Minister announced after the event, in his reply to the memorandum of the 22nd of March, above quoted. The Tsungli yamen might at all events with truth rejoin, as they did, "that no proviso exists authorising foreign governments to station officials in the interior of China; and although Yunnan is conterminous with the kingdom of Burmah, the Chinese Government has never by the terms of any enactment given sanction to trade carried on within the limits of a subject state." Nor does it seem that this objection is satisfactorily met by the rejoinder of the British minister, in his despatch of the 25th of March, that the "right to remain in the interior under passport can no more be denied to British subjects, official or non-official, than it is denied to the Romish missionary." It would seem to be a strained interpretation of the treaty clauses touching passports and the right of travel or residence in the interior, to say that "if the Government of India saw fit to send a second mission under the same form of passport into Yunnan, and were to direct it to remain there for a longer or a shorter space of time as it might determine, it would be under treaty at perfect liberty to do so, should this course appear to it essential to the accomplishment of the object of the mission." They not only may fairly dispute such a forced interpretation of existing treaties, but with their knowledge of the past in India—Burmah and China Proper—be determined, so far as their power extends, to resist any attempt to introduce clauses to this effect, or otherwise sanction any steps for establishing centres of British trade in Yunnan; lest in course of time that experience should be renewed, and trade be speedily followed by quarrels, disputes, wars, and conquest.

Having thus traced the connection between the two expeditions and the apparently natural sequence of events, culminating so unfortunately in the disaster at Manwyne, and the attack by an armed force on Colonel Browne's party, we may pass on to the consideration of the advantages gained by the adventurous journey of Mr. Margary, and the lessons to be derived from the narrative he has left us in his journal. We cannot read either this, or the letters to his family, without noticing the powers of observation he brought to his task, and the freshness and directness of purpose in all he writes. These give a charm to the narrative, even when the incidents are not of any very striking character; and when trouble and danger threaten to arrest his progress and try his courage, we admire his ready command of resources, without a moment's doubt that the events are recorded exactly as they happened, and with perfect truth. This gives great value to all he tells us of the demeanour of the officials and the conduct of the people, while it throws considerable light on a subject hitherto only imperfectly known—the relations maintained between the provincial authorities and the population, at a distance from Pekin, and away from the coast, together with the amount of obedience rendered by both to the decrees of the Sovereign power at Pekin.

Passing in review the results of the expedition on both sides of the border, we are led to conclude that the best fruit is to be found in the knowledge acquired of the physical geography of the whole line of country from Hankow to Bhamô, together with the condition of the populations through which Margary passed on his way to the latter place, and Colonel Browne's party on the Burmese side. The treacherous and predatory habits of many of the intervening Kakhyen and Shan tribes extending over one hundred and fifty miles of a difficult mountain region was fully ascertained, and indeed, with so large an experience as to compel Colonel Browne to change his route after having attempted the Sawaddy line on which Li-sich-tai had gone from the Chinese side, as far as Muangmow, professedly, to meet and forward the expedition. I say professedly, because when Mr. Elias did make his way alone to the point indicated, Dr. Anderson tells us Li-Sich-tai raised insuperable difficulties, from the alleged unsettled state of the country and anxiety for his safety. Endless attempts at extortion and imposition in reference to the means of transport, delays on evershifting and doubtful pretexts, had previously convinced Colonel Browne however, that he could not safely trust his party to such keeping. The Ponline route, which had been taken on the first expedition by Major Sladen in 1868, was thus finally decided on.

In the midst of these contentions about baggage

and payments, orders came from Mandalay that the Burmese guard should escort the mission right up to the nominal frontier of Burmah and China, or to Kwotloon, instead of Mansay, as previously arranged and approved by the Kakhyens, whose opinion of the change was not given. We are not left in much doubt, however, as to the spirit in which it was received. On the morning fixed finally for a start, a number of gunshots disturbed the party at breakfast. The Kakhyens had endeavoured to remove the reserve clothes boxes from the charge of the Sikhs on guard, and to add them to the general baggage, which was resisted. The Burmese tsitkay expressed uneasiness as to the temper of the Kakhyens, and seemed to fear a collision with them, as they numbered about four hundred men armed with muskets, and there evidently existed some ill-feeling between the two. It further appeared in the course of the day, that the Paloungto chief in charge of the caravan had not entered into any convention with the other Tsawbahs or chiefs on the route who might object, and would certainly make their own terms. In the meantime, the inveterate curiosity and pilfering habits of the hillmen were exemplified by their boring holes in several provision tins, the holes being afterwards carefully stopped with cotton. "The sugar, salt, and bags of rice were all taken toll of, and sundry bottles of brandy had mysteriously disappeared. It was subsequently discovered that the screws had been withdrawn from the boxes." Dr. Anderson suggests that a number of wild hillmen detained in the place for a fortnight with scanty provisions must not be judged too severely for petty thieving—but there must have been an unpleasant want of security for their honesty in larger matters. Colonel Browne no doubt exercised a sound discretion therefore, in declining to trust himself and his party to their convoy. Returning to Bhamô, he determined to enter the upper or northern road, thoroughly explored by his predecessor six years before, and respecting which full information had been obtained, concerning its physical and social conditions. The suspicious bearing of the Paloungto chief, which was the main ground for the change, Dr. Anderson thinks may have been greatly due to his dislike of the Burmese, who were taking part in all the arrangements. He certainly, with his brother of Warrabone, gave a very friendly reception to Mr. Elias, and Captain Cooke, who had proceeded on the original line, unencumbered by baggage, the source of much delay and danger to the rest of the party. They even seemed anxious to prove the absence of any "ill-feeling." Be this as it may, it is obvious that much patient and skilful preparation would be required with all these Tsawbahs and petty chieftains,—independent, or quasi-independent, and wholly savage hill tribes,—to secure a passage through for any commerce, free from robbery or extortion.

The second start from Bhamô, by the northern route to Manwyne, seemed to commence under happier auspices. The Woon or chief Burmese officer there showed every disposition to facilitate their progress and provide for their safety. After a conference had been held with the Tsawbahs of the northern hills, it was agreed that the hire to be paid per mule should be seven rupees and eight annas, besides a fee or tax of five rupees for each animal. Many robberies had been latterly complained of by the merchants frequenting the road, and frequent levying of black mail. An agreement in Burmese accordingly was drawn up and duly signed, by which it was stipulated that the party should be conveyed in safety to Manwyne, at which place presents were to be distributed. As guarantee of good faith, the sons of three of the Tsawbahs were to be left at Bhamô as hostages. A large influx of the subjects of these chiefs came from the hills—"little scowling women and half savage men." Margary alludes to this descent of the hill people in one of his letters, who he describes as the "queerest creatures imaginable, and dirty beyond all description." He speaks of their visits, and the roars of laughter, and constant flow of merriment induced by the novel experience of the shock of an electric machine, and the grimaces and contortions which were excited. At last the preparations were all completed, and the 14th of February was fixed as the date for starting, in order that a Chinese caravan should precede them—with a view as the Tsare-daw-gyee curiously remarked —that if the Kakhyens intended to attack either party, "he would give them the opportunity to do both, that their might be no mistakes." This might not appear to be an arrangement calculated to give much assurance of safety. No more was the report that orders had been received at Manwyne from the Governor of Momein, that the English mission was to be treated "according to custom," without any explanation of what the Manwyne custom consisted? However, there were no misgivings apparently among the party, although a squabble between the associated chiefs about the mule hire, a third of which had been paid the previous day to one for the rest, who was charged with retaining it all, was not altogether satisfactory. This was followed by a violent altercation between the Kakhyen Ponsee, and the Burmese Choung-oke or guard, with threats of shooting and cutting down, but ended only in mutual abuse, in which the Burmese seems to have had the best of it by sheer strength of lungs. The muleteers, in the meantime having been delayed by these various contentions, unloaded their animals and drove them off! Finally, however, the day having a good many hours between sunrise and sunset, a start was accomplished, and the caravan "filed off, preceded by Margary and Allan, with a division of the Burmese guard," the departure having taken place from Tsitbaw, a village some few miles in advance of Bhamô. Dr. Anderson tells us that the travellers observed by the roadside, "several women sitting with " *carafes* of water, each containing a flower, from which they poured libations as they muttered prayers for our safety, and in the three succeeding villages the road was lined with women similarly occupied. So pleasantly and propitiously the expedition started on the 16th, to return six days later in full retreat,—and one, the most hopeful and active of their party—left dead with all his attendants, in Manwyne. Colonel Browne, in the rear, surrounded by Chinese troops, had been obliged to fight his way back. From the first victim in this act of treachery, we have no information after his arrival in advance at Seray, on the morning of the 20th, whither he had gone as a pioneer, to see if the road was safe, after various warnings of danger ahead had reached Colonel Browne. In a letter despatched from thence, he announced that so far the road was safe, and all the people met with were civil, and that he was about to proceed to Manwyne.

On the strength of this communication, although the Tsare-daw-gyee urged that no movement should be made until the news of Margary's reception at Manwyne reached them, Colonel Browne resolved to proceed on, and, if possible, reach that town in one march. The camp was struck, and, crossing the river Mampoung, they entered China. But after a march of eight miles they halted for the night in a clearing, where they bivouacked in the open. The Burmese guard were on the alert all night, but the Tsawbahs of Wancheoun and Ponwah visited the camp, and they had heard nothing of any suspicious movements of troops, and the other Shans who brought fowls for sale confirmed this. Their interpreter Moung Yoh, a nephew he called himself of Li-sieh-tai the Chinese general, returned to the camp in company with the Seray men, and reported that the Seray chief was dissatisfied on account of the payment of the mule tax having been made to Sala, which, however, had been done with the consent of his son. Moung Yoh then suggested that presents should be sent to Seray, whom he had discovered to be a great friend of his uncle, Li-sieh-tai, and to whose house he returned the same evening to await their arrival, but who disappeared altogether after the attack.

The morning of the 21st found them ready for a start, but the Tsare-daw-gyee had apparently determined to remain in the camp until definite news came from Margary. Colonel Browne resolved, notwithstanding, to push on to Seray, and the camp was left in charge of the Kakhyens and the Burmese. There were some incidents on the road of a disturbing character, and at Seray an uneasy apprehension of danger was apparent. A Burman messenger from the camp urged their return, and it was found that during their absence the Burmese had thrown up barricades commanding the road to Serai. The Tsare-daw-gyee announced to Colonel Browne that they would certainly be attacked by the Chinese either that evening, or on the march next day. Some men were observed peering down from among the trees on the hill brow, as if reconnoitring, and the

Burmese who were collecting firewood came running down as fast as they could.

About seven o'clock the next morning large bodies of armed men were observed on the heights hurrying downwards in the direction of Shitee, as if to cut off the retreat of the party, and there was no mistaking their hostile purpose. While preparations were in progress to resist any attack, the Tsare-daw-gyee, Dr. Anderson tells us, " appeared with a very serious countenance, and produced two letters received from the Burmese agents at Manwyne. They briefly narrated the horrible murder of Mr. Margary on the previous day at Manwyne; his writer and other attendants were also reported to have been killed. No particulars were given, but he was warned that we were about to be attacked, and that it would be for his own interest to detach himself by some miles from the English, failing which precaution he would incur the same danger, although the Chinese bore no ill-will to him and his party." Contrasting this determined hostility and open war with Margary's letter of the 13th of January previously, written on the spot scarcely a month before, at Manwyne, where he says, " I intend to seek exercise with my gun; I come and I go without meeting the slightest rudeness among this charming people, and they address me with the greatest respect "—it is difficult to account for the sudden and total change. It is true that in this same letter he says, in speaking of some delays occasioned by the arrival of a Burmese guard of forty men for his escort over the frontier, who were footsore and required rest : " There are wheels within wheels innumerable, and intrigues going on which require my most careful watchfulness. The Burmese want to thwart our expedition, and Li himself some seven years ago attacked our last expedition, and may not be entirely free from enmity. But I have a very powerful engine in the will and express commands of the great viceroy at Yunnan, who has been an almost unexpected friend and ally throughout." But as regards this suspicion or doubt in his mind as to Li-sieh-tai's enmity, he speaks of his reception, under date of the 11th, in a letter to his parents from Manwyne :—

"A furious ex-brigand, called Li-sieh-tai, who attacked our last expedition in 1867, has been rewarded lately for his services against the rebels with a military command over all this country. He is here, and I felt much curiosity to see how he would receive me. To my surprise he prostrated himself, and paid me the highest honours. I had a most successful interview. He sent for a few notable townsmen and the chieftain of the savages, and introduced me with the greatest respect. We sat in a small room, badly lighted, quite a conclave, and carried on a regular battery of mutual buttering. Li told them that I had come protected by an imperial edict, and that they had better take care of me."

The most suspicious circumstance here is the exaggerated respect paid by Li-sieh-tai. Outwardly, there was nothing but honour and respect for his mission. As regards the disposition of the Burmese king or officials to thwart the expedition, it is impossible to read Dr. Anderson's interesting and trustworthy account of both expeditions, and not believe that they are absolved from any plotting on the last occasion, and the testimony of the whole party shows that the Burmese guard fought bravely and with great loyalty. Intrigues from Bhamô on the part of the Chinese traders there, or the Chinese and Burmese together, there may have been, but these should be carefully distinguished from any action of the king or his authorities.

In the proceedings on the Chinese side, the circumstances are very different. Everything tends to implicate in the most direct manner the authorities, since troops could not possibly be moved, nor an attack of so grave a character, in a political aspect, be adventured upon by military commanders on their own responsibility, or with no higher sanction than subordinate civilians could give. Both as regards the murder and the attack, we must await the information it was the business of the Grosvenor mission to obtain, before we can safely form a judgment as to the apportionment of responsibility and guilt among the different parties. Dr. Anderson says that the attacking party undoubtedly consisted largely of the Ponsee and Seray Kakhyens, and the son of Seray was detected by the report of his double-barrelled gun, a present to his father at the time of the former expedition. The only satisfactory feature in the whole business seems to have been the staunchness both of the Burmese and the Kakhyen escort. The safety of the whole party was greatly due to the Shitee Tsawbwha and his Kakhyens with those of Woonkah, having at a critical moment fired the forest in front of the attacking party. Dr. Anderson bears willing testimony to this fact, and adds: " Our Burmese showed great spirit, and the Tsare-daw-gyee from first to last was deserving of the highest praise."

Thus ended the second of the two expeditions, of both of which, it may, I think, be truly said they were equally unfortunate in their inception and conclusion. The time chosen for both would seem to have been peculiarly unpropitious. In the first, because it was suggested by an erroneous calculation that the Yunnan rebellion had secured the province for a Mussulman dynasty, and that the Chinese Government was incapable of the necessary effort to recover it. The event proved that the mere suspicion of a desire on our part to enter into alliance, roused them sufficiently to pour army after army into the wasted province, and wage a war of extermination which scarcely left a Mussulman to tell the tale within the limits of Yunnan. While the permanent result of the questionable attempt on our part to establish friendly relations with the insurgents, is a legacy of distrust and ill-will on the part of the Chinese within the border, if not of the Government at Pekin.

After such experience, it is evident that no movement could be made in this direction with a chance of success, unless a clear understanding could have been first established with the Chinese Government as to the real object. The concurrence of both the Emperor of China and his tributary, the King of Burmah, was so plainly essential to the attainment of the ends, that one can hardly conceive the most sanguine anticipating any good result without it. The first of these expeditions was a mistake, if only because it was illtimed—but it was not followed by any serious loss of prestige, or consequent political necessity of renewing the effort to repair a defeat. Very different is the second in this respect. It has led not only to a discomfiture, damaging in the eyes of Chinese and Burmese alike, to say nothing of all the intervening Shan and Kakhyen tribes, but to an open act of war on the part of the Chinese, for which we are obliged to seek redress, and claim an indemnity for injury sustained. Nor is even the loss of a valuable life, however much to be deplored, the worst consequence of this expedition. There is a Nemesis attaching to failure in the East, which no Asiatic power can afford to disregard. However questionable might have been our right, in an international point of view, to insist on the concession of a free passage and trade with Yunnan from Burmah originally, we could have very little choice left afterwards. The *vestigia nulla retrorsum* alluded to in the introductory remarks, is too plainly written to leave any option. Clear as it may seem to some of the latest critics of our Eastern policy, and of this advance in particular, that, if our first step was an error, to extort a concession which could not in the first instance have been rightly insisted upon, would be to take advantage of our own wrong,—it must not be forgotten that an act of treachery, followed by an attack in force on the part of the Chinese, gives a right to indemnity, and imposes the obligation upon them of affording complete reparation. A reparation which in this case cannot take any better form for us, or one less injurious to the Chinese, than the establishment of such regulations for peaceable access to their territory, as the interests of mutual intercourse and commerce demand. But a right to such access, for purposes of trade or exploration did exist antecedently by the "most favoured nation clause" of our treaty, and their action in dealing with similar claims on the part of the Russians along the Siberian and Mongolian frontier as at Kiachta, Urga, and Kiuldja. It may be safely asserted moreover, that when two countries are conterminous over a great extent of territory, intercourse is inevitable. This may either be predatory and hostile, or commercial and peaceable. But in any case, several hundred or thousand miles of frontier cannot be hermetically sealed by any acts of a government, and it is therefore in the interest of both countries to establish peaceful relations and a mutually beneficial intercourse. To do this, access must be given, and a right of transit for all peaceable and legitimate purposes be duly regulated by treaty.

On these grounds I have had no hesitation in advocating elsewhere such a policy, and the right to insist upon its adoption, greatly strengthened and rendered imperative indeed, by the treachery and hostilities which have recently taken place in Western China. If it were even granted, for the sake of argument, that the expedition was unwarranted—and that they were entitled to refuse access under passports bearing the seal of the Foreign Office at Pekin, they should have said so, either at the time, or even later, when the party of Colonel Browne was passing the frontier. It was still possible to have taken effective steps to stop him, without incurring the responsibility of deliberate treachery and violence. Fifteen armed Sikhs did not constitute an army; or any force that could offer resistance, if the passage of the party had been officially refused by the local authority. Preferring to adopt a different and wholly unjustifiable course, they not only may rightly be held answerable, but they must be so dealt with, if the *jus gentium*, which governs the intercourse of civilised nations, is not to be wholly abrogated in dealing with the Chinese Empire.

But with the expediency of the expedition—its opportuneness, or the right of his government to despatch, at any time such a mission, Mr. Margary had nothing whatever to do. He had only a duty to perform, and, as it unhappily proved, a dangerous one. In the preceding narrative and letters will be found a record full of interest showing that, apart from its dangers, his task was both arduous and difficult. The information afforded on many points, even of an incidental nature, is as novel as it is valuable, filling up a great blank in our previous knowledge of the actual state of the central and south-western provinces of China. The commercial resources of the different districts through which he passed for a distance of some nine hundred miles; the state of the roads and means of transport; the natural or manufactured products of each district traversed; the habits and temper of the people; the disposition of the provincial authorities; the deference paid in some cases, and the manifest disregard in others, of the obligations imposed upon them by the Imperial safe conduct given to Mr. Margary,—are all noted with conscientious care, and such intelligent discrimination and keenness of observation, that we cannot help feeling his selection from the juniors of the consular service reflects equal credit on the body, and the judgment of his chief in assigning him the post. A very cursory glance through the pages will suffice to show how much may be learned from the perusal of the whole narrative. The physical geography, climate, and scenery, are all noted with no less vivacity and care, than the political condition of the several districts which pass under his observation. Nothing escapes him; and it is the more remarkable and praiseworthy from the fact that he started in bad health from the malarious climate of Shanghae, and on several occasions was absolutely incapacitated, by attacks of fever and dysentery, from all exertion for days together. Under date, August 24th, while on his way to Hankow, he writes: "I have had a long spell of bad health in Shanghae, without any positive sign of sickness. The fact is, as I know now for certain, that I have been under the wearing influence of Shanghae fever, which is very subtle. It is an intermittent fever, and if one's constitution is strong enough, like mine, to resist it, the silent enemy continues its creeping attacks, until the mischief is detected by loss of flesh, and emaciation. I have been working too hard, and sitting out too much in evening breezes, the result of which was a loss of fourteen or fifteen pounds, which I was startled to discover the other day. It is not pleasant to have to start on my stupendous journey after such a pull down, but every mile away from Shanghae has been adding strength and vigour to my spirits and frame, and I have no doubt under the quiet, regular regime of a traveller's life, I shall feel as blithe as a lark."

Again, on the 8th of October:—"Felt very much better. At 6 A.M. I tried to take a stroll, but my strength was scarcely equal to a hundred yards. I went along the cliff path and found composition of hills all quartz. Tung-wan had a lot of houses on poles, which seems their favourite style of architecture here; a number of empty pens showed where the market was held in the day. Attack of rheumatism in right side."

The spirit in which he received the first intimation of the honourable commission with which he was to be intrusted is well seen in one of his letters dated August 9: "A magnificent opportunity of distinguishing myself has just been opened to me, and I am sure it will please you very much to know how great an honour has been lately conferred upon me in connection with it. I am appointed to the very duty I was longing for and wrote about in my last letter to you, namely, that of accompanying the Indian expedition which is to enter China through Burmah and survey a new route for commerce." And further on he says, "The plan adopted is to send me overland from this side to the western borders of the province of Yunnan, there to wait at one of the passes for four Indian officers who are to come over from a place called Bhamô, near the upper sources of the Irrawaddy or Irawady. I am provided with huge Chinese despatches from the Tsung-li-Yamen at Pekin to three governor-generals who rule the vast territories through which I shall pass. These letters direct them to take every care of me, and to issue orders to all their magistrates and officers along my route to protect and help me on. I shall pass over about nine hundred miles of country of which some five hundred will be new ground. I have to keep an official journal and an itinerary, and every thing will be published. The trip is calculated to last six months. At any rate I shall be completely buried out of sight till the end of November, and shall probably hear no news of you or the world in general till next year. Only think what a glorious opportunity I shall have of seeing this wonderful country, and of bringing to light numerous facts as yet unknown from regions untrodden by foreigners. It is really splendid; you cannot think how elated I am."

In the same buoyant and confident tone he writes a few days later: "It is impossible to say when you may hear from me. I shall try and make use of the native post, which is a very efficient service, but how far it may be safe for foreign correspondence remains to be proved. It may be that not a word will be heard of me the whole time, in which case, all sorts of rumours may arise as to my fate. Let me beg of you not to believe one; rest assured I will make my way there and back, by God's help, as safe as a trivet." "I have only to pray for health and strength to carry me through, and there is no doubt I shall have had the privilege of doing some service to the world at large." He speaks with enthusiasm of the time when he may hope to be "on the heights of the Momien pass, far away on the Burmese frontier and anxiously scanning the country beyond for the first glimpse of Indian helmets approaching from the west. Then you can picture the meeting, China and India grasping hands"—"The trade route of the future," as he elsewhere says, laid down. Nor can we wonder at the sanguine nature of his anticipations, for, so far as he was aware, all necessary and preliminary steps had been taken at Pekin to ensure his uninterrupted progress to the destined goal. As he remarks in another letter: "The letters and passes furnished me by the Imperial Cabinet will command respect from all the officials high and low throughout my route; so that, though no doubt, innumerable schemes may be devised to hinder my progress, I shall be hedged around with protection." And, in effect, although he did meet with numerous obstructions both from ill-disposed officials and dangerous mobs, and a sad lack of that official protection he so confidently counted upon, he achieved the end of his journey triumphantly and in safety; it was only on his return that the catastrophe came. Looking to that end, nothing is more interesting or valuable for future guidance, than the account he has left us of the behaviour of officials and populace along the line of route. None of our experiences in China have thrown so much light on the degree of protection passports secure to foreigners, and the amount of danger and insecurity to be encountered in spite of such protection. The application of this knowledge in regard to rights of inland trade and residence, so constantly demanded by the mercantile communities, in China and at home, is obvious, and fully justifies Lord Derby's warning to the India Office already quoted when this expedition was first referred to by Lord Salisbury.

There are indeed "grave difficulties in the way of any project for establishing consulates or British communities in the far interior of China, where British protection could not be extended to them, which, in the present state of the Chinese Empire, is in some shape constantly threatening foreigners, and which the Government of Pekin, even if well disposed to do so, can often only imperfectly guard against." No better commentary in confirmation of the perfect accuracy of this statesman-like estimate of the actual position in China could possibly be furnished than the entries in Mr. Margary's journal afford; and his varied experiences during this four months' journey from the centre to the south-western frontier of the empire. On the third day after his start from Hankow, our last treaty port on the Yangtzse, he had his first experience of popular violence, when he was hustled and hooted by a mob of junk men on landing from his boat for a walk. Five days later, he had a similar experience from the inhabitants at Loshan, where "there was only a local official of no position or authority." This officer was civil enough when called upon, and sent two of his soldiers to accompany Mr. Margary back to his boat as a protection—" but their efforts were barely equal to repressing the excited crowd which had surrounded me with shouts and abusive language;" he tells us. Under date, October 5, he records what seemed a more serious danger, the way in which the magistrate at one of his resting-places acted upon his instructions from the viceroy. These were imperative, to send two officials to escort and protect him as far as the next magisterial city, and the course he took was to send a small "boat of the commonest class, and a couple of disreputable-looking rascals with the card of the Tao-yuan magistrate—a couple of dirty scullions, or some other such menials out of the nasty crowd that infest all yamens." Later on, when he passed a dilapidated city which had suffered from the Taipings, he was much disturbed by the mob, and even the efforts of the sub-prefect, "who accompanied me in a gun-boat, were fruitless in quieting them, and as for the soldiers, they positively feared the mob." On another occasion, three weeks later, when he reached a provincial city, Ch'en-yuan-fu, he proceeded on foot with his party and four men, sent by the magistrate at his request, to protect him a short distance to the inn. He writes, "a crowd quickly formed round me, chiefly consisting of soldiers, the fruitful source of trouble everywhere, and attempted to follow me into the house, but the very unsubstantial door was closed upon them, and it severely taxed the energies of the four yamen men to keep it so. Then the mob in the rear would not allow his baggage to be brought in, on which he determined to go to the magistrate. By him he was received with great rudeness; and it was only after a sharp and indignant remonstrance, backed by the production of the passport and the Tsungli yamen's letter to the governor-general of the province, that he changed his tone, and condescended, when he found he had to deal with a foreigner well acquainted with Chinese, and under especial protection from Pekin, to give orders to send men down and guard the house. But even then, and when a chair had been prepared in which the traveller attempted to return, the crowd was too great and violent for all the magistrate's men, and the party had to beat a retreat again to the magistrate's yamen, " in which ignominious plight," he observes, " I had to be carried backwards through the mob." Attempts were made to upset the chair, and one man who thrust his face in to insult him got his nose broken. He concludes the account by observing, " As an example of Chinese apathy, I may as well mention that at the very spot where I was being insulted by the mob, a military mandarin of high rank was passing by, under whose very command were half the rioters round, and yet he made no more effort to repress them than a private individual." Fortunately Mr. Margary had many other and more agreeable experiences. At Kweichou, where he arrived on the 6th of November, he was most civilly treated by the governor- "a brisk old man full of energy and intelligence," and with one or two exceptions he continued in the latter part of his route to receive great attention. Up to his arrival at Yunnan Fu, the capital of the province, he met with the greatest civility from all the authorities, from the acting viceroy downwards. A couple of mandarins were deputed to escort him thence the whole way to Ta-Li Fu, and on the 11th of December,

2 B

when near the end of his journey, he speaks in warm terms of the hospitality and great civility of the prefect of Yao-chou, who had sent down his servants a distance of sixty miles to provide for his wants. " Such incomparable civility," he observes, " proves how throughly the Viceroy is to be relied on." " His career has been marked by thoroughness," was almost the last entry in the diary ! Taking all these experiences together the impression left is decidedly to the advantage of the Pekin Government, so far as the *bonâ fides* of the safe conduct given is concerned. But there is a second conclusion not less distinct, that the best passport gives no real security in the interior, and that the provincial authorities cannot be trusted for any effective protection, nor in all cases for providing an escort according to orders to perform this part of their duty.

This last conviction is so manifestly borne out by the facts recorded in this journal, and Mr. Margary's tragic end, that no government who has any care for the lives of its subjects, or its own responsibilities, can well come to any other conclusion than that arrived at by the Earl of Derby, namely— " that there are grave difficulties in the way of any project for establishing consulates or British communities in the far interior of China."

This seems to be the moral of the whole history, and had fuller consideration been given to all that was known, even before the flood of light thrown by this most interesting journal, respecting the temper of the people and the officials, as well as the uncertain control exercised by these over a mob, even when they really desire to do their duty, it is difficult to believe it would have been undertaken.

The fate of Major Sladen's expedition in 1868 was not encouraging; but, as has been already pointed out, it left no obligation to retrieve a disaster. Up to the date of this last mission I should have entirely agreed with Dr. Anderson that the "question of opening trade routes may be left to the future." But this option is no longer ours. When he says, " the death of this young officer, and the repulse of the British mission from the frontiers of China, have left a marked impression on the minds of the various populations," he points to an effect which must be counteracted, and this can only be done by success taking the place of failure. Whether it be Burmese, Kakhyens, Shan tribes, or Chinese that are in question, it is impossible we can accept a defeat of this nature, brought on too by our own spontaneous acts. It is well known, but can hardly be too often repeated, that our position in the midst of Asiatics is one of prestige. We may often refuse to advance, if we do not choose to incur the risk of any forward step, but can seldom retreat afterwards without ruin. The disadvantages or dangers of an advance, therefore, should be duly weighed before any step is taken, and among these, the chances of failure and its conse quence. However serious or unwelcome these may prove, they can rarely be averted by acquiescence in a defeat. Renewed and successful effort is the only alternative if we would avoid a total loss of the moral power by which, far more than by superior force, we govern in the East, and enjoy both security and commercial privileges. I have serious doubts of the value of any trade route between China and Burmah in the present state of Yunnan and the intervening Shan and Kakhuen territories. Such overland commerce as can reasonably be anticipated, holds out no promise of an adequate return, for the risk and responsibility that must be incurred by any government undertaking to open up and maintain a channel of communication. No doubt such a channel has existed of old time, does actually exist now, under conditions of great insecurity; and a trade is carried on by natives between Burmah and China, despite of such drawbacks. But the question is of what value is this trade, and what are the prospects or capabilities of development, even under more favourable circumstances? And, finally, at what cost can these more favourable conditions be secured? It is very natural that mercantile communities in Burmah, China, and India should desire to see a trade route permanently opened; but it is for the government which must incur the responsibility, and bear the burden of any efforts for its attainment, to estimate the cost, not merely in money, as we see, but the consequences of failure,—the risk of war and border contentions with wild and half-savage tribes, in addition to the chances of new complications and dissensions with the Chinese. The policy of Great Britain has for the most part been, with regard to uncivilised countries, to allow traders to push their way at their own risk if they think it worth their while. And it may be doubted whether, if the prosperity of Yunnan were restored, the steamers of the Burmese rivers, as Dr. Anderson suggests, and the entrepôt of Bhamô, where the British flag assures protection, would not be sufficient to furnish the best means of bringing up supplies to the border land, and opening up a continuous trade in the first instance. However, as we are now committed, and are likely to find ourselves forced into a policy we might not deliberately or voluntarily have chosen, the question of relative value and cost may be dismissed. But it would certainly seem that the only course which can with any safety be followed after recent events, must be direct negotiation with the Chinese Government, without concealment or disguise as to what is required, and the real object in view. As to the choice of routes between Burmah and China, that is rather a question of detail, and time may be taken for fuller information to be obtained as to which would be best. We can only hope that whichever may be chosen, a satisfactory settlement will in the end be effected by peaceable means. In any case the narrative of this journey from Hankow to Bhamô and the information Mr. Margary has afforded throughout his journal, will make the present work one of special interest and permanent value.

INDEX.

A

Adventure, exciting, 6.
"Ah-a-ah," 302.
"Ai-yahs," 52.
Alcock, Sir Rutherford, 11; notes by, 329; first meeting with Mr. Margary, *ib.*
Allen, Mr. Clement, 316.
America, railway travelling, 31, 37.
American Consul-General, 88.
Amur, Russian settlement in the, 14.
Anam and-Ton-Quin annexations, 334.
Anderson, Dr., 101, 216, 309, 322, 324, 325; note, 331, 335, 337.
An-hsün, 204.
An-ning Chow, 246.
Asbestos, 44.
Associated Chambers of Commerce, memorials of, 332.
Athens, Acropolis, resemblance to, 89.
Azaleas, profusion of, 79.

B

Bamboo rope manufacture, 151.
Beauty, Chinese beau ideal of, 42.
"Belle-Vue" temple, 57.
Bhamô, 98, 243, 293, 307, 312; treaty signed at, 1769, 333.
Blue Book information, 342.
Bombazine, 107, 171, 192, 238, 294, 306.
British goods, market for, 255.
Browne, Colonel, 101, 173, 234, 241, 293, 307, 309, 313; present from, 319; mission under, 330, 354.
Buddhism, 56; mockery of worshippers, *ib.*
Buddhist, priests and gods, 2; temple, 56.
Buffalo, a sacrificial, 325.
Burmah, 100; inhabitants, 298; portrait of king of, 243.
———— and China route, 326.
Burmese, opposed to expedition, 304; guard, 307; houses, 310; dress of women, 312.
Burney, Colonel, 333.

C

Calcutta, telegram from, 122.
Cambodia, inhabitants, 298.
Canton Province, Governor of, 110.
Cart, agricultural, 127.
Cave, remarkable, 225.
Chair-bearers, 214.
Ch'ang-tê, 144; river, front of, 145, 238.
Changtch, 112.
Chan-i Chow, 227.
Chao Chow, 282.
"*Chu-hu shêng-k'ou,*" 244.
Chefoo, 39, 40, 70.
Chên-ch'i Hsien, 157.
Ch'ên-chou Fu, 147, 157.
Chen-nan Chow, 260.

INDEX.

Chen Ning Chow, 276.
Ch'ên-yuan Fu, 119, 147, 165, 166. 174; difficulties with mob, 175, 198.
Chiang, 298; at the fall of Ta-Li Fu, *ib.*
Chiang-Hsi, 162.
Chiang Kôu, 159.
Chia-yü Hsien, 124.
Chicago, 31.
Ch'ien-tsung, 203.
Chiang Yang Hsien, 161.
Chih Hsien, 75, 159, 162.
Chih-fu, 149.
Chi-hsia Hsien, 66.
Chih Li, province, 127.
Chi-Ini, outrage at, 68.
China, desolation of central provinces, 54.
Chinese teachers, 5; New Year, 43; cemetery, *ib.*; garments, 48; inns, 49; proofs of pluck in, 53; cupidity, 59; pride in composition, 71; troops on the war-path, 72; quarrel with French, 74; management of boats, 80; theatre, 81; postal system, 97; curiosity, 131, 135; food, 138; mode of reception, 168, 195; etiquette, 259, 280; distrust, 310; Foreign Office and mission, 342.
Ching-chen Hsien, 201.
Ching-ch'i Hsien, 201.
Ching-k'ou, 122.
Ch'ing-p'ing Hsien, 181.
Chinkiang, 100, 103, 109.
Chou-t'ung, 125.
Chow, 213, 253.
Christmas dinner, 288, 290.
Ch'u-hsiung, 258.
Chung-chia, 216; classes of, 217.
Chung-khing, 105.
Chün-shan Island, 142; tea of, 143.
Chusan Islands, 88.
Cigarettes, value of, 137.

Circus, 86.
Coal, abundance of, 212, 261.
Confucius' tomb, 72.
Cooke, Captain and Mrs., 308.
Cooper, Mr., 243.
Copper Cash, 213.
Cotton cultivation, 114, 144.
Crawford, 333.
Cricket, 87.
Crosse and Blackwell, 290.

D

Deer, 54.
Derby, Earl of, and the consuls, 342, 366.
Despatch, important, 331.
Dodd, 19, 24; bravery of, 25; fight with looters, 28.
Dog escort, 262.
Duck, wild, 279.
Dutch, massacre of, at Formosa, 16.

E

Elias, Mr. Ney, 101, 309, 348.
Elk, the, 22.
Expedition of 1867, 301, 309, 317.

F

Fforde, Mr., 309, 312.
Fishing, mode of, 160.
Flail, use of, 185.
Foochow, 21.
Formosa, 13; Dutch forts at, 15; beauty of, 17; tea, 19; soldiers *en route* to, 140.
Forsyth's, Sir Douglas, expedition of 1870, 340.
French and Chinese quarrel, 71; action of the English police, 75.

INDEX.

French Bishop, visit to, 239.
Fytche, General, and the Bhamô trade route, 336.

G

Garnets, 44.
Garnier, Lieutenant, 150.
Geese, 279, 322.
"Gin-rick-a-sha," the cab of Yedo, 36; in Shanghae, 74; mode of guiding, 86.
"Goggles," 310, 315.
Gold mines, 44.
Gordon, Colonel, 109.
Griffiths, Mr., 3.
Grosvenor, Mr., 326; mission under, 330, 337.

H

Hai-tzŭ P'u, 226.
Han dynasty, 216.
Hankow, 14, 97.
Hanlin, or Forest of Pencils, a member of the, 13.
Hannay, 334.
Hirado, the, 102.
Holland and Holland, 17.
Hong-Kong, 14.
House building, 208.
Hsia, 224.
Hsia Chwang, 278.
Hsiao, magistrate of Lu-feng Hsien, 252.
Hsaio-hua-pai, 124.
Hsias Lou Tsai, 160.
Hsien, a, 209.
Hsien Niao, 163.
Hsin Chow, 179.
Hsin T'i, 125.
Hsin Tsai Tâng, 165.
Hughes, Mr. Consul, 118, 238.
Hughes, Mrs., 288.

H'ua-king, 212.
Hu-hsin Chou, 124.
Hu Kwang, viceroy of, 119.
Hu Nan, route, 118, 142, 150, 166.
Hung Chiang Ssŭ, 161.
Hu Pei carts, 127.
Hwang Chow, 164.
Hwang-kwo-su, 207.

I

I-ch'ang, rapids of, 105; gorge, 255.
I-lung Ssŭ, 230.
Imperial badges, 13.
Indian mission, 293; Government despatch, 331.
Indians, appearance of, 37.
Indigo, 122.
Inns, misery of, 49; charges, 50.
Irrawaddy the, or Irawady, 98, 317.
Iron, 44.

J

Jade, 44.
Japan coast, beauty of, 35.
Japan, the, 32.
Jasper, 44.
Joss-sticks, 62.
Junks, timber, 90.

K

Kakhyen, hills, 307, 324; tribes, 310; in treaty with, 312; Pawmynes, or deputy chiefs, 320; Tsanbwas, 321; women, 323.
Kaoliang or Sorghum, 122.
Kelung, 18, 20; typhoon at, 21; shipwrecks, 24; earthquakes, 28.
"Khang," 67.
Kilt, the, 17.
King, Mr. Vice-Consul, 100, 111, 117.
Kinkiang, 100, 104, 111.

INDEX.

Kobé, or Hiogo, 39.
K'o-t'ou, 213.
Kow-tows, 56, 62.
Koxinga, 16.
Kung, Prince of, and the mission, 341.
Kuanging, 12.
Kuang-t'ung Hsien, 256.
Kung-kuan, 253.
Kwei-chou, province, 112, 206; route, 118; climate of, 218.
Kwei-yang Fu, 189, 191; plain, 205.
Kwe-ting Hsien, 184.
Kwotloon, 349.
Ky-oung, or priest's house, 321.

L

Lai Yang, 60.
Lake Spirit, army of the, 143.
Lang-tai, 209.
Lao-ya Kuan, 250.
Lao-yeh, 245.
Lee-see-tai, charges against, 337.
Leila, 107, 134.
Letters from Augustus Raymond Margary to—
  Brother, 316.
  F. E. R., 29, 32, 34, 39, 70, 111, 113, 152, 166, 185, 189, 198, 262, 281, 287, 293, 302, 308, 313, 320.
  Layard, Rev. J., 1, 12, 18, 192.
  Layard, Mrs. J., 36.
  Parents, 4, 21, 98, 101, 127, 171, 235, 271, 290, 296, 298, 307.
" Li " (courtesy), 53.
Li (measurement), 49.
Liao Ya Tsui, 144.
Li-chou, 145.
Lien-p'êng, 269.
Li Hsieh Tai, ex-brigand, 300; his attack on 1867 expedition, 301, 303, 356.

Li Hung-Ch'ang, 148.
Lin, 60; his bravery, ib.; his daughters, ib.
Li Pi-shêng, 146, 148, 153.
Li-Sieh-tai, 348.
" Longhaired Rebels," 157.
Lo-shan, 122, 125, 112; theatrical troop at, 133.
Lotus cultivation, 141.
Lou-ch'i Hsien, 157, 158.
Lu-ch'i-k'ou, 124.
Lu-fêng Hsien, 251.
Lung-chi-kou, 164.
Lung-li Hsien, 188.
Lung Wang Sang, work at, 1.
Lung-yang Hsien, 144.
Lytton, Bulwer, 115.

M

Magoung, 314.
Mahommedans, 271.
Ma-lung Chow, 228.
Mantchooria, 72.
Mandalay, 314.
' Mandalay to Momien,' by Dr. Anderson, 325.
Mansey, 309.
Manwyne, 298; semi-savages at, 300.
Man-yang-hsien, 165.
Margary, Augustus Raymond, at Lung Wang Sang, 1; visit to temple of Ta-pei-su, 11; at Formosa, 13 (see, also, Introduction); Kelung, 20; conduct during typhoon at Kelung, 25; return to England, 29; at Niagara, 29; on board the Japan, 32; misery of American railway journey, 33; Yokohama, 34; at Yedo, 36; sent to Chefoo, 39; visit to the Tao-Tai, 40; trip to

INDEX.

hills of the Shantung province, 47; at Lai Yang, 158; curious visitors, 65; at Chi-hsia Hsien, 66; an affable host, 67; return to Shanghae, 73; an interrupted rehearsal, 77; trip to Ningpo, 79; visit to monastery, *ib.*; work at Shanghae, 85; visit to the Chusan Islands, 88; at Napier Island, 91; return to Shanghae, 92; appointed to Colonel Browne's Mission, 95; preparations for journey to Hankow, 99; start for Hankow, 102; route, 105; at Hankow, 111; at Tung-kua-nao, 122; wind-bound at Lu-ch'i-k'ou, 125; at Lo-shan, 127; leave Lo-shan, 142; on the Yuan river, 143; at Ch'ang-tê, 145; ill, 156; notes from private journal, 158; at Hung Chiang Ssu, 161; disturbance with crowd at Yuen Chow Fu, 162; at Yü-ping Hsien, 165; an old friend, 167; a sad incident, 169; reach Ch'ên-yuan Fu, 174; visit magistrate at Shihping Hsien, 178; trouble with bearers, 185; at Ching-Ch'i Hsien, 201; at An-hsün, 204; Chên Ning Chow, 205; Lang-tai, 209; reception at P'ing-i Hsien, 224; Chan-i Chow, 227; arrive at Yunnan Fu, 232; at Au-ning Chow, 247; Lu-fêng Hsien, 252; Kuang-t'ung Hsien, 256; reach Ch'u-hsiung, 259; at Chên-Nan Chow, 262; reception at Chen Ning Chow, 276; sport, 279; at Ta-Li Fu, 285; Yung-ch'ang Fu, 292; an alarm, 295; to join mission at Bhamô, 296; Momien, 297; Tu Wen Hsin, 297; Manwyne, 298; meets Colonel Browne at Bhamô, 307; with Captain and Mrs. Cooke at Sawaddy, 308; break up camp at Bhamô, 313; in camp at Tsikaw, 316; murder of, 325 (*see*, also, Introduction); letters from (*see* Letters).

Medhurst, Mr. Consul, 97, 107, 117, 122.
Mê-k'ou, 212.
Miao-tzu, 216; distinctive dress of, *ib.*
Miaotsze, the, 178, 183, 271.
"Mihiloongs," the, 85.
Mission, *see* Yunnan.
Missionary question, 71.
Momien, 105, 235, 297.
Monastic service, 79.
Mormons, the, 33.
Mosquitoes, 138.
Moung Yoh, 354.
Mountains of Kwei-chou province, 211.
Muangmow, 348.
Mule litters, travelling by, 47.
Murder, attempted, 164.

N

Nan-chai, 143.
Nankin, 103; destruction of the porcelain tower, *ib.*, 109.
Nanny and the orchid, 295.
Nan-tien, 304.
Napier Island, 90, 91.
New Year, in China, 43, 45, 59; worship, 62.
Niagara, 29; hotels at, 30; falls, *ib.*, 37.
Ni Hsin T'ang, 144.
Ningpo, 88, 89.
Ni-Ssŭ-yeh, 161.
Northbrook, Lord, 193, 316, 342.
North Walsham, 194.
Nuikong River, 302.

O

Octopus dish, 264.
Ogden, Mormon settlement at, 34.
Opium smoking, 246.
Otto des Granges', Baron, 'Survey,' 335.

P

P'ai-chou, 123.
Pai-ma t u, 147.
Pai-shui, 225.
Pai-tzŭ Pu, 229.
Paloungto, the, chief, 349.
Pan-ch'iao, 231.
Panthays, the, 336.
Passport question, 343.
Pa-tsung, 139, 253.
Payi tribe, 298; picturesque dress of women, 299.
Peacocks, 322.
Pekin, storm at, 4. 54.
Pekinese, 5; mode of fighting, 6.
Pemberton, 334.
Pepohwan tribe, 183.
Persimmon tree, 189.
Phayre, Sir A., 334.
Pheasants, 54.
Piccadilly lamps, 135.
Pi-chi K'ou, 245.
Pidgeon English, 192.
Pien, magistrate of Yunnan Fu, 234.
Pigs, wild, 54.
P'ing-i Hsien, 224.
Players, strolling, 133.
Pouline route, 348.
Pottery trade, 147.
Prairie dog, 37.
Pŭ-an Chow, 221.
Pu-erh-ch'a, 200.
" Pulpit Rock," 34.
Pŭ-p'êng, 269.
Pu-shih, 157.

Pu Ssu, 161.
Pwai, a, 309.

Q

Queen Victoria, Her Majesty, 246.

R

Rafts, timber, 126, 172.
Rain, effect on wind and waves, 35.
Rangoon, 113, 122; interest in object of mission, 331.
Revue des Deux Mondes, 49.
Rice cultivation, 141.
Richthofen's, Baron, report, 219.
Ritual, 62.
Roads, how formed, 4.
Rocky Mountains, 37.
Roman Catholics successful as missionaries, 2.

S

Sai-tsŭ, 254.
Sa-li-ju, 237.
Salisbury, Marquis of, 331.
Salt, 221, 219.
Salt Lake City, 34.
San Francisco, 38.
San Men Tân, 164.
Sankoi river, route by, 335.
Sa-tui, 159.
San-o-bay, 22.
Sawaddy, 308.
Saw-teeth Mountains, 55.
Sea discoloration by rivers, 90.
Seng-Yuen-Fu, or Momein, 105.
September, first of, 12.
Sha-ch'iao, 268, 270.
Shan Valleys, 310.

INDEX. 381

Shanghae, 14, 36, 40, as a place of residence, 73; French and Chinese riot at, 76; fire at, *ib.*; further alarms, 77; theatre, 81; recreation grounds, 84; circus, 86; cricket ground and race-course, 87; the Maloo, *ib.*
Shans, the, 298, 336.
Shansi, the, 88.
Shantung province, 47.
Sha-shih, 145.
Sha Yang, 287.
Shenchow, 112.
" Sherroo," 323.
Shê-tzŭ, 253.
Shih-ma P'u, 144.
Shihping Hsien, 178.
Shih-yeh, 221.
" Ship stone," 70.
Shui-ch'i, 148.
Siam, inhabitants, 298.
Sierra Nevadas, the, 37.
Sikhs, guard of, 320.
Silver Island, 104.
Singapore, 15.
" Sing-song," a, 298.
Sladen, Major, 330 and *note*; 336; and the expedition of 1868, 341.
Soo-ah, 306.
Spirits, banquet to, 62.
Ssŭ Ch'uan, 255; province, 268.
Ssŭ-yeh, 160.
Storks, 225.
Sträng leäng, 76.
Sulphur baths, 44.
Sunday, a day of rest and enjoyment, 3.
Swanfield, 194.
Symes, Colonel, 333.
Sz'chuen province, 105, 331.

T

Ta-ch'i-k'ou, 146.
Ta-fêng T'ung, or Cave of the Winds, 181.
Taiping rebels, 109, 143, 157; rebellion, 217.
Ta-jên, 203, 239, 245.
Tale, 44.
Ta-li Fu, 241, 243, 265; the magistrate of, 276; plain, 283; lake, *ib.*, 332.
Ta-loa-yeh, 245.
Tamsuy, fort of, 16, 18.
Tao-Tai, the, 40.
Tao-t'ai, 125.
Tao-Tai of Yunnan Fu, 163, 173.
Tao-Tai Wu, 196.
T'ao-yuen Hsien, 146.
Ta-pei-su, visit to temple of, 10.
Tapeng, camp by the, 321; view of from Kakhyen hills, 324.
Tau, 5.
Taoist temple, visit to, 6.
Ta Wan, 159.
Tea trade, activity of, 14; at Formosa, 19.
T'êng-yueh Chow, 258, 287, 293, 302.
Theatre, Chinese, 81.
Theatrical performances, 82.
Thrupp and Maberly, 47.
Tientsin, pugnacity of, men, 5, 40.
Tigers, pursuit of, 283.
T'ing, a, 209.
Ti-tu, 161.
Tobacco cultivation, 184.
Tomatoes, 187.
Towns, walled, mode of building, 57.
Trade routes, 331; the object of residents in Burmah, 334.
Treaty of Bhamô, 1769, 323.
Tsare-daw-gyce, the, 353.
Tseng-shih, 145.
Tsikaw, 313, 316; start of caravan from, 352.
Tsung-li-Yamen of Pekin, the, 98, 118; memorandum of, 312.

Tsungping, 149.
Tuin Qun, 161.
Tumuli on Kwei-yang Fu plain, 204.
Tung-kua-nao, 122.
Tung Ling Lake, 128.
Tungting Lake, 112, 114, 123.
Tung Shing, 72.
Tung-wan, 160.
Twain, Mark, 109.
Typhoon, 22, 34.

U

"Undefined persuasion," the, 68.
Utah, the "promised land," 34.

V

Van Eyk, Professor, 81.
Verrey, 11.

W

Wade, Sir Thomas, 98, 101, 113, 122, 128, 272, 330, 341.
"Walking Beam," the, 103.
Wang, 44.
Wen, 5.
Westward Ho! the, 25.
Wilcox, 333.
Williams', Dr., map of China, 100; journey to Bhamô, 334.
Woon, the, 309, 324, 351.
Wu, 181.
Wu-ch'ang Fu, 121, 149.
Wu Tao-Tai, 181, 196.

Y

Yakob, 340.
Yakob Beg, 340.
"Yamen," 78.
Yang, 243, 253.
Yang-lin, 230.
Yang-shun, 220.
Yangtsze, the, 39, 79, 104, 268.
Yang-tzŭ, 255.
Yao-chan, 258.
Yao-chou Fu, 123, 142.
Yao-chow, prefect of, 271.
Yedo, 36, 38.
Yin Ho Hsiang, 144.
Yo-chow, 112.
Yokohama, 24, 38.
Young, Brigham, 34.
Yuan river, 143; journey up, *ib.*
Yu-chi, 125.
Yuen Chow Fu, 162.
Yule, Colonel, 213.
Yung-ch'ang Fu, 105, 235, 241, 258, 278, 287; mandarins, 296.
Yunnan Fu, 105, 113, 171, 231; reception at, 233; province, 98, 106; Mission, origin of, 330; object of, 331; Mahommedan rising in, 335; attack on mission, 355, 357.
Yü-ping Hsien, 165.

Z

Zebra, H.M.S., 21.
Zui-hi, 108.

THE END.

LONDON: PRINTED BY WILLIAM CLOWES AND SONS, STAMFORD STREET AND CHARING CROSS.

www.ingramcontent.com/pod-product-compliance
Lightning Source LLC
Chambersburg PA
CBHW050851300426
44111CB00010B/1212